BEHIND THE smile

Unmasking the Silent Battles
We Hide and the Strengths We Find

BEHIND THE smile

ROB GODDARD

First published in 2025 by Dean Publishing
PO Box 119
Mt. Macedon, Victoria, 3441
Australia
deanpublishing.com

Copyright © Rob Goddard

All rights reserved. No part of this publication may be reproduced, stored in a retrieval system or transmitted in any way or by any means, electronic, mechanical, photocopying, recording or otherwise, without the prior written permission of the author and publisher.

Cataloguing-in-Publication Data
National Library of Australia

Title: Behind The Smile
ISBN: 978-0-6489386-2-0
Category: Self-help/personal growth

Cover design: Meng Koach

The views and opinions expressed in this book are those of the author and do not necessarily reflect the official policy or position of any other agency, publisher, organisation, employer, medical body, psychological body, or company. Assumptions made in the analysis are not reflective of the position of any entity other than the author(s) — and, these views are always subject to change, revision, and rethinking at any time.

The author, publisher or organisations are not to be held responsible for misuse, reuse, recycled and cited and/or uncited copies of content within this book by others.

The ideas within this book are coaching creations by the author and are not intended to replace any professional advice or diagnose or treat any health or mental issues. This book is not intended to solve interpersonal relationships or psychological issues but act as a reflective resource for personal development. Personal development and 'masking' is a multi-faceted subject with many different opinions and recommendations, the reader is advised to always seek professional advice according to their specific needs.

The stories and ideas in this book stem from the author's personal experiences and are created from memory. The reader is encouraged to seek professional help in regards to experiences or traumas related to their own sexual identity or interpersonal relationships as themes in this book may trigger or evoke emotion in some readers. Although the details in this book are based on the author's life experiences and unique worldview, some names and identifying details of others have been changed to protect the privacy of individuals.

To my mom,

Thank you. Thank you for the strength you instilled in me. Your love was complicated, but it was real. Through the chaos and the pain you endured, through the moments we were apart and the ones we shared—you remained one thing: my mother.

Every mask you wore, every struggle you faced, you never let it steal your light.

This book, in many ways, is a reflection of the journey we walked together. The ups, the downs, the lessons I learned through you, because of you, and sometimes in spite of you. You continue to be part of my journey every day, in everything I do.

I wish we had more time. I wish things had been different. But I have made peace with what was and hold on to what will always be—you were loved, and you loved in the best way you knew how.

To my younger self,

The little boy who struggled to find his voice, who navigated the unpredictability and chaos. The boy who kept standing back up, no matter how many times he was knocked down. The boy who believed—despite everything—that there was more waiting for him in this big world.

I'm proud of you.

You kept fighting, kept pushing, kept believing. Because of that, this book was born. This book is your voice—the one you couldn't find back then. The words within it hold the messages you were too afraid to speak. But now, your voice is heard.

And through these pages, it will help others find theirs too.

This book is for you!

CONTENTS

Introduction: It Always Starts Somewhere – 1

Chapter 1: The Masks We Wear – 5

Chapter 2: The Mask of Tradition – 17
Navigating Cultural and Societal Norms

Chapter 3: The Mask of Adaptation – 35
Shape-shifting to Survive

Chapter 4: The Mask of Conformity – 51
Blending in to Fit In

Chapter 5: The Mask of Isolation – 71
Withdrawing to Avoid Connection

Chapter 6: The Mask of the Rescuer – 93
Carrying the Weight of Others' Struggles

Chapter 7: The Mask of Defense – 109
Guarding Against Emotional Pain

Chapter 8: The Mask of Approval – 127
Hiding from the Fear of Judgment

Chapter 9: The Mask of the Seducer – 153
Using Charm to Deflect Depth

Chapter 10: The Mask of Independence — 181
Shielding from Dependency

Chapter 11: The Mask of Normalcy — 211
Coping with Life's Challenges

Chapter 12: The Mask of Perfection — 229
Hiding Behind Flawlessness

Chapter 13: The Mask of Survival — 257
Persevering Through Life's Challenges

Chapter 14: The Mask of Cynicism — 279
Defending Against Disappointment

Chapter 15: The Mask of Control — 299
Controlling to Feel Secure

Chapter 16: The Mask of Invulnerability — 337
Shielding from Fear of Vulnerability

The Last Chapter: Moving Forward — 361

Acknowledgements — 387
About the Author — 393
Testimonials — 394
Endnotes — 397

INTRODUCTION

IT ALWAYS STARTS SOMEWHERE

One of my earliest memories is bittersweet, tied to the day my parents' relationship truly ended. It's strange to think about now, how two people who must have shared so much love could have left me with just one memory of them in the same place. And it wasn't a tender moment, or even something mundane like a family dinner. No—it felt like a battle. **A sword fight.**

I was barely three or four years old, too young to understand what was happening but old enough to feel the tension. I remember sitting in the back seat of the car as Mom, her friend John beside her, drove us up to Dad's property. It wasn't a visit, though. It was more like a retrieval mission. We were there to pick up some of Mom's things.

To close this chapter. When the car stopped, my mom stepped out and walked toward the garage, her movements quick, like she wanted to be in and out as fast as possible. I watched from the window as she came back with her fishing rod and a few other things. But then Dad appeared, storming out of the house, gripping a hockey stick in his hand. His face was red with frustration, his body tense with anger.

That's when it happened. To my young eyes, what unfolded wasn't just an argument between two adults—it was a duel. My mom, holding her fishing rod like a spear. My dad, wielding the hockey stick like a sword. Their voices clashed, sharp and cutting, but I couldn't understand the words. All I could see were the weapons they held in their hands and the way they squared off like two people fighting for something much bigger than mere possessions.

It felt like I was watching the world split in two. My heart pounded in my chest, and even though I was safe in the car, I felt like I was in the middle of their fight—like their anger could tear everything apart. It wasn't just their marriage dissolving in front of me. It was the idea of family, of security, of home.

Years later, I learned that their fight was about belongings—who would take what. But back then, it looked like something far more dramatic. It was a battle for control, for closure, for who would walk away with the least damage. And I was caught in the middle of it. **The only memory I have of my parents together is the day they tore our family apart.**

What you just read is one of my earliest memories—a moment that shaped how I came to understand the masks we wear in life.

When I started writing this book in the beginning of 2022, I hadn't even begun venturing down the life coaching path. I've been in the health and wellness space for over 10 years, and I've definitely implemented my fair share of different coaching styles. But it wasn't until January 2023 that I made the decision to dive deeper into understanding not only myself but also how I could help others through life coaching, taking the knowledge I already had and amplifying it.

This book stems from a deeply held belief that everyone's experiences—whether they be joyful, painful, or somewhere in between—hold valuable lessons that can light the path for others. My journey has been eventfully rich with diverse experiences that have not only shaped me into the coach I am today but also into a person who deeply values the transformative power of sharing stories and being vulnerable. This book began as me sharing some significant events in my life and the lessons I learned along the way. But since starting my coaching journey, learning what I've learned not only about myself but also from others I've had the pleasure of working with, I chose to add even more value to this book and truly give you something—tools, lessons, insights—you can use on your own journey, whether you relate to my stories or not.

I wrote this book because, for years, I hid behind different masks—masks that often came in the form of a smile. Whether it was pretending I had everything together or avoiding emotional intimacy, these masks stopped me from fully living and truly connecting with others. It wasn't until much later that I realized how many of us do this, silently struggling beneath the surface.

This book is both a personal journey and a practical guide. It's an invitation to explore the hidden struggles that many of us face but keep to ourselves. Through my own stories and those of others, I hope to inspire you to take off your own masks—one by one—and step into a more authentic, connected life.

Behind the Smile is more than a collection of personal stories; it's an exploration of the hidden struggles many of us face but hide behind a mask. The aim is to bring these stories to light, offering you and others a chance to see the common threads that unite us in our human experience and for you to know that you're not alone. Through these pages, I hope to inspire you and offer solace while providing practical tools that have helped me navigate through some of life's darkest and brightest moments. This book is what I held behind my own smile. The truths of what went on behind the scenes. The stuff you didn't see on social media. The dark, the ugly, the sad but also some of the most beautiful moments in my life. I'm grateful for my journey, as I can now look back and identify the lessons I learned, and I hope, through reading this book, it will help you do the same and find peace.

Throughout the book, you'll learn how to identify *your* masks, understand why you wear them, and take the steps to begin shedding them. Whether it's the Mask of Control, where we try to manipulate our surroundings to feel safe, or the Mask of Normalcy, where we pretend everything's fine when it's not, you'll find insights, reflections, and practical exercises to help you break free.

So let me take you through my journey—the moments of joy, pain, and everything in between—that ultimately led me to uncover the masks I was wearing. Along the way, I hope you'll discover your own.

Let's begin.

CHAPTER 1

THE MASKS WE WEAR

It's no secret that, in today's world, it's becoming more acceptable—perhaps even expected—that we open up and share our feelings. Especially among men, we're seeing this shift toward emotional vulnerability. In urban centers, this openness is increasingly celebrated, but in more rural or traditional settings, and within certain cultural contexts, there remains a significant journey ahead. Even as mental health becomes more openly discussed, a question still remains: Why do we hide? Why do we put on a front and pretend that everything's OK when, deep down, it isn't? Why do we wear these masks?

At the core, it's about protection. We put on these masks to shield ourselves from hurt, from judgment, and from the raw vulnerability that comes with letting others see us as we truly are.

> **Sometimes it feels easier to wear a mask—to pretend we're OK, to downplay our struggles, or to adopt an identity that feels more "acceptable" to the world.**

If you've ever seen Jim Carrey's movie *The Mask*, you know exactly how powerful a mask can be. The protagonist, Stanley Ipkiss, starts out as a timid, self-doubting man. He's walked over at work, unlucky in love, and constantly apologizing for simply existing. But when he stumbles upon an ancient mask, everything changes. The mask transforms him into a wildly confident, unstoppable force of nature. Suddenly, he has the charm, boldness, and fearlessness he always dreamed of.

At first, the mask is thrilling—it unlocks parts of himself he didn't even know existed. It gives him abilities and confidence that feel like freedom. But the more Stanley wears it, the more it begins to consume him. His relationships suffer, his actions spiral out of control, and the line between the mask and his true self starts to blur. The mask, once a tool of empowerment, becomes a prison.

Sound familiar?

Many of us walk through life wearing our own version of Stanley's mask. It may not be a physical object, but we all have ways of hiding—whether it's pretending to be fine when we're not, putting on a brave face, or playing the role we think others want us to play.

At first, the mask serves a purpose. It protects us from pain, shields us from rejection, and helps us navigate situations where we feel unsafe. Like Stanley, it gives us abilities we didn't know we had—confidence, resilience, composure. But over time, if we're not careful, the mask can take over. It becomes less about protection and more about avoidance. And just like in the movie, the longer we wear it, the more it starts to affect our relationships, our decisions, and even how we see ourselves.

THE COST OF WEARING MASKS

When we wear these masks, we may gain short-term approval or avoid discomfort, but the long-term effects are far more damaging. Wearing a mask denies us the chance to be fully seen, fully accepted. It keeps us from forming deep, meaningful relationships. And more than anything, it creates a disconnect between the image we project and the person we truly are underneath.

By holding up these masks, we miss the chance for real connection—both with others and with ourselves. We forget that true strength comes not from avoiding emotions but from facing them head-on. The more we hide behind the masks, the more we distance ourselves from the opportunity for growth, healing, and transformation.

THE MASK OF TRADITION

Navigating Cultural and Societal Norms

The Mask of Tradition is worn by those who feel the weight of family, cultural, or societal expectations. This mask encourages adherence to established norms, even if they conflict with personal desires or values. It can provide a sense of belonging, continuity, and identity, but also restrict personal growth and freedom. The pressure to uphold tradition often leads to internal conflict, as the individual struggles between following their heart and meeting the expectations of their community. While tradition can offer structure and meaning, wearing this mask too tightly stifles individuality and prevents the wearer from exploring their true self.

THE MASK OF ADAPTATION
Shape-shifting to Survive

The Mask of Adaptation is worn by those who have had to continuously change and adjust to survive in challenging environments. Whether it's adapting to a difficult family dynamic, a hostile workplace, or an unpredictable world, this mask allows the wearer to blend in, be flexible, and do whatever's necessary to fit in or survive. The person behind this mask is often highly adaptable, but at the cost of their own identity. Constantly adjusting to others' expectations can leave the wearer feeling lost, unsure of who they truly are outside of the roles they play. While this mask can help navigate difficult situations, it also creates internal conflict as the individual struggles to balance their own needs with the demands of their environment.

THE MASK OF CONFORMITY
Blending in to Fit In

The Mask of Conformity is about blending in to avoid standing out. It's about doing what's expected, rather than what feels authentic. This mask often appears in environments where individuality is seen as a threat or where cultural norms are strict. The wearer finds safety in fitting in, adhering to expectations, and following the crowd.

This mask keeps the individual from expressing their true identity and living authentically. While it provides a sense of belonging and acceptance, the cost is high—it can lead to a loss of self, a suppression of individuality, and an internal conflict between who the wearer is and who they feel they must be.

THE MASK OF ISOLATION
Withdrawing to Avoid Connection

The Mask of Isolation is worn by those who choose to distance themselves from others to avoid vulnerability or emotional pain. It's a defense mechanism often rooted in fear—fear of rejection, fear of judgment, or fear of being hurt. This mask allows the wearer to retreat into their own world, where they feel safe from the emotional risks that come with human connection. While isolation can provide a sense of security, it also leads to deep loneliness and disconnection. The longer this mask is worn, the harder it becomes to remove, as the individual becomes more accustomed to being alone and less willing to take the emotional risks necessary to build meaningful relationships.

THE MASK OF THE RESCUER
Carrying the Weight of Others' Struggles

The Mask of the Rescuer is worn by those who feel compelled to save, fix, or care for others, often at the expense of their own emotional well-being. This mask is rooted in a desire to feel needed, valuable, or in control, and often stems from early experiences of taking on the role of a caregiver. While helping others can bring fulfillment, it also allows the wearer to deflect attention from their own struggles and vulnerabilities. Over time, this mask can lead to burnout, resentment, or a lack of boundaries, as the rescuer becomes so consumed with helping others that they lose sight of their own needs and identity.

THE MASK OF DEFENSE
Guarding Against Emotional Pain

The Mask of Defense is a shield worn by those who have been emotionally wounded and fear further pain. It's a protective barrier, often built after experiences of rejection, betrayal, or trauma. The wearer uses this mask to keep others at a safe distance, making sure they can't get close enough to hurt them again. Common defenses include sarcasm, humor, anger, or emotional aloofness, all of which serve to deflect vulnerability. While this mask can keep emotional pain at bay, it also isolates the wearer, preventing deep emotional connections with others. Over time, the constant defense mechanism can become a lonely, isolating experience, as genuine intimacy is sacrificed for self-protection.

THE MASK OF APPROVAL
Hiding from the Fear of Judgment

The Mask of Approval is worn by those who crave validation and acceptance from others. The need for approval drives the wearer to conform to societal expectations, often at the expense of their own identity. This mask can manifest as people-pleasing, avoiding conflict, or constantly seeking external validation through accomplishments or appearance. It stems from a fear of rejection or not being enough. While the Mask of Approval may make the individual feel temporarily accepted, it becomes exhausting as they suppress their true self in favor of being liked or praised. Over time, the mask can erode self-worth, as the wearer becomes disconnected from their authentic self, relying instead on the opinions of others.

THE MASK OF THE SEDUCER
Using Charm to Deflect Depth

The Mask of the Seducer is a captivating and deceptive defense, one that draws people in while keeping true vulnerability at bay. At first glance, this mask might appear harmless—even flattering. It allows the wearer to use charm, wit, and physical allure to maintain a sense of control in their relationships. But beneath this seductive exterior lies a much deeper struggle: the fear of letting anyone get too close, of allowing someone to see the real, imperfect self behind the charm. Wearing this mask often stems from past emotional wounds, especially those involving rejection or feelings of unworthiness. By seducing or charming others, the wearer receives validation without the risk of being emotionally vulnerable, keeping relationships surface-level and emotionally distant.

THE MASK OF INDEPENDENCE
Shielding from Dependency

The Mask of Independence is worn by those who have learned to rely only on themselves, often because they've been let down by others in the past. This mask allows the wearer to feel in control, self-sufficient, and strong. However, it also prevents them from forming close relationships or asking for help when needed. Independence becomes a source of pride, but it can also become a prison, keeping the wearer isolated and disconnected from others. While this mask can offer a sense of empowerment, it also comes with a sense of loneliness, as the fear of dependency keeps others at a distance.

THE MASK OF NORMALCY
Coping with Life's Challenges

The Mask of Normalcy is worn when the individual pretends that everything is fine, even when they're struggling. This mask is common in a society that values strength and resilience, often leading the wearer to hide their struggles to avoid being seen as weak or vulnerable. It helps them maintain a facade of stability, but it also prevents them from seeking help or expressing their true feelings. The Mask of Normalcy allows the wearer to keep up appearances, but it also leads to internal conflict, as the pressure to maintain the illusion of "normal" can become overwhelming. Over time, this mask can prevent the wearer from addressing their challenges and finding real solutions.

THE MASK OF PERFECTION
Hiding Behind Perceived Flawlessness

The Mask of Perfection is worn by those who believe that being flawless is the only way to be accepted or loved. This mask pushes the individual to strive for unattainable standards, masking insecurities and imperfections behind a polished, seemingly perfect exterior. While it may win approval and admiration, the constant pursuit of perfection is exhausting and unfulfilling. The fear of failure or being seen as imperfect leads to burnout and anxiety. The Mask of Perfection also prevents authentic connection, as the need to appear flawless keeps others from seeing the real, vulnerable person underneath.

THE MASK OF SURVIVAL
Persevering Through Life's Challenges

The Mask of Survival is worn by those who have been through extreme hardship and have had to rely on their resilience to get through. This mask reflects the drive to push through life's most difficult moments, often at the expense of emotional and mental well-being. The wearer becomes a master of endurance, able to soldier on when others might give up. While this mask provides the strength needed to navigate tough times, it also blocks the individual from acknowledging their vulnerabilities and asking for help. The Mask of Survival can create a sense of invincibility, but deep down the wearer may be exhausted, longing for relief and connection. Over time, this mask becomes a heavy burden, as the constant need to survive prevents the wearer from thriving.

THE MASK OF CYNICISM
Defending Against Disappointment

The Mask of Cynicism is worn by those who have been let down by life, relationships, or society. This mask shields the wearer from disappointment by making them skeptical or negative about the world. It offers protection from further emotional pain by preemptively dismissing hope, trust, and optimism. While it may feel like wisdom, cynicism narrows the wearer's perspective, preventing them from experiencing the full range of life's possibilities. It creates emotional distance in relationships, as the fear of disappointment keeps the wearer from being vulnerable or open to new experiences.

THE MASK OF CONTROL

Controlling to Feel Secure

The Mask of Control is worn by those who fear unpredictability and chaos, often stemming from early experiences where life felt out of their control. This mask reflects the need to manage every detail, relationship, and outcome to maintain a sense of safety. The wearer may attempt to control their emotions, surroundings, or even other people as a way to avoid vulnerability, uncertainty, or failure. At its core, the Mask of Control is about creating a sense of order in a world that feels overwhelming.

THE MASK OF INVULNERABILITY

Shielding from Fear of Vulnerability

The Mask of Invulnerability is often worn by those who fear emotional exposure, vulnerability, and being hurt. This mask creates a barrier between the wearer and the world, protecting them from perceived emotional threats. For many, it's developed early in life, particularly after experiencing rejection, betrayal, or loss. Over time, it becomes a defense mechanism, a way to keep others from getting too close. Wearing this mask helps the individual feel in control and safe, but it also means they can't connect with others on a deeper level. While it offers a sense of security, it comes at the cost of intimacy, leaving the wearer feeling isolated, even when surrounded by others.

BREAKING THE CYCLE

In the pages that follow, we will explore these masks in greater detail—their origins, how they manifest, and how to begin the process of removing them. It's not easy work, but it is necessary. By becoming aware of the masks we wear, we take the first step toward breaking the cycle. When we dare to take off the mask, even for a moment, we give ourselves the gift of being truly seen.

The journey toward authenticity begins with understanding that the masks we wear were never meant to be permanent fixtures in our lives. It's time to take them off, one by one, and experience the freedom that comes with embracing our true selves.

CHAPTER 2

THE MASK OF
TRADITION

NAVIGATING CULTURAL AND
SOCIETAL NORMS

The Cycle of Tradition

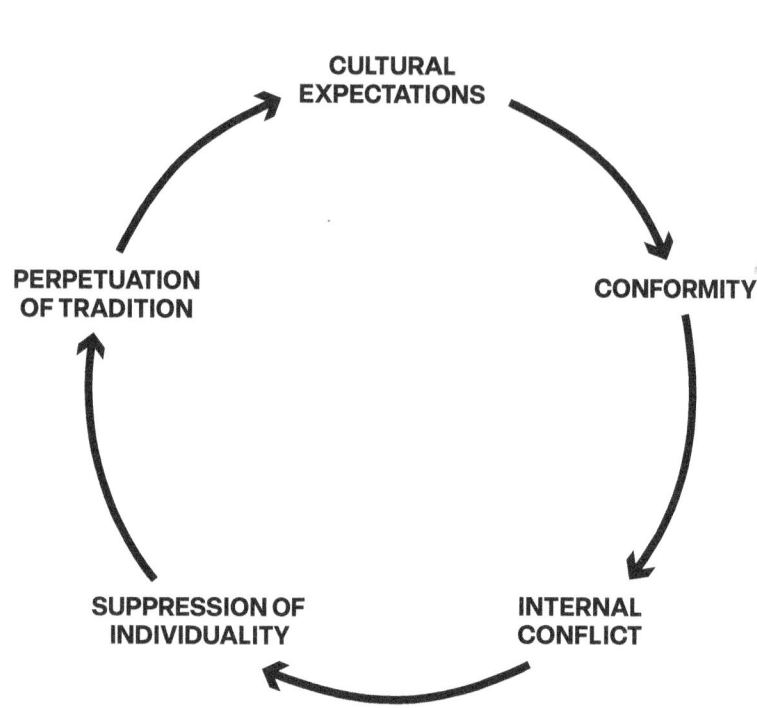

I remember vividly standing by the lake outside my dad's house, staring across the water as the sun dipped behind the mountains. I must have been no older than 10, but even at that age, I could feel the weight of expectations settling heavily on my young shoulders. The wind was cool, carrying the scent of pine and earth, and the lake was calm, reflecting the fading colors of the sky, but my mind was anything but peaceful. As I stood there, I repeated a mantra I had convinced myself I needed to believe: *wife, kids, white picket fence, wife, kids, white picket fence.* Over and over, I whispered it, as if saying it enough would make it true.

It wasn't my dream. It wasn't something that naturally came from within me. But growing up, this was the ideal that had been etched into me—by family, by society, by tradition. This was the life I was supposed to strive for, the life that would prove that I had made it, that I was enough. The Mask of Tradition was already being molded to my face, and I wasn't even aware of it.

I told myself this was what it meant to be a man: stability, a family, a perfectly structured life. There was no room for deviation from the script. Anything else felt like failure, or worse, rebellion. And yet, even as I tried to make myself believe in this vision, there was a quiet voice within me—one I wasn't ready to fully listen to—that questioned whether any of it would truly make me happy.

Growing up in a small town, expectations were amplified. The traditional values of the community—get a good job, settle down, start a family—were ever-present, and I quickly realized that stepping outside those lines could invite judgment. The idea of success was well-defined and rigid: follow the well-trodden path or risk being labeled an outsider. At home, there were unspoken rules, too, shaped by the way my parents navigated their lives and relationships. These family traditions molded my early worldview.

But with time, I began to notice the cracks in the foundation—how these rigid traditions didn't always fit who I was becoming. I started to feel the tension between the life I was expected to lead and the person I truly was. The more I tried to conform, the more I realized I was wearing a mask, one that made me appear as though I fit the mold of tradition, but left me feeling disconnected from myself.

THE ORIGINS AND STRANGLEHOLD OF TRADITION

We're all born into some sort of tradition, whether culturally, societally, or within the family unit. These traditions shape our earliest understanding of life—what's expected of us and how the world's meant to be. Growing up, we rarely question these norms because, to us, they're simply "the way things are." Depending on where you're born, the scale of your town, and the specific cultural circumstances of your upbringing, these traditions can vary significantly. But no matter where you are, one thing is consistent: tradition feels like a rulebook for how life should unfold. It's passed down to us, a hand-me-down worldview from our parents, shaped by what they were taught and what society demands.

Back in the day, it was harder to challenge or even see past these traditions. Without the internet or a way to easily access different perspectives, people often lived and died adhering to these cultural or societal expectations. In small towns, it might have meant inheriting the family farm, working the land as your ancestors did. In other parts of the world, it might have meant accepting an arranged marriage because "that's just the way it's done."

> **Tradition often provides comfort, a sense of continuity with the past. But it becomes a mask when we wear it too tightly—when it prevents us from becoming who we truly are, stifling our growth and individuality.**

Tradition becomes a facade, a role we feel obligated to play, even if it no longer fits the person we're growing into.

GROWING UP IN THE MASK OF TRADITION

I was born on September 20, 1989, adding to a family of three that included my parents and my older sister, who was three at the time. My birthplace was a picturesque small town called Smithers, nestled in the Bulkley Valley of northwestern British Columbia, Canada. From the moment you drive into Smithers, you're greeted by a striking view: the towering Hudson Bay Mountain to the west and the Babine Mountain Range to the east. It's breathtaking, and even now, whenever I return, it still takes my breath away, as if I'm seeing it for the first time.

Smithers is a town with a vibrant, adventurous spirit. It caters to nature lovers and thrill seekers, and the alpine theme that runs through its architecture adds a sense of charm and old-world tradition. Driving down Main Street, you're welcomed by a statue of a man with an alpine horn, a reminder of the town's deep-rooted connection to its heritage. It's a place that proudly displays its traditions, especially during the winter months when tourists flock to the local ski resort on Hudson Bay Mountain.

Growing up in Smithers felt like living in a constant adventure playground. Nature wasn't just something we appreciated from a distance—it was our backyard. My love for the outdoors was cultivated by the endless opportunities for skiing, hiking, fishing, and exploring the vast landscapes. These early experiences laid the foundation for my love of nature and later shaped my career, where I often encourage clients to seek the peace that nature can offer.

In many ways, tradition defined the path that seemed laid out for me. My dad was the embodiment of rugged masculinity. He was an outdoorsman, and our life in Smithers reflected that. We lived 15 minutes out of town, in a house that he had built on top of a hill, surrounded by nature. It was a remote retreat, with views of the valley below and the Hudson Bay Mountains standing tall in the distance.

The house overlooked a private lake, surrounded by towering Douglas fir, spruce, aspen, and birch trees. In the fall, the vibrant colors of the trees mirrored off the lake, creating a beautiful, peaceful haven. This was the backdrop of my childhood—the place where I learned the importance of resilience, nature, and simplicity. But beyond the physical beauty, there was an undercurrent of tradition, a set of unwritten rules I was expected to follow.

My father's property was more than just a retreat—it was a working farm. We had chickens, ducks, and pigs. My favorite was a giant sow named Charlotte. On hot summer days, I'd climb onto her back while she lay in the mud, scratching her ears. It was one of my favorite memories, at least until one evening at dinner when Dad casually asked, "How's Charlotte taste?"

At the time, I didn't understand the deeper implications of these traditions. All I knew was the world I grew up in—country life, small town, masculine outdoorsman for a father, and church on occasion. It wasn't until I grew older that I began to question the path laid out for me and whether it truly fit the person I was becoming.

HOW TRADITION SHAPES US AND HOLDS US BACK

In many small towns like Smithers, tradition is worn like a badge of honor. It's passed down, from father to son, mother to daughter, often without question. You inherit not just the family name but also the family's way of doing things—the expectation to follow in their footsteps, live life by their rules, and maintain the legacy they've built. In my case, it was the expectation to embrace the outdoors, become independent, and carry on the masculine ideals my father upheld.

But the Mask of Tradition, while offering a sense of belonging and continuity, also has a way of stifling personal growth.

For many people, breaking away from tradition feels like betrayal—betrayal of family, culture, or community. It's like stepping off a path that's been laid for you for generations and wandering into uncharted territory.

This tension between honoring tradition and finding our own way is something many of us face, especially when the traditions no longer serve us. But as I grew older, I realized that the Mask of Tradition was just that—a mask. And while it provided comfort and stability, it wasn't the only path. There was room for me to carve out my own path, one that honored where I came from but also allowed me to grow into who I was meant to be.

THE FLIP (POSITIVE) SIDE OF TRADITION

For me, tradition wasn't just about grand cultural or religious rituals. It was also the small, quirky family celebrations and rituals that shaped my sense of belonging and identity. Pokémon, one of my earliest obsessions, became a staple in my personal traditions. Every Thursday, without fail, Mom would pick me up from school and take me to the local 7-Eleven to buy a new packet of Pokémon cards. Over time, I ended up collecting 'em all. This obsession wasn't lost on my family, and birthdays and Christmases quickly became Pokémon-themed extravaganzas, with every gift connected to this one passion.

Birthdays were a big deal in our household. Most of my birthday parties were held at my mom's house, with around 15 or so school friends. Mom's best friend, Barry—whom we called "Uncle Barry"—was always the life of the party. He was a magician and would show up dressed as a clown or some other whimsical character, performing magic tricks that captivated us kids. But the most memorable part of those birthday parties was a quirky tradition Mom and her partner Gary invented: They would fill a giant garbage bag with random items of clothing from around the house—ski goggles, socks, my mom's bras and underwear, even Gary's old sweaters. Each kid would blindly reach into the bag and pull out an item, putting it on no matter how ridiculous or oversized it was. By the end, we all looked absurd—an ensemble of misfits marching down the street, waving at passing neighbors. It was our little tradition, our unique way of celebrating, and while it may have seemed silly, it brought joy and a sense of belonging.

Rob and his mom during a traditional birthday celebration.

Traditional birthday party dress-up (Rob and friends).

Tradition also played a significant role on my dad's side. Every Sunday, without fail, he would pile all of us kids into the car and take us to the pool. It was a simple but consistent way of bonding—splashing around, playing games, and just being together as a family. But Sundays weren't just limited to pool time. During hunting season, those family outings took a different turn. Dad, an avid hunter, would take us out into the wilderness, and it was there that I first learned about patience, precision, and the rituals of hunting. He would carry the big guns and handle the larger game, like moose and deer. I, on the other hand, was given a little .22 rifle. At the time, it felt like the perfect size for me. Though, looking back now, it seems almost toylike. But to me then, it was everything. When a grouse wandered into view, Dad would let me take aim and practice, teaching me how to shoot and instilling in me a sense of responsibility.

THE MASK OF TRADITION: WHY WE WEAR IT

Tradition tells us who we should be, what we should value, and how we should act. As children, we absorb these traditions without thinking; they become the lens through which we see the world. But as we grow, there can be a conflict between who we are and what tradition tells us we should be.

One of the most powerful traditions in my family was our observance of Remembrance Day. Every year, my father, being the commanding officer of the Sea Cadets, a position he held after his time in the navy, led the parade. I would stand in silence alongside my family as the town gathered to honor those who served and died in conflict. Wearing our poppies and standing still on the 11th hour of the 11th day of the 11th month, it was a day to remember those who had fought in World War I and all wars thereafter. I would watch my father lead the cadets down the main street, and later, when I became a cadet myself, I joined in, marching in tribute.

This tradition was deeply ingrained in me from a young age. It wasn't just about honoring the fallen; it was about respecting the past and the values my family, especially my father, held dear. It was a powerful symbol of the importance of remembering our history, of showing respect, and upholding a sense of duty.

Traditions like this—whether they're family customs or cultural practices—shape who we are. But the Mask of Tradition can also come with its own set of challenges. While these customs connect us to our heritage and provide a sense of belonging, they can also create pressure to conform, even when those traditions no longer align with our true selves.

THE IMPACT OF TRADITION ON PERSONAL EXPRESSION

Traditions can provide stability, comfort, and a sense of continuity. They ground us in something bigger than ourselves, linking the past to the present. But there are times when these traditions limit our ability to express our individuality. Growing up, I felt the pressure of living according to the traditions and expectations of my father, of adhering to what was considered "normal." Even at the age of 10, repeating to myself, *Wife, kids, white picket fence,* I felt the weight of expectation, even though deep down I knew it didn't fully resonate with who I was.

This isn't something that solely affects men; women, too, are heavily impacted by the Mask of Tradition. I've watched women in my community and beyond navigate the pressures of traditional gender roles—roles that often confine them to certain expectations around marriage, motherhood, and appearance. Whether it's the expectation to be a caregiver, to prioritize family over personal ambitions, or to follow the path laid out for them by their parents, women also wear this mask, and the pressure can be suffocating.

For example, in many cultures, women are expected to get married by a certain age, bear children, and prioritize their roles as wives and mothers above all else. In some cultures, there's a tradition of arranged marriages, where women have little say in choosing their life partner. They wear the Mask of Tradition, sacrificing their personal desires for the sake of upholding family honor and societal norms. Even in more progressive societies, there's often an unspoken pressure for women to "have it all"—a career, a family, a perfect home—while maintaining societal standards of beauty and composure.

Many women grow up internalizing the belief that their worth is tied to their ability to meet these traditional expectations. Even when they have other dreams—whether it's pursuing a career, delaying marriage, or choosing a different life path—breaking away from these norms can feel like betraying their family or dishonoring their culture, fueling an underlying struggle for autonomy and self-expression.

STEPS TO REMOVE THE MASK OF TRADITION

While traditions can offer comfort and structure, they can also feel limiting when they no longer serve who we are today. Recognizing when it's time to remove the Mask of Tradition can be a challenging but liberating experience.

1. **Reflect on your values:** Start by asking yourself if the traditions you uphold truly align with your values. Are they enriching your life? Or are they expectations passed down that no longer resonate with you? Take a moment to reflect on whether you're living according to what truly matters to you or if you're conforming out of fear or obligation.
2. **Identify what serves you:** Not every tradition needs to be discarded. Some can still bring joy, connection, or a sense of belonging. Consider which traditions bring fulfillment, and let go of those that feel restrictive or disconnected from your true self.
3. **Give yourself permission to evolve:** It's OK to outgrow certain traditions. Evolution is part of the human experience. Breaking away from long-established customs doesn't mean dishonoring your heritage; it means you're allowing yourself to

grow authentically, creating room for new experiences.
4. **Communicate with loved ones:** Many of us fear judgment or rejection when stepping away from tradition. Open conversations with loved ones can pave the way for understanding and reduce the pressure to conform. You may even find that others are also seeking change but feel too afraid to speak up.
5. **Balance honoring and redefining:** Finding a balance is key. It's possible to honor meaningful traditions while creating new ones that reflect who you are today. By doing this, you maintain a connection to your roots while staying true to your evolving identity.
6. **Practice self-compassion:** Breaking free from tradition can stir up feelings of guilt or fear. Be kind to yourself as you navigate these emotions. This journey toward authenticity isn't easy, but it's one filled with growth and self-discovery.
7. **Embrace the unknown:** Finally, embrace the uncertainty that comes with change. Tradition provides a sense of security, but stepping into the unknown can offer personal transformation and a renewed sense of purpose. Trust in your ability to handle whatever lies ahead.

REFLECTIONS AND LEARNINGS: THE MASK OF TRADITION

Reflecting on Traditions in Your Life

My story: Growing up in Smithers, I experienced a range of traditions—from birthday parties filled with magic and laughter to Christmases spent hopping between my parents' homes. These traditions shaped my sense of belonging and structure, even when they conflicted with my deeper personal desires.

Your reflection: Think about the traditions that shaped your upbringing. Were they comforting or restricting? How did these traditions influence the way you see the world today?

Exercise: Write down a tradition from your childhood. Reflect on how it made you feel at the time and whether it still holds meaning for you today. Is it something you want to continue, or is it time to let it go?

Navigating Cultural and Societal Expectations

My story: The weight of societal expectations often conflicted with my personal sense of self. As a young boy, I felt the pressure to follow a certain path—one defined by my father and the larger community. The "wife, kids, white picket fence" mantra echoed in my mind, even though it didn't feel right to me.

Your reflection: Have you ever felt pressure to conform to societal or familial expectations that didn't align with your true desires? How have you navigated these expectations?

Exercise: Identify one area in your life where you feel pressured to conform to a tradition or expectation. How does this affect your happiness and fulfillment? What steps can you take to align more closely with your true values?

Balancing Tradition with Personal Identity

My story: As I grew older, I began to realize that some traditions no longer served me. The traditions passed down by my family provided a sense of stability, but they also stifled my sense of individuality. This internal conflict between honoring the past and embracing who I truly was became a defining challenge.

Your reflection: Reflect on how traditions have shaped your identity. Have they helped you feel grounded, or have they limited your personal growth? How do you balance honoring your heritage with being true to yourself?

Exercise: Write about a time when you felt torn between following a tradition and following your own path. What did you decide? How did that choice impact your sense of self?

Understanding the Role of Tradition in Relationships

My story: Watching my father and the men in my community struggle with traditional masculine expectations had a profound impact on how I viewed relationships. I saw firsthand how these traditions created barriers to vulnerability, love, and authenticity.

Your reflection: Have the traditions or expectations passed down to you influenced how you approach relationships? How do they impact your ability to connect with others on a deeper level?

Exercise: Think of a relationship where traditions or societal expectations have played a significant role. How do these expectations shape your interactions? What changes might be needed to foster more authentic connections?

Letting Go of Traditions That No Longer Serve You

My story: There came a point when I realized that adhering to tradition out of fear or obligation was holding me back. Letting go of certain traditions allowed me to embrace my own identity and create new, more meaningful practices.

Your reflection: Are there traditions in your life that no longer align with your personal values or desires? What fears or barriers keep you from letting them go?

Exercise: Identify one tradition or expectation that no longer serves you. What steps can you take to release it? How will doing so create space for new growth and opportunities?

MASK OF TRADITION
KEY TAKEAWAYS

- **Tradition and identity:** Traditions can offer stability and a sense of belonging, but they can also limit personal growth if they conflict with your true self. Reflect on which traditions serve you and which you may need to let go.
- **Balancing heritage and authenticity:** Honoring the past doesn't mean you must conform to every tradition. Find a balance that allows you to respect your heritage while staying true to your personal values.
- **The power of reflection:** Taking time to reflect on the traditions you follow allows you to gain clarity

on whether they align with your authentic self. Give yourself permission to evolve and redefine what tradition means to you.

- **Challenging societal norms:** Traditions often come with societal expectations. It's important to recognize when these expectations are limiting your personal expression and to have the courage to challenge them.
- **Creating new traditions:** As you grow and evolve, creating your own traditions can offer a sense of grounding and purpose. Embrace the freedom to forge new paths that reflect who you are today.
- **Connection and support:** Tradition can both connect and divide us. Seek support when breaking free from traditions that no longer serve you, and surround yourself with people who honor your journey toward authenticity.

CHAPTER 3

THE MASK OF ADAPTATION

SHAPE-SHIFTING TO SURVIVE

The Cycle of Adaptation

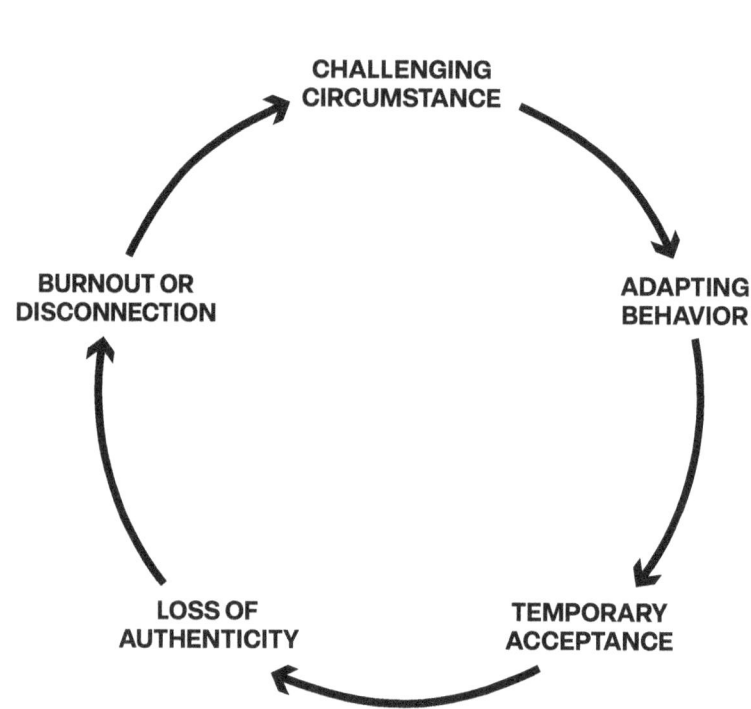

After my parents' divorce, my life and my sister's life were split in two—living between two homes, two personalities, chaos and quiet. Not only did I learn to adapt to the physical spaces I was shuffled between each week, but I also had to adjust to the revolving cast of adults and siblings who entered and exited my life. New aunts, new uncles, new stepmoms, new stepdads—all bringing different energies and dynamics, and with each new arrival, I had to find my place all over again.

I never questioned it at the time. It was just how life was. But looking back now, I see how often I wore the Mask of Adaptation—shifting my behavior, my attitude, even my identity to keep up with the constant change. Molding myself to fit whatever environment or relationship I was in became second nature, even though I didn't realize it at the time.

> **As kids, we don't get a say in what happens between our parents. Where we live, what we eat, who our new family members are—these decisions are made for us. We're simply told, "This is your new life now," and we're expected to adapt.**

Looking back, I realize that the constant changes and unpredictability of my childhood shaped me in ways I didn't fully understand until much later. I believe that the Mask of Adaptation first formed during these early years, when I had to quickly adjust to the new realities life threw my way. Adapting became a survival skill, one I carried into adulthood.

A TALE OF TWO HOMES

Despite the turbulence, each home offered its own form of escape. My father's property was an expansive playground where my siblings and I deeply engaged with nature. It was a haven of rugged adventure—countless hours were spent building tree forts, swimming in the lake, skating on it during the winter, and joining my dad on moose or grouse hunts. His world was a raw, unfiltered experience of the outdoors, where you learned the value of resilience through action.

My mother's home, on the other hand, provided a different kind of adventure. It was more intimate, nestled in a bustling neighborhood full of kids, animals, and winding roads, which I explored with wild curiosity. The absence of cell phones and social media meant our adventures were tangible and real—scraping our knees, getting our hands dirty, and creating entire worlds with just our imaginations.

Rob's mom's house in Smithers (back view).

Mom's house was a sanctuary, a beautiful log home just five minutes from town, surrounded by five acres of land. The drive to her house was like stepping into a postcard. The high windows reaching up to the roof, offering breathtaking views of the Hudson Bay Mountains, and the large brick fireplace added to the rustic charm of our home. She had a love for gardening, and our summers were spent with our hands in the dirt, nurturing life. This experience planted the early seeds of my love for the outdoors. Mom's neighbor, Ann, had a collection of animals, turning her property into something of a sanctuary. We'd often drive down "rabbit road," named for the bunnies that littered the area. It was like being in a world untouched by time.

Rob's mom's house in Smithers (side view).

In these two vastly different homes, I learned to adapt—quickly. The shift from the rugged wilderness of my dad's house to the more communal, structured atmosphere of my mother's home created a blueprint for resilience. I became fluent in the art of change. These constant transitions made me nimble, flexible, and open to new experiences, but they also carried an emotional weight, a reminder that my life didn't fit the traditional mold. There wasn't a "normal family" to look up to or a consistent set of rules. The concept of tradition was more fluid, and I found myself learning to navigate what many would consider a broken home.

WHEN RELATIONSHIPS END, OTHERS BEGIN

The divorce was just the beginning of the constant shifts in my life. My dad quickly entered into a new relationship with a woman named

Kate, and soon my world, and our family, expanded with the arrival of my two half-sisters. Sundays became ritualized with church visits, dressing up in our Sunday best, attending mass, and trying to fit into this new life.

However, when their relationship dissolved, so did the churchgoing. Following their separation, my interactions with my new sisters became sporadic, relegated to them visiting every other weekend. They were homeschooled on a farm with their mother and her new partner, which added another layer of separation. This shift in family structure, the sporadic interactions, the shuffling back and forth—it all felt more like scheduled playdates than building actual relationships. This transient, patchwork family dynamic only deepened my need to adapt, highlighting how relationships—especially early in life—can be fleeting and disconnected.

While my dad's relationships were evolving, my mom found Gary. Gary's lifestyle was worlds apart from what I was used to. His life was a mix of chaos and disorder—a cluttered house that reeked of cigarettes, filled with beer cans, with stacks of rock records scattered everywhere. To a young kid, it felt like another world—gritty, dark, and nothing I aspired to.

Yet, despite the disorder, Gary had his good moments. He stepped up and took us on camping trips, down to the river with the dogs, and joined in family walks, with our cats and dogs trailing behind us.

On the other side of my life, my dad's next partner, Michelle, brought a completely different energy. She was the mother of three boys, a homemaker, and her arrival turned our family dynamic into a bustling, joyful mess. With her sister and two kids often around, family dinners and chaotic playtimes became the norm. I was no longer the youngest, which gave me a strange kind of freedom—I didn't get into as much trouble. And with a house full of boys and cousins, adventure was never far away. Weekends were alive with activity, and there was a sense of inclusion that came with being part of such a large extended family.

Two years after they met, Dad and Michelle got engaged, and their wedding took place in a backyard ceremony where everyone dressed in white. My sisters all carried bouquets of wildflowers—paintbrushes and fireweed—symbolizing both the simplicity and beauty of our new family unit.

Michelle was also part of the Society for Creative Anachronism (SCA), a medieval reenactment group that opened up an entirely new world for me. I participated in archery competitions, dressed up in armor, and even wrote poetry to woo a princess. I also took on the name Legolas from *The Lord of the Rings* to match my archery skills. These experiences gave me the space to experiment with different parts of myself, allowing me to escape reality for a while and step into different roles. It was through these events that I found a channel for creativity and expression, providing me with moments of respite where I didn't have to adapt to anyone else—I could just be someone entirely new for a few days.

Each new relationship in my parents' lives introduced me to different versions of family. From Kate and the church-filled Sundays, to Gary's chaotic but occasionally heartwarming presence, to Michelle and her vibrant extended family, I learned that family was fluid. These experiences shaped my understanding of how relationships work, how people come and go, and how adaptability wasn't just a skill, but a necessity. I didn't have a choice but to keep changing, learning to navigate these different personalities, environments, and dynamics.

THE EXPERT ADAPTER

The Mask of Adaptation is worn by those who have learned to adjust to every situation in order to fit in or survive. It's a mask that shifts depending on the environment, the people around us, or the expectations placed upon us. While adaptability can be a great strength, when this mask is worn too tightly, it can lead to a loss of self—our true identity buried beneath the versions of ourselves we present to the world …

At a young age, I became an expert at reading the room, understanding who I needed to be in any given situation, and making sure I didn't disrupt the flow. But this constant shape-shifting came at a cost. Over time, I realized that I didn't know who I truly was. I was so busy adapting to everyone else's needs and expectations that I never had a chance to explore my own. This is the danger of the Mask of Adaptation—it helps you navigate difficult situations, but it also distances you from your authentic self. We become chameleons, constantly shifting our identity based on what we think others want or expect from us, never fully comfortable in our own skin.

The benefit of this mask is that it allows us to navigate difficult environments or relationships with ease. It can be a survival tool, enabling us to blend into different situations and relationships seamlessly. We can be the person others need us to be, ensuring our acceptance or survival. This adaptability can feel like a strength, giving us the flexibility to adjust to life's curveballs. But the downside is that we often feel disconnected from our own desires, values, or identity. When worn for too long, it becomes difficult to peel back the layers and rediscover the person beneath. We may start to question who we are without the influence of others, constantly wondering, *Who am I, really, when no one else is around?* We become exhausted from shape-shifting, emotionally burned-out from the effort it takes to keep up. Relationships formed while wearing this mask may lack depth because they're built on inauthentic foundations.

It's funny when I think about my ability to adapt to different environments and situations—I've always seen it as a massive strength, and to this day I still think it is. But looking back, I see how the skill of adaptation was forced upon me, born out of the constant changes happening around me as a little boy. I know this is common for many children, especially in households where parents separate, siblings leave, or even in situations of loss. We're often left feeling different, and we learn to adapt to survive.

For me, as a little gay boy, adapting to my surroundings became second nature. All throughout life, it wasn't just about the big moments—like moving to a new school, starting a new job, or even immigrating to Australia—it was about constantly adjusting to whatever life threw my way. Whether it was a new family dynamic or a shift in culture, I had to adapt. This mask of adaptation forms in response to environments where we feel we must change ourselves to fit in, survive, or avoid conflict.

I always come back to the image of the vine tree when thinking about this mask. I even have one tattooed on my torso.

> **The vine tree represents fluidity, adaptability, and growth. No matter where it's planted, it flourishes. That's how I've always felt—able to adapt and thrive no matter what environment I find myself in. Even in the toughest times, I've adapted; I've thrived.**

Over time, as we wear this mask, we may feel unworthy of acceptance for who we really are. We may internalize feelings of inadequacy, questioning whether our true self is enough. We become so skilled at adapting that we lose sight of who we are, making it incredibly difficult to reclaim our authentic identity.

Research from John Bowlby's attachment theory provides significant insights into how children adapt to their environments, particularly in unpredictable or unstable settings. In the field of developmental psychology, it has been found that children who grow up with constant changes—whether it's moving homes, changing schools, or experiencing family conflict—develop adaptive social behaviors to manage the ongoing flux around them. According to a study on adaptive social behaviors in childhood development, these strategies, while protective in the short term, can lead to long-term challenges, particularly in establishing a stable sense of self.[1]

As a child, I was so accustomed to shifting to meet the demands of my surroundings that, as I grew into adulthood, I continued to mold myself to cater to the needs of others. It became second nature, to the point where I started losing touch with my own sense of identity. I never questioned it. But as I reflect now, I see how deeply rooted this pattern was. Bowlby's study highlights how children who adapt to family instability often grow into adults who struggle with boundaries or understanding their emotional needs. When I read that, it hit close to home. I struggled with setting boundaries in relationships and fully understanding my own emotional needs because my ability to adapt became so ingrained that I rarely stopped to ask myself, *Who am I beneath this mask?*

STEPS TO REMOVE THE MASK OF ADAPTATION

As much as the Mask of Adaptation may have served me growing up, I eventually realized that continuing to wear it was holding me back from fully embracing my true self. While adaptability can be a powerful tool, it should never come at the cost of our identity. The key to shedding this mask lies in recognizing when it no longer serves us and taking steps to rediscover who we truly are.

1. **Acknowledge your authentic self:** Recognize that constantly adapting to fit others' expectations comes at the cost of your true identity. Take time to explore who you are without the pressures of outside forces. This could involve journaling, self-reflection, or talking with trusted friends or therapists about your true desires and values.
2. **Identify the situations that trigger adaptation:** Observe when and why you tend to put on this mask. Is it around certain people or in specific environments? By identifying these triggers, you can start to understand the underlying fears driving your need to adapt.
3. **Start small with authenticity:** Practice showing up as your

authentic self in small, low-risk situations. Begin to express your true thoughts, desires, and feelings, even if it feels uncomfortable. Over time, you will build confidence in being yourself, even in more challenging environments.

4. **Learn to trust in acceptance:** Recognize that true belonging doesn't come from blending in—it comes from being accepted for who you are. Gradually allow yourself to be seen, even if it means risking rejection or conflict. Trust that the right people and environments will embrace you, flaws and all.

5. **Create stability internally, not externally:** Instead of seeking external stability by adapting to your surroundings, work on cultivating internal stability through mindfulness, self-care, and personal boundaries. This inner foundation will allow you to remain authentic, even when external circumstances are uncertain.

REFLECTIONS AND LEARNINGS: THE MASK OF ADAPTATION

Reflecting on Your Early Adaptations

My story: From the constant shuffling between my parents' homes to the presence of numerous adult figures, I had to adapt quickly to new environments and personalities.

Your reflection: Think about the situations in your life where you've felt the need to adapt. What were the circumstances that pushed you into that space?

Exercise: Take a moment to write down one or two instances where you felt you had to adapt to fit in or survive. How did that shape who you are today?

Recognizing the Power and Cost of Adaptability

My story: While my ability to adapt became a superpower, it also masked my true self. Over time, I lost sight of my own desires and identity.

Your reflection: In what ways has adaptability served you? In what ways has it limited you?

Exercise: Write down the pros and cons of being adaptable in your life. How can you leverage the benefits while staying true to yourself?

Learning to Be Yourself in Every Environment

My story: I learned that constantly adapting to others' expectations made me lose touch with my authentic self.

Your reflection: Are there environments or people that still trigger you to wear this mask? How can you begin to show up as your authentic self in those situations?

Exercise: Write about a time when you felt like you weren't being true to yourself. How can you start to show up more authentically in that environment or relationship?

Building Inner Stability

My story: Over time, I realized that true stability doesn't come from changing who I am to fit into my surroundings, but from building a strong sense of self within.

Your reflection: How can you create internal stability in your life?

Exercise: Reflect on what practices, boundaries, or self-care routines could help you stay grounded and authentic, no matter the environment.

Learning from the Past—Boundaries and Emotional Needs

My story: Looking back, I realized that my childhood—constantly moving between homes and adjusting to the ever-changing dynamics around me—may have contributed to my struggles with setting boundaries and understanding my emotional needs as an adult. The constant adaptation created a pattern where I focused more on others' needs than my own, leaving me disconnected from my personal emotional boundaries.

Your reflection: Reflect on whether your own childhood experiences have impacted your ability to set boundaries or express your emotional needs. How has this shaped your relationships or personal growth?

Exercise: Identify one area of your life where you struggle with boundaries or expressing your emotions. What small step can you take this week to better understand and communicate your needs in that area?

MASK OF ADAPTATION KEY TAKEAWAYS

- **Adaptability is a strength, but not at the cost of your identity**: Adaptation is crucial for survival in changing circumstances, but losing yourself in the process isn't a solution. There's power in knowing when to adapt and when to stay true to who you are.
- **The importance of inner stability**: True stability doesn't come from your external environment; it comes from building a strong foundation within. Developing personal boundaries and learning to trust in your own identity can provide a sense of grounding, even when the world around you is uncertain.
- **Authenticity over blending in**: The need to adapt often stems from a desire for acceptance, but true belonging happens when you're accepted for who you truly are, not for who you become to fit in.
- **Identify your triggers**: By understanding what situations or relationships make you feel the need to adapt, you can begin to challenge those patterns and show up more authentically.
- **Start small and build confidence**: You don't have

to completely discard this mask overnight. Begin with small steps toward authenticity and gradually build the courage to show up fully as yourself.

- **Boundaries and emotional needs**: Recognize the impact of your upbringing on your current ability to set boundaries and understand your emotional needs. Reflect on areas where you've neglected these aspects and start making conscious efforts to assert your needs and establish boundaries.

CHAPTER 4

THE MASK OF
CONFORMITY

BLENDING IN TO FIT IN

The Cycle of Conformity

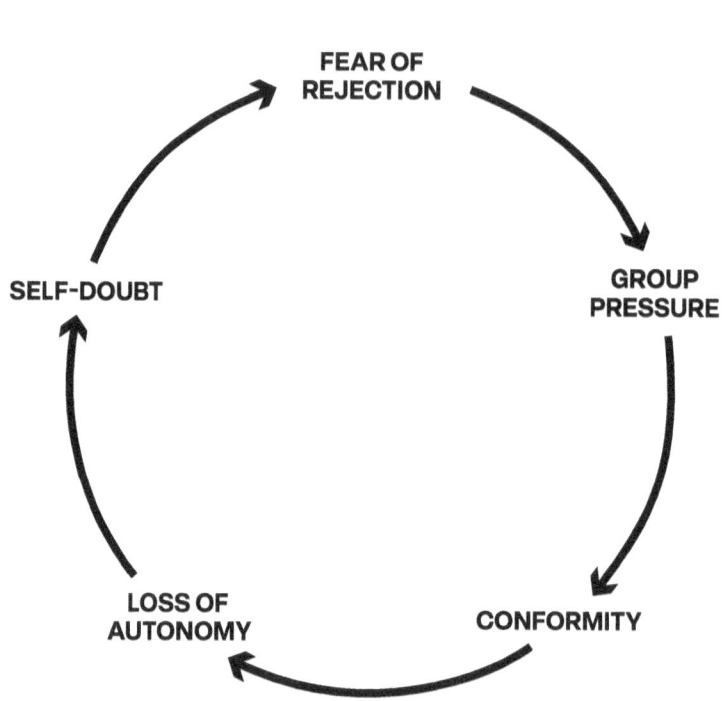

My first school was St. Joseph's Catholic school, a place where conformity wasn't just encouraged—it was ingrained. Like any school, there were cliques that formed early on: the sporty guys, the geeks, the pretty girls, and the misfits. But I never really felt like I belonged to any specific group. I floated somewhere in between, observing how others fit into their roles while I tried to figure out where I stood. Even now, as an adult, I often feel like I'm standing on the outside, looking in at the tight-knit bonds that some people formed in their early years. You know the type—those childhood friends who grow up together, stay together, and carry their friendship into adulthood. That was never me.

By the time I reached grade six, I was curious about a lot—especially about myself. Another boy and I would have sleepovers, where we would experiment, exploring feelings that were confusing yet exciting. During school, we'd even sneak into the bathroom, hiding in a stall and, well, having a little "fiddle." It was innocent at the time, but the thrill of it—the rush of possibly getting caught—added another layer to the mask I was wearing.

I didn't talk about these feelings or experiences, though. The Mask of Conformity was always there, telling me to keep those parts of myself hidden, to blend in with the expectations of what boys should be like. The fear of being different, of standing out in a way that could lead to judgment or rejection, kept me from being open. That mask was like a shield, protecting me from the world's scrutiny, but it also kept me from fully understanding and accepting myself. It wasn't just about blending in with the boys at school or following the rules at St. Joseph's; it was about hiding parts of myself, even from me. And the longer I wore the mask, the harder it became to recognize who I really was beneath it.

THE CONSEQUENCES OF CONFORMITY

Have you ever done something so out of character just to blend in and be part of the pack? Many of us have, and with that we've adopted behaviors that clash with our deepest values simply to avoid standing out. The desire to fit in can lead to poor choices, especially in our formative years. Think about young kids experimenting with drugs or young adults indulging in behaviors driven more by peer pressure than personal choice. *Everyone else is doing it, and I don't want to be the odd one out, so I'll do it too.* It becomes a very common, yet dangerous justification.

It goes even deeper than risky behaviors. For some, the Mask of Conformity leads them to deny their true identity, whether it's their sexual orientation, religious beliefs, or even political views, just to fit societal expectations. In professional settings, employees may suppress their innovative ideas or genuine opinions, not wanting to stand out—just blending into the team rather than shining individually.

This pressure is reflected in a study from the American Psychological Association, which revealed how perceived masculinity among different racial groups plays into the Mask of Conformity. The study found that participants with strong racial essentialist beliefs—those who think racial characteristics determine individual qualities—viewed masculinity differently among Asian American, Black American, and White American men. Black American men were viewed as the most masculine, while Asian American men were perceived as less masculine compared to their White counterparts.[2] This perception, heavily influenced by physical and athletic stereotypes, illustrates how societal pressures push men to conform to traditional masculine standards, often at the cost of their mental health and well-being.

SCOTT'S STORY OF CONFORMITY— BREAKING THE MASK

The profound impact of societal expectations can lead us down unhealthy paths. This isn't just my story—I've seen it echoed in the lives of many people I've worked with. One client, Scott, had been bullied from a young age for being different. The constant teasing and rejection taught him early on that blending in, wearing the Mask of Conformity, was a way to avoid harm. He learned to hide his true self out of fear of rejection and judgment. Over time, this mask became a defense mechanism, protecting him from further pain but also shaping how he interacted with the world.

Scott told me how he would wear this mask with everyone, adjusting himself to fit into whatever environment he was in. Whether it was with friends, family, or at work, he buried his authentic self beneath layers of conformity. It became a habit—a survival tactic he relied on to prevent judgment or rejection. But with every adaptation, he felt a deeper sense of disconnection from who he really was.

As we worked together, Scott began to realize that while the mask had provided temporary safety, it was also reinforcing a sense of alienation. Each time he adjusted himself to meet someone else's expectations, he strayed further from his true identity. The fear of standing out, of being rejected, had led him to create a life that didn't reflect his own desires or values.

One of the pivotal moments in our sessions came when Scott identified the origins of this mask. He could trace it back to his school years, where the bullying began and where the need to conform to avoid being singled out took root. Acknowledging this was the first step in learning to remove the mask. Through our work, he slowly started to unpeel the layers, recognizing when and why he was putting on the Mask of Conformity and taking small steps to be more authentic in his interactions. Scott came to understand that true belonging doesn't come from blending in—it comes from embracing who we are, even if it means risking rejection or standing out.

FORCED DOWN THE PATH OF CONFORMITY

Growing up, I felt the constant weight of conformity—especially with a strict father who instilled fear in all of us. I was expected to follow a path that didn't leave room for who I was or what I was feeling inside. There was no space for exploration, no room to question or express what was happening with me. All I knew was that I had to suppress it. There was a time when my younger brother and I were in the field, and we had lit a small fire to burn some grass. Since we were unsupervised, Dad got angry. He told us to go into the woods and find a stick. When we brought it back to the house, he hit us with it. I ran up to my room, crying, holding onto my pillow, feeling the sting from where the stick had struck me. As I lay on my bed sobbing, Dad came in to talk. The moment he entered, I jumped out of bed and ran to the bathroom, curling myself into a ball beside the toilet, facing the corner, still crying. Dad followed me in, knelt beside me, and apologized. "I'm sorry for hitting you, I overreacted," he said, realizing he had crossed a line.

My dad's anger was something we were used to. If it wasn't the stick, it would be the belt. He sent us to his room on numerous occasions to fetch his brown leather belt, which he used to spank us. And when neither the stick nor the belt was within reach, it would be his hand. I lost count of how many times I had to climb those stairs to retrieve my own punishment weapon, crying all the way up and down, knowing what was coming. For cursing, we were fed a bar of soap—after a while, as I got older, the taste didn't bother me as much.

Before the internet came to life, on weekends at my dad's house, after everyone was asleep, I'd sneak downstairs to watch *Red Shoe Diaries*—the erotic drama led by David Duchovny's character, Jake, who explored love, betrayal, and desire through letters sent to him. This became my routine 9 p.m. fix, captivated by the character Jake and exploring the feeling inside of me.

As the internet became available, my self-curiosity deepened, and I began to explore my feelings further. I started searching online—anything related to being gay, trying to understand what was happening inside of me. I found myself getting more and more drawn to the content I discovered, and it became like a drug. Every chance I had, I was on the computer at Dad's, getting my fix. I even invited my stepbrother Garrett to watch with me a few times. We were young—just eight or nine years old—exploring things that were really more about my own need to understand myself.

At Mom's house, things weren't much different. She had an old boxy computer with a floppy disk drive. I had memorized Mom's credit card PIN after ordering pizza a few times and began using it to pay for webcam shows, paying men to perform on camera. The more I watched, the more I wanted—it became an obsession.

Of course, being young, I didn't consider the consequences—like clearing the browser history or worrying about the charges on the bank statement. Eventually, the day came when Mom saw her statement. I have no idea how I got away with it for so long, but when she confronted me about the numerous charges labeled "porn," I panicked. Fear washed over me, and the first thing I blurted out was,

"It's straight porn, I swear! It's just straight porn." Over the course of a few months, I had spent over $1,000 on her credit card, but I did eventually pay it all back.

Not long after that, Dad called both me and my brother into his office. There, on the computer screen, were all the gay porn sites I had been visiting. "What's this?" he asked. I froze, terrified. I didn't know what to say, and my heart raced as I tried to come up with something.

My stepmom Michelle chimed in, saying, "Garrett would never watch this." She knew, at least on some level, that I was gay or working through something, but her words still stung. I could have used a bit more support in that moment instead of being singled out.

But then something inside me snapped, and I stood up to my dad for the first time. "What are you going to do, huh? Kick me out if I was gay? What are you going to do?" I demanded.

"Yes, maybe," he responded.

Anger coursed through me, and I stomped out of the room. I had never raised my voice to my dad before, but I felt cornered. Michelle later had words with him, telling him he needed to accept the fact that his son was gay. He dismissed it, claiming it was just a phase. The tension between Dad and I only grew from there. I avoided him, spending weekends in my room or outside to stay out of his way.

Not long after that confrontation, Dad called me into the kitchen one morning. He placed a stack of papers in front of me and told me to read them. As I scanned the documents, I realized they were about AIDS and STIs. I didn't know if he was trying to scare the gay out of me or if this was his awkward attempt at education, but either way it made me feel even more uncomfortable. It created more fear and pushed me further away from him. I wanted nothing to do with him after that.

Michelle, however, made an effort to bridge the gap. She once visited me at school, and we sat on a bench to talk. She could see how much I was struggling, and I still remember her words: "Rob, it's not about *who* you love, it's *that* you love." Those words stayed with me, even in the midst of all the chaos.

In 2002, Dad and Michelle went through a rocky separation. She moved out temporarily, came back, and then moved out again, with the third time being the final separation. Michelle relocated to Telkwa with her boys, and I started spending weekends with her to avoid being at my dad's place. Once again, the Mask of Adaptation was in full force. Despite the constant upheaval, I found myself falling back into survival mode, trying to adapt to the ever-changing dynamics.

THE WEIGHT OF THE MASK

During this time, the weight of trying to live up to societal expectations, to play the part of the "good son" or the "normal kid," took a toll. My grades slipped; I stopped eating, and I went to school less and less. It wasn't just the pressure from my dad; it was the pressure from everyone. I had girlfriends because that was what I was supposed to do, but it never felt right. It was like I was living someone else's life, trying to meet the expectations of a society that didn't understand me.

Mom began to notice these changes. On days when I couldn't handle going to school, she would bring me to work with her. There, she'd let me sit at her computer to write letters to my dad, pouring out my feelings and frustrations. Writing became a way to release the anger and confusion that had built up inside of me.

In this difficult time, my relationship with my mother grew stronger. At the same time, my bond with Michelle deepened. I felt more comfortable around her than I did with my father. After her final move, I often spent weekends with her, where I could relax and feel supported.

The Mask of Conformity often begins as a response to societal or environmental pressures. For many of us, the need to fit in starts during our formative years—at school, within families, or among peers. Society teaches us, either directly or indirectly, that standing out can lead to criticism, judgment, or exclusion. This belief fosters a deep-seated fear of being different, causing us to hide aspects of ourselves that might set us apart.

From childhood, we begin to notice what's "acceptable" and what's not—whether it's the clothes we wear, the opinions we hold, or even the emotions we express. Children who experience ridicule or exclusion for being different often internalize the message that it's safer to blend in. This mask then follows us into adulthood, where it can affect everything from career choices to personal relationships. As we grow, it becomes more difficult to identify where the mask ends and our true selves begin.

The Mask of Conformity doesn't just impact individuals; it also sustains cultural norms. Whether it's a school setting where uniqueness is stifled or a workplace where creativity is undervalued, this mask helps uphold systems that prioritize sameness over individuality.

In environments that favor conformity, the fear of standing out often outweighs the desire to express our authentic selves, perpetuating cycles of social uniformity.

In some families, the Mask of Conformity is enforced by cultural or traditional expectations. For example, many cultures have rigid ideas about gender roles, career paths, and family dynamics. Individuals who step outside these norms may face rejection, criticism, or even ostracism. As a result, they wear the mask to appease their families and communities, ensuring they "fit the mold."

Take, for example, my own upbringing. Growing up, I felt pressure to conform to the idea of having a "traditional" life: wife, kids, white picket fence. I convinced myself that this was what I wanted because it was what was expected of me. The Mask of Conformity makes us believe that, by conforming, we're protecting ourselves from judgment and rejection, often at the cost of our happiness.

These expectations are not just familial. Society as a whole reinforces the idea that, to be accepted, we must blend in. Whether it's through media, social circles, or workplace environments, we learn early on that standing out can be risky, and the safer choice is to conform.

In some cases, wearing the Mask of Conformity can lead to a lifelong struggle with self-esteem and self-worth. Many people who constantly conform experience a growing disconnect between their internal desires and the external life they lead. Over time, this disconnect can lead to feelings of depression, dissatisfaction, and even resentment. When our value is tied to how well we fit in, we lose the ability to trust ourselves and our instincts. The longer we wear this mask, the more difficult it becomes to take off, as the fear of rejection or failure grows stronger with time.

THE ROLE OF THE MASK IN MODERN SOCIETY

In today's world, social media amplifies the pressure to conform. The need to appear a certain way, live a specific lifestyle, or present a curated version of ourselves can be overwhelming. This constant drive to fit in can lead to superficiality. When we prioritize blending in over authenticity, we create a cycle in which real emotions, thoughts, and struggles are hidden. It almost becomes a "sheep mentality," where we follow the crowd just to belong.

One of the most striking examples of how powerful conformity can be comes from the famous Asch conformity experiments, conducted by social psychologist Solomon Asch in the 1950s. Asch's experiments revealed that individuals could be influenced to go against their own perceptions and judgments to align with the group, even when the group was clearly wrong.

In the experiment, participants were shown a set of lines and asked to choose which one matched the length of a given line. The task was simple, but the twist was that all but one of the participants were actors instructed to give incorrect answers. The results were astounding—many of the real participants conformed to the group's wrong answers, even when the correct choice was obvious.[3]

Asch's work highlights how the desire to fit in and avoid standing out can lead individuals to suppress their own truth in favor of blending into the crowd. The experiment illustrates a core truth about the Mask of Conformity: it's not just about dressing or behaving like others; it's about the deeper psychological pressure to align with group norms, even when it conflicts with our inner sense of right and wrong.

When I reflect on my own experiences growing up, particularly in a small town with rigid traditions and expectations, I see how easy it is to fall into this trap. Like the participants in Asch's study, I often chose the comfort of conformity over the discomfort of standing out—even when it came at the cost of suppressing my true self. This is the essence of the Mask of Conformity: acting not out of personal choice or belief but out of a desire to fit in and avoid judgment.

Conformity isn't always an obvious act; it can be subtle and unconscious. Whether it's following social norms, hiding opinions, or choosing a career that feels safe but uninspiring, conformity is something we all deal with in one way or another. The key is recognizing when the Mask of Conformity has taken over and assessing whether it's still serving us or holding us back.

THE EVOLUTION OF THE MASK

As I moved into middle school, the Mask of Conformity took on new shapes. I started dabbling in things like smoking weed—not because I was particularly drawn to it at first, but because it seemed like the "cool" thing to do. I was doing it to fit in, to appear like I belonged. Over time, though, I came to enjoy it, and eventually became a huge pothead.

I wore the Mask of Conformity well into my adult life, shaping the way I interacted with people and the world around me. It was a survival tool, something I relied on without even realizing it. As you'll soon learn, many of the masks I wore continued to influence my decisions and relationships, often hiding the parts of me that longed to be authentic and true.

STEPS TO REMOVE THE MASK OF CONFORMITY

Recognizing the Mask of Conformity is the first step toward removing it. When you begin to notice the ways you've shaped yourself to fit the expectations of others, you can take conscious steps to rediscover your true self.

1. **Self-awareness:** Begin by reflecting on the areas of your life where you feel pressure to conform. This could be at work, in social settings, or even online. Ask yourself: *Am I acting from a place of authenticity? Or am I conforming to meet expectations?* Journaling or meditation can help you gain clarity around these patterns.
2. **Identify core values:** Take time to identify your personal values—the things that matter most to you, regardless of what society or your peers may expect. When you have a clear sense of your values, it becomes easier to live in alignment with them rather than following the crowd.
3. **Practice vulnerability:** Removing the Mask of Conformity requires courage and vulnerability. Start small—share an authentic thought or feeling with a trusted friend or family member. Over time, this practice will help you feel more comfortable being your true self, even in situations where conformity is the norm.
4. **Challenge the status quo:** Conformity thrives when we don't question the norms. Start challenging the "shoulds" in your life, whether it's about how you dress, how you speak, or how you live your life. Ask yourself if these behaviors truly reflect who you are, or if they've been adopted to blend in.
5. **Surround yourself with authentic people:** Seek out people and communities that encourage authenticity. When you surround yourself with individuals who value you for who you really are, the pressure to conform lessens. Authentic connections create a safe space for self-expression.
6. **Take risks:** Conformity often stems from a fear of rejection

or failure. To remove the mask, you need to take small, intentional risks. Say what you truly think in a meeting, wear something that reflects your style, or share an unpopular opinion. These small acts of authenticity build confidence over time.

7. **Celebrate your uniqueness:** Embrace the fact that standing out isn't a weakness; it's a strength. Your uniqueness is what sets you apart and makes you valuable. Celebrate the parts of yourself that you've hidden or downplayed in the past, and let them shine in your daily life.
8. **Set boundaries:** Sometimes, conformity is driven by the fear of disappointing others. Learning to set boundaries with people who expect you to conform is essential. This could mean saying "no" to things that don't align with your values or limiting your exposure to environments that pressure you to fit in.

REFLECTIONS AND LEARNINGS: THE MASK OF CONFORMITY

Conforming to Expectations

My story: Growing up, I conformed to the unspoken rules of my environment—from the way I dressed to the roles I played. The fear of standing out always lingered beneath the surface.

Your reflection: Think back to a time when you conformed to a group. What were the unspoken expectations? How did they shape your behavior?

Exercise: Write down one or two instances where you felt compelled to conform. How did this affect your sense of self?

The Cost of Conformity

My story: Even though conformity gave me a sense of safety and belonging when I was younger, it also stifled my true self. As I grew older, I lost sight of my personal values and desires, hiding behind the need to fit in.

Your reflection: In what ways has conformity helped you? In what ways has it limited your ability to be your authentic self?

Exercise: List the pros and cons of conformity in your life. Reflect on how the conformity you experienced as a child may have carried into your adult life. Consider where you might still be sacrificing your true identity for acceptance.

Embracing Authenticity

My story: As I've grown, I've learned that while conformity offers comfort, it comes at the cost of individuality. As I began to embrace my true self, I started to feel more aligned and fulfilled, even when it meant standing out.

Your reflection: Are there areas of your life where you still feel pressure to conform? How can you start showing up as your authentic self in those situations?

Exercise: Reflect on a time when you felt like you weren't being true to yourself. What small steps can you take to express your authentic self in that environment?

Challenging the "Shoulds"

My story: Breaking away from conformity didn't happen overnight. The Mask of Conformity formed early in my life, and I wore it well into adulthood. It took time to recognize the societal and peer pressure that shaped my decisions. Once I began to challenge the "shoulds" in my life, I could start making choices that aligned with my values.

Your reflection: Are there any "shoulds" in your life you frequently adhere to? Do they stem from your own authentic beliefs? Or are they the result of external pressure?

Exercise: Write down one "should" you've been following that doesn't align with your true self. What is one action you can take to break away from this expectation?

Authentic Connections

My story: When I began shedding the Mask of Conformity, I started attracting relationships based on authenticity rather than superficial acceptance. This gave me a greater sense of belonging and connection.

Your reflection: Who in your life encourages you to be yourself? Are there relationships that still pressure you to conform?

Exercise: Identify one relationship where you feel safe being your true self. Nurture that connection and consider how you can bring more authenticity to other relationships.

MASK OF CONFORMITY KEY TAKEAWAYS

- **Conformity provides temporary comfort but long-term disconnect:** While fitting in can feel safe in the moment, the long-term effects of hiding your true self can be disconnection and dissatisfaction.
- **The power of authenticity:** True belonging happens when you're accepted for who you are, not for who you pretend to be. Authenticity is a path to deeper fulfillment and connection.
- **Challenge the norms:** Questioning societal or group norms isn't easy, but it's essential for shedding the Mask of Conformity. Start by identifying the areas where you've been conforming and make a conscious effort to break free.
- **Start small and build confidence:** You don't have to remove the mask all at once. Begin with small steps—express an opinion, embrace your style, or take a stand in situations where you would typically conform.
- **Your true self is worth the risk:** There's always a risk in stepping away from conformity, but the reward of living an authentic life far outweighs the

temporary discomfort of standing out.
- **Surround yourself with authentic people:** Seek relationships and environments that encourage authenticity, and you'll find that the pressure to conform gradually diminishes.

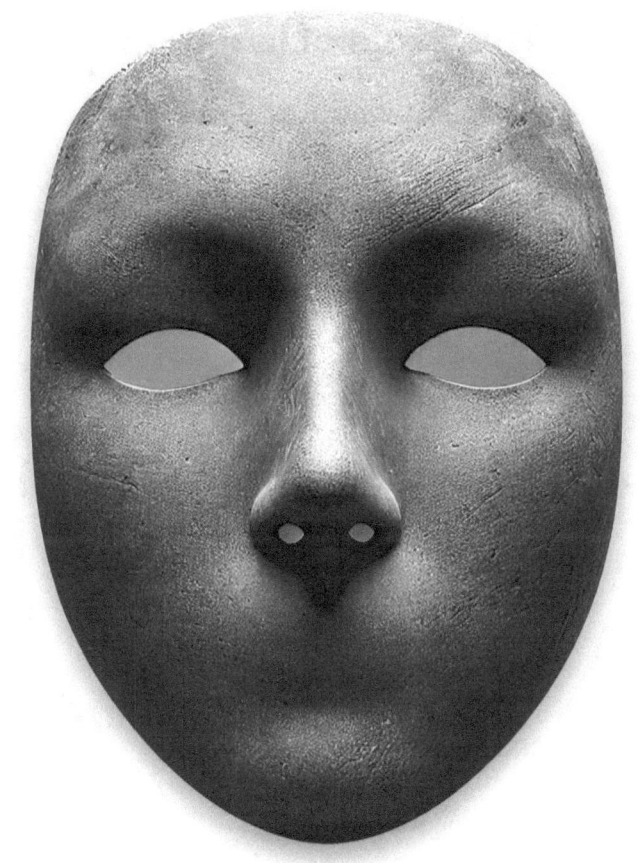

CHAPTER 5

THE MASK OF ISOLATION

WITHDRAWING TO
AVOID CONNECTION

The Cycle of Isolation

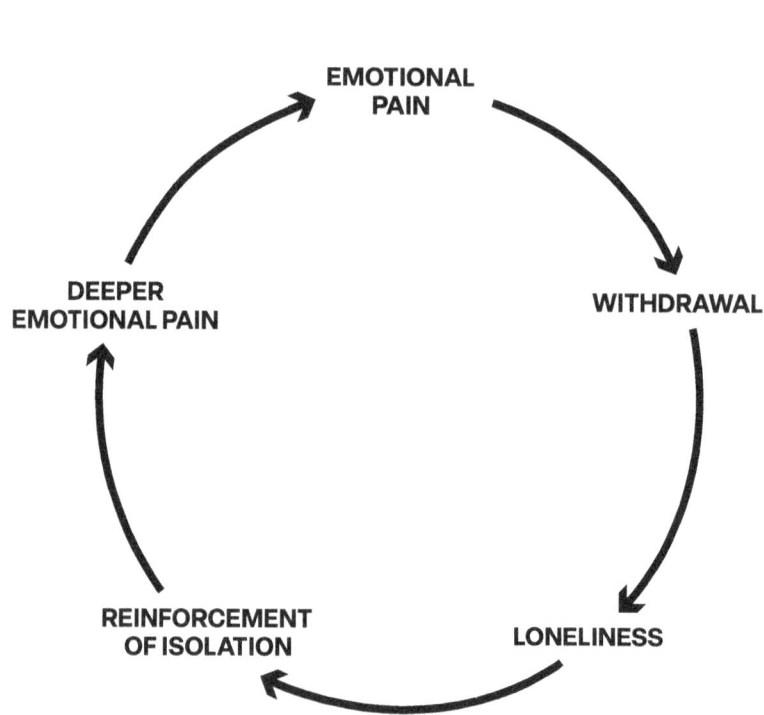

A rt became my escape, my way of communicating without words. To an outsider, it might have seemed like a dark representation of suicidal thoughts, but to me it was a vivid expression of the profound loneliness I felt—a visual metaphor for the internal turmoil I couldn't express in any other way.

A MASK OF DISTANCE, SEPARATION, AND INSULATION

The Mask of Isolation is often born from emotional pain—whether it's rejection, betrayal, or a deep sense of not belonging. It acts as a shield, protecting us from the vulnerability that comes with connection. For me, it started with a mix of feeling different from my peers and the ongoing tension at home. I floated between social groups but never truly felt like I belonged anywhere.

The more disconnected I felt, the more I withdrew—building walls to shield myself from rejection or judgment. Growing up, I didn't realize it, but that mask was shaping my relationships and my ability to be vulnerable. I hid behind it, convincing myself that I didn't need anyone. Smoking weed and spending time alone became my way of coping. At the time, it felt safer to isolate than to confront the emotions that were stirring inside me.

For me, isolation wasn't just about physically retreating; it was emotional. I kept my feelings and struggles locked away, not letting anyone truly see what was going on inside. While I hung out with different groups and floated through social circles, I always felt a sense of distance. No matter where I was, I couldn't shake the feeling of being on the outside, looking in.

Isolation is a double-edged sword. While it may protect us from the pain of connection, it also deprives us of the joy, support, and growth that come from authentic relationships.

Loneliness, anxiety, and depression often lurk beneath the surface of isolation. When we wear this mask, we may appear strong and self-sufficient on the outside, but inside we are craving the connection we've convinced ourselves we don't need.

I experienced this firsthand. I believed that being alone was the safer option—that if I didn't let anyone too close, they couldn't hurt me. I told myself I was fine being independent and I didn't need the emotional complications that come with deeper relationships. But in truth, that solitude began to feel more like a prison. The longer I wore the Mask of Isolation, the more it drained me. On the outside, I seemed fine—managing school, drifting through different social groups—but inside I was drowning in a sea of loneliness that I didn't know how to escape.

This internal conflict worsened the more I kept my true self hidden. The more I avoided vulnerability, the heavier the mask became. The weed helped numb the pain, but it also deepened the disconnect, creating a cycle of isolation that was hard to break free from.

NAVIGATING THE ROCKY ROAD OF ADOLESCENCE

My journey through middle and high school was a relentless quest for self-discovery amid the turbulent dynamics of adolescence. In middle school, I entered my first relationship with a girl named Alice. It was brief, but as I moved into high school, I dated two more girls, Lucy and Samantha, both figure skaters. Consistency, it seems, was my unintended theme. Deep down, I knew it was a facade. I was wearing the Mask of Isolation, masking my true self from the public, concealing what I did behind closed doors as if it were something shameful. All throughout middle school, the Mask of Isolation stayed firmly in place, keeping me withdrawn from the people and connections I needed most.

Transitioning into high school, the stakes seemed higher, the social labyrinth more intricate. I drifted among groups, never fully committing to any, reflecting the instability I experienced at home. This period was filled with challenges: grappling with my sexual identity, struggling to balance conformity with the urge to break free, and navigating familial conflicts that left me feeling isolated and misunderstood.

Starting high school also meant joining the Sea Cadets. It was there that I met Fred, a fellow cadet from the nearby town of Terrace. He was a charismatic individual who was openly gay—something rare in our circle—and someone who, by simply being himself, challenged social norms.

One evening, gathered at a friend's house, the casual atmosphere led to a more personal interaction between us. As we watched a movie, subtle touches escalated, unnoticed at first by our friend Joe. Sensing the changing dynamics, Joe discreetly left the room, leaving Fred and me alone. The intimacy that followed was new and exhilarating but also terrifying. It was the first time I allowed myself to explore the feelings I had been suppressing. Kissing each other, fondling each other, a little foreplay here and there, but that was the extent of it.

With the morning came panic—guilt, fear, and shame crashing down all at once. The Mask of Isolation wrapped itself around me even tighter. Adding to the pressure, Samantha, the girl I had previously dated, showed up unexpectedly that morning, heightening my confusion and anxiety about what had transpired. Fearful of being discovered, I adopted a harsh homophobic facade, speaking negatively about gay people in an attempt to protect my secret.

Unfortunately, rumors about that night spread quickly, altering how I was perceived by my peers. The taunts and jokes were relentless, with students singing, "Rob and Fred, sitting in a tree, K-I-S-S-I-N-G." My days at school were filled with wandering the halls in isolation, haunted by anxiety. The Mask of Isolation became my shield against the mockery and judgment, but it also locked me in a state of loneliness. The quiet corners of the library became my refuge, where I ate lunch alone, surrounded by books rather than the stares and whispers that followed me through the halls.

Now, I'm not saying that my entire high school experience was terrible, or that I spent every day wandering the halls in isolation, or that I spent most of my lunch hours in the library eating by myself. I still did things any normal kid would do. I was quite athletic and took part in the morning basketball games before school. A mix of parents, teachers, and students would always get together around 6:00 a.m. to play basketball. I also participated in track and field, where I was pretty fast and frequently competed in the 100-, 200-, and 400-meter races.

During my high school years, it felt like I had so many things going on both externally and internally. Externally, I was dealing with relationships with my parents, experimenting with drugs, and being a sporty, athletic kid. But on the inside, I was holding onto this big secret, battling feelings of isolation that only grew stronger as high school went on.

FROM REJECTED TO CONNECTED

The Mask of Isolation also manifests in how we communicate—or rather, how we don't. Instead of reaching out for help or expressing what's really going on inside, we retreat. We keep our thoughts, our pain, and our emotions to ourselves, avoiding vulnerability at all costs. We tell ourselves that others won't understand, or worse, that they wouldn't care even if they did. Over time, this mask becomes so ingrained that it feels like a part of us—being alone becomes our normal, and the silence turns into a shield.

Turning to art as a way to escape, I'd find images online—animals, anime, landscapes—and recreate them with pencil and paper. But as the weight of my emotions grew heavier, so did the expression in my drawings. One piece in particular captured my emotional state more vividly than anything I had ever drawn before. It was a desolate scene: a forest reduced to stumps, under a gray, gloomy sky. Among the remnants stood a small solitary tree, from which a doll hung by a noose. To someone else, it might have looked like a dark symbol of suicidal thoughts, but to me it was something different. It wasn't about wanting to die—it was about feeling completely alone, about being cut off from everything and everyone. The doll hanging from the tree wasn't an expression of wanting to end things, but a symbol of my deep, internal struggle. It was the loneliness I couldn't put into words, a visual metaphor for the turmoil I kept buried beneath the surface.

This drawing was my silent cry for help, even if I didn't fully understand that at the time. I was pouring out the emotions I couldn't voice to anyone around me. I didn't expect anyone to notice or care—it was just something I did to survive. But then Mr. Smith, my high school principal and mentor of sorts, noticed.

Recreated drawing of a doll hanging from a tree in a desolate landscape.

As I sat in the school's round room, sketching as usual, he approached and quietly took in the drawing. I didn't hide it but rather let him see it. He didn't say much at first, but I could tell by the look in his eyes that he saw more than just a sketch on paper. He saw me—the part of me I had been hiding behind the mask. Without drawing any attention, he gently guided me to the counselor's office, offering me a way to talk about the things I had been burying for so long.

It was in that moment, sitting in the counselor's office, that I realized how deeply the Mask of Isolation had shaped me. I had become so used to keeping everything to myself, convinced that no one would understand, that the idea of opening up felt foreign and terrifying. But that small act of being seen, of someone noticing the pain I had been hiding, started to crack the mask I had worn for so long.

Over time, my relationship with drugs deepened—it wasn't just weed anymore; other substances found their way in. With the drugs came a different crowd, a group of kids who were always up for mischief. We called ourselves "Rejected." We weren't just hanging out to get high; we were part of an online community that turned stunts into a global competition, almost like something straight out of the movie *Jackass*. The adrenaline, the attention—it all fueled us.

The competition had a list of stunts, each one crazier than the last. For every stunt completed, you'd earn points. The goal? Film yourself, upload the video, and claim your points. It was chaotic, but we thrived on it. I can't even remember what the winner got—maybe it didn't matter. It was more about pushing the limits, proving yourself to the group, and chasing that rush.

One stunt in particular still stands out. My friend Jim sat on a bicycle at the top of a hill, ready to do something truly reckless. We doused him in gasoline, just enough to make a statement, and, as I set him on fire, he coasted down the hill. The flames caught fast, and, for a few seconds, Jim was literally a human torch. As planned, he quickly jumped off the bike and threw himself into a nearby creek to put out the fire. The whole thing was surreal, watching him burn and then seeing the relief as he splashed into the water. That stunt ended up going viral—everyone was talking about it. It even made the local newspaper. For a while, we felt invincible, like we were making a name for ourselves, even if it was for all the wrong reasons.

As my exploration of drugs intensified, it wasn't long before it caught up with me. When my sister mentioned it to my counselor, the decision was made. The next thing I knew, I was being sent to rehab in Terrace, B.C. for a month.

Rehab became more than just a break from the chaos. It was a period of deep introspection and growth. Located in the quiet, natural setting of Terrace, the facility offered me a space to detox and disconnect from the pressures of my life. Unexpectedly, it also became a place where I began to reconnect—with myself and with others.

One of the most significant connections I made during that time was with my uncle Dave, who visited me often. He didn't lecture me or try to fix me—he simply listened. Our conversations during walks around the nearby hot springs weren't forced or heavy, but they had a way of helping me make sense of everything I was going through. In a way, Uncle Dave became a mentor, offering me the kind of quiet, grounding support I didn't even know I needed. His presence was a stark contrast to the strained communication I had with my father. Where my father pushed, Dave simply connected.

DOWNWARD SPIRAL INTO FURTHER ISOLATION

The remainder of my high school years was a blend of being bullied, using drugs, and constant conflicts with my parents. By grade 12, things had escalated to the point where I was kicked out of home due to my disrespectful behavior and acting out. This only deepened the sense of isolation I had been carrying for years.

Looking back, I can trace the roots of the Mask of Isolation to several origins: childhood neglect, emotional abandonment, and bullying. Growing up in an environment where emotional expression was discouraged, I learned early on to keep my feelings buried, believing that opening up would only lead to rejection or betrayal.

The pain of being misunderstood or overlooked as a child left me afraid of vulnerability, and by the time I reached high school, isolation had become my mask, my way of coping.

The climax of my high school experience came when I threw a massive house party at Michelle's place where I was staying while she was away. At the time, I was selling pot, so I was popular among the other kids. What started as a good time quickly spiraled out of control. The police eventually showed up, and the aftermath was a harsh phone call from Michelle that ended with the words, "Get the fuck out of my house."

In that moment, the Mask of Isolation felt suffocating. I had worn it for so long to avoid the pain of rejection, to maintain control over my emotions, and to protect myself from dependency on others. But now, it had left me completely isolated, without a stable home, without real connections, and without the support I so desperately needed.

NEW CONNECTIONS—AN ANTIDOTE TO ISOLATION

One day, my friend Chris messaged me asking if I wanted to join him at a drop-in gymnastic night. When we arrived, there were three male coaches. They were new to town. Mike, Brent, and Keiran. They had recently moved to Smithers from Ontario, and they all lived under the same roof in Telkwa. Over time, Mike and I started to build a bit of a connection. I was doing really well at gymnastics, and I was even helping him coach some of the younger boys. I had some self-taught skills before receiving any official training. I had started off doing little back flips off my couch onto some cushions, which evolved into doing standing back flips and more.

I soon discovered that Mike and Brent were gay, so we started hanging out. I would occasionally visit them at their house. Over time, the connection between Mike and I grew stronger. We ended up sharing kisses in the car, and one night I stayed at their place. They shared a bed, which I didn't quite understand, and the second room had just a mattress on the floor, which was where I slept.

After going to bed, I lay awake for about 30 minutes before my door opened, and Mike slipped in beside me. We started kissing—slowly, deliberately—our connection deepening in a way I had never experienced before. It was electrifying yet safe, a mix of excitement and familiarity.

The chemistry had been building for weeks, lingering in glances, the kissing in the car. Now that it was happening, it felt right. Natural. Like something I had been waiting for without fully realizing it. But it wasn't some idealized, romantic first time like in the movies. We were on a single mattress in a spare room, trying to stay quiet so we wouldn't wake anyone. There was no candlelight, no grand gestures—just us, figuring it out in real time.

As things progressed, I let myself surrender to the moment, trusting him, trusting myself. I had never been this intimate with a man before, never allowed myself to fully embrace what I had always felt deep down. As he held me, I felt a quiet reassurance in his touch. "Just breathe," he whispered, grounding me in the moment. I closed my eyes and did just that—letting go of hesitation, of years of questions.

* * *

After a few weeks, tensions started to build between Mike and Brent. It came to light that they were actually engaged. Suddenly, I was in the middle of this domestic battle of the gays. Team Mike one min, and then team Brent the next, bouncing back and forth like a ping-pong ball.

One day, I got a phone call from Brent. Mike had been arrested for charges laid on him back in Ontario. Charges that involved him and a boy he used to mentor. Suddenly, it was front-page news. Mike's face and ... *Gymnastics coach charged with sexual assault of a minor*. He was facing 14 charges, and he had to stay in jail waiting to be transported back to Ontario.

Brent was losing his shit. Mike said he didn't do it, and I believed him. During several phone calls with Brent, he explained there was evidence supporting his innocence and the mother of the child had set him up using fake emails.

During all this craziness, I started a Facebook page to support Mike and get him out of jail. Ironically, my sister, I believe, started a page to keep him in jail. I figured she and my dad teamed up on this one. I was reading some of the comments on the page, and I saw that Dad had made a comment mentioning that he knew I was hanging out with Mike. I was shocked. Outing me like that, his own son. It felt like a betrayal.

Eventually, Mike was sent back to Ontario where he awaited trial, while Brent scraped together money, selling what he could to move back to support him. Once I graduated in September, I wanted to see Mike. I was in love with him. He was my first love.

A NEW BEGINNING: ACKNOWLEDGING MY IDENTITY

As the end of the school year approached, the pressure of upcoming graduation loomed large. Despite the academic challenges, I managed to scrape through, thanks largely to a few understanding teachers who recognized my struggles and supported me beyond the confines of their classrooms. It was during this tumultuous period that I began to truly embrace my sexuality. After confiding in my friends Nadine and Jen, it felt as though a weight had been lifted. Their acceptance was a balm, and it encouraged me to open up to more people. The responses were unexpectedly positive, which bolstered my confidence further.

Then came the moment to tell my stepmom Michelle. Her reaction was simply, "Fantastic," delivered with such genuine enthusiasm that any residual fears I had about acceptance evaporated. She didn't just acknowledge my truth; she celebrated it, which deepened our bond significantly.

The following morning at school marked a turning point. As I walked through the corridors, I was greeted with smiles and hellos—a stark contrast to the isolation I had felt for so long. It seemed that my coming out had not only changed how others saw me but had altered my social landscape. This newfound respect was bewildering yet exhilarating. For years, I had been the target of bullying and exclusion, but now I was being acknowledged for my courage to be true to myself. The acceptance was empowering and transformative, making the school environment feel less like a battleground and more like a community.

Internally, I felt a profound sense of relief and freedom. Being open about my identity allowed me to interact with others more authentically, and the fear of judgment that had once stifled my self-expression began to dissipate. I walked taller, spoke more freely, and engaged with peers and teachers with a new openness—it was liberating.

As graduation neared, I realized that coming out was just the beginning of a new chapter in my life. It wasn't just about acknowledging who I was, but also about embracing the journey ahead with honesty and integrity. I was ready to face the world as both a graduate and a proud, openly gay man, not just advocating for myself but also for others who might still be struggling in silence.

THE LONE WOLF RARELY THRIVES

While the Mask of Isolation may feel like it's protecting you, it comes at a heavy cost. I wore it for years, convincing myself it was shielding me from the emotional pain and rejection I was so afraid of. At times, the mask even gave me the space to pull away from the chaos of my life, to think and regroup. It can feel comforting, like a refuge. But that sense of protection—it doesn't last.

The truth is, the Mask of Isolation only drove me deeper into loneliness. Even though I was often surrounded by people—at house parties or hanging out with my "Rejected" crew—I never let anyone in. The emotional walls I built were meant to protect me, but they kept me from forming real, meaningful connections. Maybe you've felt this too—surrounded by people but still feeling completely alone.

> **When we wear the Mask of Isolation, we're not just protecting ourselves from pain; we're also cutting ourselves off from joy, from any real sense of belonging.**

By keeping the mask on, I thought I was being strong, but in reality I was becoming more detached and isolated than ever. The mask did its job too well, and, in the end, it was suffocating.

STEPS TO REMOVE THE MASK OF ISOLATION

The first step to removing the Mask of Isolation is to acknowledge the trade-offs. Yes, the mask offers some protection. It can make you feel independent, safe from rejection, and in control. However, the cost is often loneliness, emotional numbness, and an inability to reach out when you need help the most. It's a high price to pay for something that only gives the illusion of safety.

1. **Acknowledge the fear behind isolation:** Isolation is a defense mechanism, often born out of fear—fear of rejection, betrayal, or emotional pain. Recognizing this fear is the first step toward removing the mask. It helps to understand why you've been wearing it and to face the fact that the mask isn't really keeping you safe—it's just keeping you disconnected.
2. **Take small steps toward connection:** Removing the Mask of Isolation doesn't happen overnight. It begins with small steps toward reconnection. Whether it's reaching out to an old friend, joining a group, or even just being more open in casual conversations, these small actions can help rebuild trust.

Taking those first steps can feel terrifying, but they're crucial to break the cycle of isolation.

3. **Learn to be vulnerable:** True connection requires vulnerability, and for someone who has been wearing the Mask of Isolation, it can feel nearly impossible. It's OK to take this process slowly. Start by sharing small, manageable parts of yourself with others. You don't have to reveal everything all at once. For me, learning to be vulnerable was a gradual process that involved letting go of control and allowing myself to be seen for who I really was, bit by bit.
4. **Practice asking for help:** One of the hardest things for me was asking for help. Try reaching out for support in small ways, whether it's emotional support from a friend or practical help from a colleague. It can feel uncomfortable at first, but asking for help is a crucial step in breaking the cycle of isolation.
5. **Engage in community activities:** Another way to slowly remove the mask is to engage with a community. It doesn't have to be anything deep at first, just participating in activities or joining groups where you can meet people who share your interests. Over time, these casual connections can develop into deeper, more meaningful relationships.

REFLECTIONS AND LEARNINGS: THE MASK OF ISOLATION

Reflecting on Your Early Experiences with Isolation

My story: Much of my isolation stemmed from the bullying I faced in high school and the dysfunctional home environment I grew up in. These experiences taught me to retreat, to keep my emotions hidden, and to build walls around myself.

Your reflection: Think back to your own life. Were there moments when you felt the need to retreat or withdraw from others? What were the circumstances that led you to wear the Mask of Isolation?

Exercise: Take a moment to write down one or two experiences where you felt isolated or disconnected from others. How did those experiences shape the way you engage with people today?

Recognizing the Protection and Cost of Isolation

My story: The Mask of Isolation provided me with a sense of safety—it kept me from being hurt. But over time, I realized that while it was protecting me from pain, it was also keeping me from joy, connection, and growth.

Your reflection: In what ways has isolation served you? Has it kept you safe from emotional pain? At what cost?

Exercise: List the pros and cons of isolation in your life. Where might you be sacrificing connection or happiness in order to avoid vulnerability?

Learning to Let Others In

My story: I discovered that the more I opened up and allowed others into my life, the more fulfilling my relationships became. The walls I had built were keeping me safe, but they were also keeping me alone.

Your reflection: Are there people in your life now that you've kept at a distance? What might happen if you let them in, even just a little?

Exercise: Reflect on a relationship where you've been holding back emotionally. What small step could you take to be more open and vulnerable in that relationship?

Breaking the Cycle of Self-Reliance

My story: Asking for help felt like weakness, but I learned that true strength comes from knowing when to rely on others. Letting go of the need to do everything on my own allowed me to build stronger, more meaningful connections.

Your reflection: Do you struggle with asking for help? What might it feel like to reach out to someone for support, even in a small way?

Exercise: Identify one area of your life where you've been trying to handle everything on your own. Consider one small way you could ask for help this week, whether from a friend, colleague, or family member.

Rebuilding Connection through Vulnerability

My story: It wasn't easy, but learning to be vulnerable and rebuilding connections brought me a sense of belonging I hadn't felt in years. The more I showed my true self, the more I found that people could connect with me on a deeper level.

Your reflection: Are there parts of yourself you've been hiding? How might your relationships change if you allow yourself to be seen, flaws and all?

Exercise: Reflect on a recent moment where you felt like you were holding back or wearing a mask. What's one small way you can show up more authentically in that situation next time?

MASK OF ISOLATION
KEY TAKEAWAYS

- **Isolation may protect, but it also limits:** While isolation might protect you from the immediate pain of rejection or betrayal, it also cuts you off from the deeper joys of connection, intimacy, and personal growth. In the end, the Mask of Isolation often causes more harm than the hurt it's trying to prevent.
- **True strength comes from vulnerability:** The Mask of Isolation makes you feel like you're strong for keeping your emotions to yourself, but true strength lies in the courage to be vulnerable. When you allow yourself to be open, you open the door to meaningful relationships and emotional healing.
- **Small steps lead to big changes:** Removing the Mask of Isolation doesn't require huge, dramatic actions. It's a gradual process that starts with small steps—like reaching out, being open in a conversation, or asking for help. Over time, these small changes can lead to profound shifts in your life.
- **Self-reliance can become a trap:** It's important to be independent, but isolation can trap you in

self-reliance, preventing you from leaning on others when you need it most. True connection requires allowing yourself to receive support as much as you offer it.

- **The mask of isolation can be removed:** Though it may feel like a part of your identity, the Mask of Isolation isn't permanent. It can be removed, piece by piece, as you begin to trust others again and let yourself be seen for who you really are. With time, vulnerability, and effort, you can break free from the patterns of isolation and rediscover connection.

CHAPTER 6

THE MASK OF THE
RESCUER

CARRYING THE WEIGHT
OF OTHERS' STRUGGLES

The Cycle of the Rescuer

I was 16 the first time I rode in an ambulance with my mom. Watching her slumped and unsteady, her voice slurring as she insisted she was "just fine," I realized I wasn't just her son that day—I was something else, something heavier. It was the first time I felt the weight of having to be the strong one, stepping into a role I'd never asked for.

While I found solace and acceptance in my own journey, the same period marked deepening struggles within my family, most notably my mother's battle with alcohol addiction. My personal victories were often set against the private battles that raged within our home.

As I navigated my identity, my mother fought her own demons, her addiction casting long shadows over our family.

In this interplay of light and darkness, my story continued to unfold, reflecting the dual nature of our lives: moments of triumph interwoven with times of turmoil.

Despite the challenges of a turbulent upbringing, I've always felt a special connection with my mom. I was a "mama's boy," and I'd proudly admit it. My mother was a beautiful woman with striking blue eyes, long brown hair, and a spirit that was endlessly giving. She was a woman of remarkable strength, known throughout the community for her work and for her adventurous side. Growing up, I heard stories about her time in mountain search and rescue, her passion for hiking, and her love of skydiving. She had over 300 jumps to her name—her friends even called her "Boulder Boisvert" because of her tendency to land hard.

Growing up, I only ever knew her as one thing: she was a dedicated nurse, working in both the ER and home care, caring deeply for her patients and giving endlessly to the community. After her divorce from my dad, she purchased her first home: a beautiful log house on five acres, just 10 minutes from town. That house became a symbol of her independence. Even though parts of it remained unfinished, it had five bedrooms, two in the loft, two on the main floor, and one in the basement. It was her sanctuary, a place that represented freedom.

But as much as that house meant to her, as much as she loved it, her personal battles took a toll on both her and our family. My relationship with my mother was full of love, connection, and respect, yet it was also defined by the complicated role I took on to support her through struggles that were bigger than either of us. It was there, in the shadow of that log house and the life she built, that my relationship with the Mask of the Rescuer truly began.

A RESCUER IS BORN—THE FORMATION OF THE MASK

For many, the Mask of the Rescuer begins forming in early childhood, particularly in unstable or challenging environments. In situations where family members struggle with instability, addiction, or trauma, children often step up to provide the stability they lack, becoming a grounding force. Once established, this pattern frequently extends into adulthood, affecting relationships in friendships, romantic partnerships, and even professional settings.

In my case, this dynamic played out in my relationship with my mom and her partner, Gary. Through this experience, I learned to navigate two distinct roles within what's known as the Drama Triangle, a model developed by psychiatrist Stephen Karpman in the 1960s. The triangle consists of three roles—victim, rescuer, and persecutor—that people unconsciously adopt in response to conflict.[4]

While I primarily took on the *rescuer* role, constantly stepping in to fix problems and shield Mom from pain, I found myself shifting between roles depending on the situation. At times, I felt like the *victim*, overwhelmed by circumstances I couldn't control. Other times, I played the *persecutor*, acting out of frustration when my efforts to help weren't enough. I adapted to whatever role I thought might keep the peace or offer Mom the support she needed, unknowingly staying trapped in a cycle that never truly resolved anything.

But what I eventually came to understand is that this cycle wasn't just exhausting—it was unsustainable. The Drama Triangle keeps people stuck in unhealthy patterns, reinforcing dysfunction rather than resolving it. It wasn't until I learned about the Empowerment Dynamic, the alternative model that shifts people from reacting to challenges to actively creating change, that I saw a way forward.

The Empowerment Dynamic, created by David Emerald as a response to Karpman's model, reframes the three roles in a way that fosters growth rather than dysfunction:

- **Victim → Creator:** Instead of feeling powerless, the creator takes ownership and seeks solutions.
- **Rescuer → Coach:** Rather than fixing everything, the coach supports and empowers others to take responsibility.
- **Persecutor → Challenger:** Instead of blaming or controlling, the challenger holds people accountable while encouraging growth.[5]

Once I made this shift, I started seeing my relationships through a new lens. I began stepping out of the rescuer role and focusing on empowering, rather than enabling, those around me—including Mom. It was a difficult but necessary transformation.

THE KARPMAN DRAMA TRIANGLE

PERSECUTOR

The person doesn't value other people's views and integrity.

- Angry (opening and passively)
- Aggressive
- Judgmental
- Bullying
- Demanding
- Spiteful and scornful

RESCUER

The person doesn't value other people's capacity to help themselves.

- Appear self sacrificing
- Over helpful and facilitative
- Like to be needed
- Prone to meddling unnecessarily

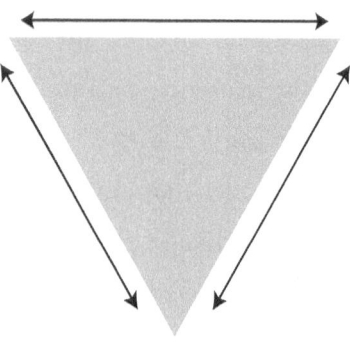

VICTIM

The person doesn't value self and defers to others.

- Manipulative
- 'Poor me' syndrome
- Helpless and needy
- Complaining and whinging
- Downtrodden
- Blaming others

THE EMPOWERMENT DYNAMIC[6]

CREATOR

Realize they have power and think about the alternatives.

- Problem solver
- Vulnerable

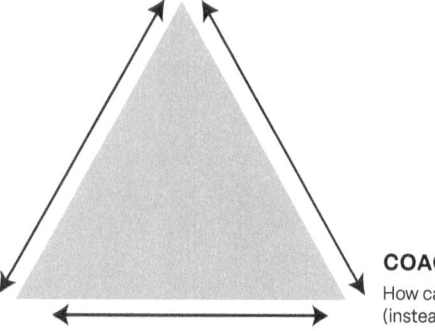

CHALLENGER

Constructive way of getting needs met (without punishing).

- Assertive
- Grows others

COACH

How can I help you (instead of taking over)?

- Caring
- Listens

As a nurse, Mom worked long hours, first in the hospital and later as a home care nurse. On days when I didn't want to go to school, she'd let me tag along as she did the patient rounds. I remember the thrill of holding her stethoscope, playing with it, and feeling a sense of pride in what she did.

Outside of work and school, she made time for camping and fishing trips. One summer, she even took me, my sister, and our best friends, Kristy and Kayla, to a ranch resort tucked away in the mountains. These moments were filled with her kindness, warmth, and thoughtfulness, creating memories I still hold close.

Yet, alongside these moments of light, there were also shadows. Gary came into our lives when I was around five. When he was home, he'd spend his time on the couch, drinking and watching sports, his presence heavy in our home. His constant absence and detachment seemed to amplify Mom's loneliness, adding to the emotional weight she already carried.

Beneath her radiant energy, my mom held deep scars from trauma she rarely spoke of—scars I didn't learn about until I was older. Her childhood had been marked by abuse from her grandfather, and she experienced further betrayal from a past partner. She also endured the loss of two sons before my sister and I were born, both to premature births. One had passed shortly after birth, while the other was lost after a difficult decision, knowing he would face a life of complications. The weight of these losses, coupled with her past trauma, contributed to the mask she wore, and it left a mark on both our lives.

* * *

By the time she had my sister in 1986, she was cautious, determined to protect her pregnancy by staying still and careful. My sister's birth represented a moment of light amid her journey through trauma. Three years later, in 1989, I came into the world.

When my sister moved out, I didn't get any explanation—she just stopped staying at Mom's house. We used to spend alternate weeks with Mom and Dad, but suddenly she was living with Dad full-time. Over time, her room grew emptier and emptier, her belongings disappearing one by one. It left just me, my mom, and Gary. I didn't fully understand the reasons behind my sister's absence, but I felt the emptiness she left behind.

With her gone, I found myself swinging between different emotions. Some days, I was angry with my mom, frustrated with her choices, and I'd yell that I hated Gary and that she should leave him—though I couldn't really say why. Other days, I'd be mad at my sister, telling Mom she should just marry Gary already. As a kid, I didn't have the words for it, but I was struggling to make sense of the fracture in our family, torn between loyalty and resentment.

The older I got, the more I noticed about Gary. He was an overweight guy who seemed content with a cycle of work, drinking, and watching hockey. I started to see how he was influencing my mom's lifestyle, dragging her away from the active life she'd once led—skydiving, hiking, ski patrol—and settling her into a slower, less active routine.

It was around this time I started to feel an instinct to protect my mom, to somehow counter the hold Gary had on her. But she was infatuated with him, afraid of being alone. In her eyes, Gary could do wrong, and I felt like she was prioritizing him over me.

* * *

By the time I hit my early teens, I could see Gary's impact more clearly, and he seemed less like a neutral presence and more like a poison seeping into our family. He wasn't a role model; he was a burden, a weight pulling us down. My frustration with him turned into full-on hatred, and my relationship with Mom grew more strained. I started acting out, arguing with her constantly. I was kicked out of her house more than once.

Despite my outbursts and resistance, a part of me still felt responsible and wanted to protect my mom. Even as I acted out, I found myself pulled back into the role of the rescuer, sensing that Mom needed stability and feeling like it was up to me to provide it, even though I felt powerless to change anything. This conflict between wanting to rebel and feeling the weight of responsibility sent me in a loop—angry, resentful, yet still deeply loyal.

* * *

The day the mask fully formed, I was sixteen. I woke up that morning and went upstairs, where I was greeted by Mom's best friend Nicole. She told me she'd called an ambulance for my mom and it was on its way. Mom was sitting on the couch, clutching an ice pack to her head, her voice wavering as she repeated, "I'm fine, I'm fine." But she didn't sound fine. She was slurring, disoriented, and, as I quickly realized, drunk. She had fallen and hit her head, and I had no idea what was going on. It all happened so fast. The next thing I knew, the medics were at our door, checking her over and insisting she needed to go to the hospital. She resisted, of course, but eventually relented, and I was asked to ride along in the ambulance.

I'd never felt more unprepared in my life. One moment, I'd just woken up, and the next, I was sitting in an ambulance, watching my mom—my strong, independent mom—arguing with the medics as they tried to reassure her. I sat there in silence, trying to process everything, but the reality of it all seemed too big to grasp. The ride felt endless as I watched her, not acting like herself, telling the medics that she didn't need to be there, that she was fine. They spoke to her calmly, assuring her it was just to get her checked out.

When we finally arrived at the hospital, they wheeled her in, settling her in a curtained-off section while I stayed by her side. She kept repeating, "I want to go home. I'm fine. I want to go home." And I kept telling her she needed to be there, but inside I felt like a kid again—helpless, scared, trying desperately to keep it together. I'd messaged Michelle, letting her know what was happening, and she replied that she'd be over to pick me up. Gary eventually showed up too, though, by that point, everything felt like a blur.

When Michelle messaged me that she'd arrived, I exited the hospital and saw her waiting. The moment I reached her, the walls I'd been holding up collapsed. I broke down in tears, all the fear and confusion spilling out in one overwhelming rush. She held me until I'd calmed down, and then told me to wait by the car. I later found out she'd gone back in to confront my mom, furious that she'd put me in that situation, having to see her like that.

From that day on, everything changed. It was as though the roles had shifted overnight. I was no longer the child. That 16-year-old kid had to grow up even faster, taking on the weight of responsibility and stepping into the role of the parent, the role my sister had been playing to protect me. Mom, in many ways, had become the child, and I the protector. The Mask of the Rescuer had fully taken shape, marking the beginning of a journey that would define so much of who I became.

THE RESCUER—A DOUBLE-SIDED MASK

Parentification—the role reversal I described—can occur when children assume adult responsibilities to stabilize family dysfunction, often due to addiction or mental health challenges. In my life, it took the form of both emotional support and practical tasks around the home. Studies led by Dr. Jacinda Dariotis emphasize the profound impact of parentification, which can lead to self-worth and boundaries becoming closely tied to caregiving.[7]

As adults, many parentified individuals find themselves drawn to relationships where they can "rescue" others, often to their detriment. I saw my relationships echo this dynamic—love felt like caregiving, a duty to fix or protect. Asking for help felt impossible; I sought people who, like my mom, seemed to need me. This pattern blurred boundaries and made intimacy difficult, leaving me caught between my own needs and the role I'd taken on.

> **For me, the path of the rescuer led to both resilience and inner conflict as I juggled the drive to protect or rescue others while managing my own struggles.**

Recognizing the effects of parentification has been part of my healing journey. By understanding the cost of my role, I've gained insight into the value of boundaries and self-care. This journey has allowed me to see the Mask of the Rescuer for what it is: a protective layer that once defined me but doesn't have to.

By wearing the mask, I learned how to stay composed and provide support in difficult situations. The constant requirement to be tuned in to my mother's needs fostered a deep sense of empathy and compassion, making me sensitive to the struggles of others. My role as a dependable figure became known to those around me. Friends, family—everyone could count on me in times of crisis, which helped build trust in those relationships.

However, the Mask of the Rescuer comes with costs that can be hard to recognize at first. When you're constantly focused on others' needs, it's easy to lose sight of your own well-being. Over time, this mask often leads to burnout—both emotionally and physically—as the energy spent in "rescue mode" drains even the most resilient. It can become nearly impossible to set boundaries or say no, even when you're stretched too thin.

This pattern often creates relationships based on dependency, where others lean heavily on the support you give, making it difficult to find balance. Focusing so intently on others' needs can also be a way to avoid facing your own vulnerability or struggles. For some of us, this mask becomes a protective layer, allowing us to focus outward rather than looking inward at our own pain and needs.

STEPS TO REMOVE THE MASK OF THE RESCUER

The Mask of the Rescuer can be both a comfort and a barrier, helping you feel needed while also keeping you from exploring your own growth. Recognizing the costs is the first step in understanding when and how to set the mask down, to be present not just for others but also for yourself.

1. **Recognize your motivations:** Understand why you feel compelled to step in and "fix" things. Reflecting on past experiences can reveal how early caregiving roles shaped this pattern.
2. **Set small boundaries:** Practice saying "no" in manageable situations. Starting small helps you build confidence in maintaining boundaries without feeling guilt.
3. **Reclaim self-worth:** Remind yourself that your value isn't tied solely to helping others. Explore activities or hobbies that fulfill you personally, without focusing on anyone else's needs.
4. **Allow yourself vulnerability:** Sharing your own struggles and being open with trusted people can foster balanced connections, reducing the need to "rescue" as a form of emotional self-protection.
5. **Seek support:** Working with a therapist or counselor can provide tools to help break the cycle of over-responsibility. Therapy offers a space to explore healthier boundaries and self-care practices.
6. **Celebrate progress, not perfection:** Remember that change takes time. Celebrate each step you take toward balancing your needs with those of others, knowing that learning to set down this mask is a journey.

REFLECTIONS AND LEARNINGS: THE MASK OF THE RESCUER

Recognizing Early Patterns of Rescue

My story: Looking back, I realize that I felt an early sense of duty to help my mom manage the chaos at home. I thought that, by "rescuing," I could help keep her safe.

Your reflection: When did you first feel responsible for others? Reflect on whether there are patterns that led you to take on a rescuer role.

Exercise: Write about one instance where you felt you needed to rescue someone. Consider what motivated you in that moment.

Balancing Self-Care with Helping Others

My story: Over time, I learned that focusing only on others left me drained, making it hard to be present with my own needs and emotions.

Your reflection: Are there times you neglect self-care in favor of helping others? How does this impact you?

Exercise: Commit to two self-care practices this week. Write down how it feels to set these boundaries and focus on your own well-being.

Breaking the Dependency Cycle

My story: I found that being the "fixer" created a cycle where people came to rely on me, but it also led to one-sided relationships.

Your reflection: Do you find yourself feeling more like a caretaker than an equal in relationships? Consider how this affects the relationship balance.

Exercise: Identify one relationship where you feel overly responsible.

Reflect on a small boundary you could set to encourage balance.

Embracing Vulnerability for Growth

My story: By focusing only on others, I avoided my own vulnerability. Letting people see my true struggles became a step toward healthier relationships.

Your reflection: Do you find yourself hiding your own struggles from others? Think about how openness might create deeper connections.

Exercise: Practice sharing a small personal challenge with someone you trust. Note how it feels to be vulnerable.

Redefining Self-Worth Beyond Helping

My Story: I used to believe my value lay in how much I could help others. Over time, I learned that my worth isn't dependent on how much I can "fix."

Your reflection: How much of your self-worth is tied to helping others? Reflect on where your worth might come from beyond caregiving.

Exercise: Write about three qualities you value in yourself outside of being a caregiver. Revisit this list to remind yourself of your full worth.

MASK OF THE RESCUER
KEY TAKEAWAYS

- **Balance is key**: Recognizing that you don't have to be the rescuer in every situation frees you to build more balanced, reciprocal relationships.
- **Boundaries build balance:** Setting boundaries allows others to step up and grow while giving you the space for self-care.
- **Your worth is more than what you give:** Your value isn't tied solely to helping others. Finding fulfillment outside of the rescuer role enriches your life.
- **Vulnerability opens new connections**: Allowing others to see your own needs builds trust and allows for genuine connection beyond caregiving.
- **Celebrate small shifts**: Every small boundary and moment of self-focus is a victory toward finding balance and healing from the rescuer role.

CHAPTER 7

THE MASK OF DEFENSE

GUARDING AGAINST EMOTIONAL PAIN

The Cycle of Defense

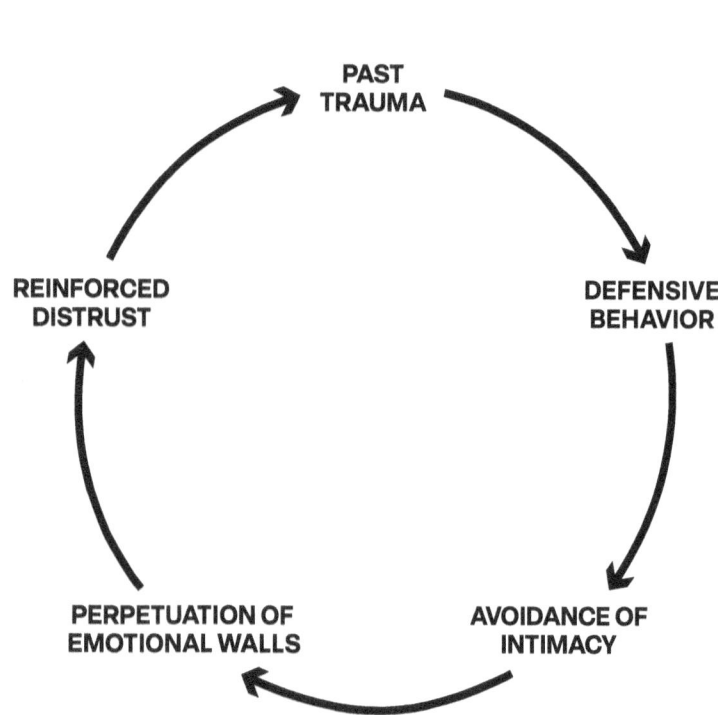

Early in my coaching career, I began working with a client named Corey. Corey and I had known each other for some time and became friends. We'd even met in person while I was back in Canada, where he shared a bit about his life. I knew he'd been through something difficult about 10 years earlier, but it wasn't until we began working together in a coaching setting that more details came out.

As Corey opened up, I started to see just how much this past incident had affected him. The defenses he'd built to protect himself from reliving that trauma were always present, even in our early conversations. But his protective instincts weren't just about guarding himself from physical pain or harm—they were about keeping his emotions contained, safe from anyone who might hurt him again. He didn't let people in easily, and he maintained a safe distance from relationships and situations that could make him feel vulnerable.

The Mask of Defense isn't just about creating barriers against others; it's about building walls to protect our inner world, keeping it safe from the vulnerability and emotional risks that relationships inevitably bring.

The mask forms when we've experienced hurt or betrayal and don't want to experience that pain again. For many, it becomes a reflexive shield—a constant effort to avoid closeness, to stay in control, and to prevent others from getting too close.

A DEFENSIVE RESPONSE TO EXTREME TRAUMA (COREY'S STORY)

Corey's journey of healing and self-discovery began with a long-held dream—to recover from a spinal fusion surgery, work through extensive physiotherapy, and eventually return to the body and life he once had. His recovery inspired him to take a long-awaited solo trip to Greece in the summer of 2013. This trip was meant to be an escape, a reward, and a way to reconnect with himself after months of hard work and dedication. But instead, it turned to an event that altered his life forever.

Once in Greece, Corey spent most of the trip exploring, meeting people, and reveling in the beauty of the nation's islands. One night, as he was nearing the end of his trip, he went out with a vacationing family he'd befriended. They invited him to a dance bar near the harbor for a night of celebration.

After finishing a drink bought by two strangers at the bar, Corey began feeling increasingly unwell. Dizzy, hot, and numb, he stumbled out toward a secluded area beyond the bar's back deck, hoping some fresh air would help clear his head. But as he reached the trees, the situation took a dark turn. Now on all fours, he could hear footsteps approaching, which he assumed belonged to someone from the family checking on him. As he looked up, he received a sudden, powerful punch to the face. While he remembers most of what happened next, some parts remain fragmented, forever locked away in his memory.

The next morning, Corey woke up in pain, both physical and emotional. Scared, ashamed, and overwhelmed, he avoided the main paths and chose a rocky, secluded route down to the shoreline, hoping to wash away not just the physical pain but also the shame he felt. He returned to his hotel discreetly, avoiding any possibility of being seen by others.

Later, he gathered the strength to visit a local surgeon to have his jaw set back in place—another blow that required both physical and emotional endurance. Yet, even after enduring so much, Corey chose to keep this experience to himself. He returned home without telling anyone, carrying this wound in silence, afraid of the judgment or pity it might bring.

When Corey and I began coaching, I saw the toll that 10 years of isolation had taken on him. The Mask of Defense had formed as a way for him to protect himself from future harm, keeping others at a distance so he could feel safe. The walls he built made him feel like he was in control, but they also became his prison. The trauma and shame he carried weighed on him, creating emotional barriers that kept even his closest family and friends at arm's length. Corey avoided intimacy, shrank from vulnerability, and became guarded in every interaction, even with me. It took time, trust, and patience for him to lower his defenses and confront the pain he had hidden away.

Corey's journey illustrates how the Mask of Defense forms as a response to deep emotional pain, rejection, or betrayal, convincing us that keeping others at a distance will protect us. But Corey's story also shows that, over time, this mask can become suffocating, leaving us isolated and disconnected from the very support we need to heal. Working together, Corey and I began the difficult process of peeling back that mask, helping him reconnect not only with others but also with the parts of himself he had been hiding for so long.

A MASK, A SHIELD, A BARRIER IS FORMED

The Mask of Defense often originates from past emotional wounds, trauma, or painful experiences where vulnerability led to hurt, betrayal, or rejection. For many, this mask begins early in life, serving as a shield to protect from further harm. It becomes a way to avoid intimacy or connection, ensuring that no one gets close enough to cause pain.

From childhood, there are often signs of this mask beginning to form. Rejection, abandonment, or betrayal by loved ones can leave deep scars that lead to emotional withdrawal. For some, it comes from a single traumatic experience; for others, it forms from the accumulation of smaller wounds, like bullying or social rejection. In my own life, this was particularly true during high school. Bullying made me defensive, and my home life left me feeling as though vulnerability was a weakness. Growing up, I believed I had to live up to the example my father set—the strong, stoic "manly man"—which meant keeping my feelings hidden.

As Corey's story shows, the Mask of Defense is often rooted in shame, pain, and a fear of being hurt again. Corey became adept at hiding his trauma. He avoided mirrors, unable to look into his own eyes. He started showering with his clothes on, struggling to feel comfortable even in his own skin. To cope, he tried to change his appearance, growing his hair, keeping a beard, and even wearing colored contacts, hoping that, by altering his appearance, he could somehow change what he felt inside.

The Mask of Defense, once a means of self-preservation, became a prison. Corey tried to numb the pain in ways that felt increasingly desperate. Twice he attempted to overdose on old pain medication, but, each time, he survived. Friends and family reached out with messages of concern, but he avoided them, unable to share the pain he carried. The mask he wore kept him protected, but it also kept him isolated.

Corey's journey illustrates the power and the trap of the Mask of Defense. By acting tough, distant, or detached, we try to protect our wounded inner self from being exposed. This mask offers a sense of control over relationships, allowing us to dictate the level of intimacy and guard our emotions from further harm. But in the process, it can leave us profoundly alone, disconnected from others and, ultimately, from ourselves.

Research published in *Frontiers in Psychology* reveals that individuals who rely on defense mechanisms, such as denial and repression, to cope with trauma may actually worsen their psychological distress.[8] These mechanisms can reduce immediate discomfort, but by preventing proper emotional processing and healing, they ultimately keep the trauma unaddressed. Over time, this contributes to increased isolation—as was the case with Corey, who withdrew further into himself, unable to trust or open up. The very defenses he thought would protect him became barriers to the connections he needed, trapping him in a cycle of defensiveness and fear.

Then there's the issue of trust—or the lack thereof. For Corey, the trauma he endured led him to believe that others couldn't be trusted, and over time he became more and more entrenched in this defensive stance. In his mind, people, even those close to him, were a potential source of pain. He was convinced that only by staying distant could he avoid betrayal. This lack of trust became one of the main reasons he wore the mask, reinforcing the barriers he had built over the years.

Avoidance of vulnerability is another common reason for wearing the Mask of Defense. Vulnerability often feels synonymous with weakness, and by maintaining a defensive front, individuals can avoid being seen as fragile or exposed. For Corey, his self-protective instincts were so strong that vulnerability became something he couldn't risk. The thought of revealing his pain was terrifying, and the mask became his way to avoid that discomfort.

> **Ultimately, the Mask of Defense serves as a means of self-preservation. By not allowing others in too deeply, individuals feel they can protect their emotional well-being, even if it means sacrificing true connection.**

DISMANTLING THE MASK OF DEFENSE

Now, I want to be clear—I wasn't the only one who worked with Corey. In the months following the traumatic incident, a few close friends of his—friends who knew the full story—recognized how much he was struggling and stepped in to help. They found a psychologist willing to see Corey on weekends, arranging appointments so he could come and go discreetly, away from the watchful eyes of anyone who might recognize him. Corey described those early sessions as incredibly difficult, a place where he would just shake and cry, feeling as though he was right back in the morning after his trauma. It took months before he could even begin to express his pain, but, over the next eight years, therapy became a lifeline.

By the time Corey and I began working together, he had made immense strides through years of therapy. My role wasn't to replace the work he had done but to help him build on it—to further dismantle the barriers he'd created, to help him push out of his comfort zone, and to support his efforts in confronting the last remaining shadows of his trauma.

Corey was ready for a new chapter. He had developed tools to calm himself in triggering moments, and while the occasional nightmare still arose, it no longer debilitated him the way it once had. For Corey, this work was about moving beyond survival and embracing a life where he no longer had to hide, where he could finally begin to live without the mask.

During my work with Corey, I focused on helping him become clear on the meanings he had assigned to different aspects of his life. Over the years, he had built stories around his experiences—stories that kept him isolated and safe within the confines of his home, which he called his "safe house." Our sessions involved a lot of reframing, gradually chipping away at the layers of protection he had built up. Corey wanted to break out of his comfort zone and be more adventurous and engage in activities outside of his familiar surroundings. He knew this would be challenging, but he was ready for a new chapter.

By wearing the Mask of Defense, Corey was missing out on genuine emotional connections and the richness of intimate relationships that could have brought more meaning to his life. The toll was exhausting. The effort required to constantly guard himself was draining, leading to emotional fatigue and burnout. He began to understand that his defensive posture wasn't just keeping others at bay—it was preventing his own personal growth. Without vulnerability, Corey realized he was stalling his own emotional and spiritual development, missing opportunities to learn from his emotions and from those around him.

Through it all, Corey remained dedicated. He knew that breaking free from the Mask of Defense would be difficult, and some sessions were particularly tough and emotionally draining. But he persisted, knowing the value of the process. After spending years sitting in the past, haunted by old wounds, he was finally ready to embrace a new chapter, one that allowed room for connection, trust, and the richness of authentic relationships.

Corey's journey didn't end with our sessions; they were just the beginning of a new chapter. Today, he stands with renewed confidence and openness. He's able to face challenges that once seemed overwhelming, and his relationships have deepened as he's become more assertive and comfortable with vulnerability. His life is no longer marked by avoidance and isolation, but instead by meaningful connections and a sense of personal empowerment.

While Corey continues to work with his psychologist, he now approaches these sessions from a place of growth rather than survival. He's found excitement in taking new risks, like attending events he once avoided and opening up more to those close to him.

> **Corey's journey has shown him that change doesn't mean erasing the past—it means moving forward with a renewed sense of self, courage, and purpose.**

STEPS TO REMOVE THE MASK OF DEFENSE

Removing the Mask of Defense takes time, patience, and a commitment to personal growth, but the benefits, which include a newfound ability to build meaningful connections, are well worth the effort.

1. **Acknowledge your wounds:** Recognize the past experiences that led you to put up defenses. Understanding these wounds isn't weakness—it's the first step toward healing and freeing yourself from their grip. The more you acknowledge them, the less power they have over your present.
2. **Practice vulnerability in small steps:** Vulnerability doesn't

have to happen all at once. Start by allowing yourself to be open in small, safe situations. This could mean sharing a thought, feeling, or fear with someone you trust, or letting yourself express an opinion that might expose a bit of who you really are. Observe how it feels to let your guard down, even in a small way. These gradual steps help make vulnerability feel more manageable and less threatening.

3. **Build trust:** Rebuilding trust with others is a significant part of dismantling the Mask of Defense. This may mean taking small, calculated risks in your relationships, allowing people to prove they're trustworthy. It's natural to feel hesitant after being hurt, but by giving others a chance, you begin to soften your defenses and open up to meaningful connections. Over time, these small acts of trust can help rewire your perspective on relationships.

4. **Challenge your beliefs about vulnerability:** Remind yourself that vulnerability isn't a weakness; it's a strength that allows for deeper connections and emotional freedom. Practice reframing vulnerability as an opportunity for growth rather than a threat. Vulnerability is an act of courage—it means you're willing to embrace the unknown and show up as your true self, regardless of how others may respond.

5. **Let go of the need for control:** Relationships are unpredictable, and while this uncertainty can be uncomfortable, it's also what makes them rich and dynamic. Allow yourself to experience relationships without trying to control every aspect. Accept that while opening up may come with risks, it also brings the potential for joy, connection, and

growth. By relinquishing the need for control, you allow for more authentic interactions.

6. **Seek support:** You don't have to go through this alone. Working with a therapist, counselor, or coach—like myself—can provide guidance, tools, and a safe space to explore vulnerability. Support from a trusted professional can help you break down barriers, develop healthier coping strategies, and step into a more open and empowered version of yourself.

7. **Be patient with yourself:** Removing the Mask of Defense isn't a quick fix—it's a gradual journey of self-discovery and healing. There will be times when you want to retreat behind the mask, and that's OK. Allow yourself to move at a pace that feels right for you. Be patient and compassionate as you learn to embrace vulnerability, build trust, and reconnect with the world in a way that feels genuine and open.

Removing the Mask of Defense can feel intimidating, but each step brings you closer to a life where connection and trust are possible. It's a path to discovering a truer version of yourself—one who can engage in relationships without fear, experience emotional freedom, and find strength in vulnerability.

REFLECTIONS AND LEARNINGS: THE MASK OF DEFENSE

Reflecting on Trauma and Healing

Corey's story: As Corey's story demonstrates, you can't rush the process of healing and moving past trauma. Healing takes time.

Reflection: How are you treating the trauma you're carrying? Is it like a hangnail, a sprained ankle, or a full-blown medical emergency? Recognizing the level of attention and care your trauma needs can help guide your healing process.

Exercise: Reflect on how you've approached your healing. Are there areas where you could slow down? Are there others where you might benefit from more focused attention?

Recognizing How Trauma Affects Identity

Corey's story: Corey learned that while he couldn't erase the past, he could move forward from it. The events of the past will always be a part of you, but they aren't the only part of you.

Reflection: How much of your identity revolves around your trauma?

Exercise: Identify aspects of yourself beyond your trauma. List things that make you unique and contribute to who you are today.

Understanding the Pitfalls of Comparison

Corey's story: Following his trauma, Corey changed in many ways, using the Mask of Defense to shield himself from further pain. It's important that you don't compare who you were before the trauma, during it, or after it, and don't compare your journey to that of others.

Reflection: Comparison is the thief of joy. Are you comparing yourself to who you used to be or to others with similar experiences?

Exercise: Identify where you were and where you are now. Acknowledge the small wins and achievements along the way.

Accepting the Path of Healing

Corey's story: Corey's healing journey took many twists and turns, which is expected. Healing isn't linear—it's messy but still progress.

Reflection: Are you allowing yourself to have tough days? Are you celebrating the good days? Are you acknowledging your feelings along the journey? Remember, it's OK to have hard days—it's a part of being human.

Exercise: Accept the tough days as they come. Be present with your emotions, allowing them the space they need.

Recognizing the Resilience Within

Corey's story: During his healing journey, Corey found a strength he didn't know he had. Resilience remains, even during times when you feel like you're failing. Each challenge strengthens that resilience within you.

Reflection: In what ways have you demonstrated resilience, even when you didn't feel strong? How can you honor the resilience you've shown during difficult times?

Exercise: List a few moments when you pushed through a struggle. Reflect on how each has contributed to your inner strength and resilience.

Breaking Down Big Goals into Smaller Steps

Corey's story: Tackling small tasks without expecting overnight change allowed Corey to challenge his beliefs and expand his comfort zone.

Reflection: Are you setting small, achievable tasks that allow for steady progress? Or are your goals too far out of reach?

Exercise: Break down a current goal into smaller, manageable steps. Reflect on how each step, no matter how small, brings you closer to lasting change.

> ## MASK OF DEFENSE
> ## KEY TAKEAWAYS
>
> ---
>
> - **Healing takes time:** True healing can't be rushed. Trauma is complex and often needs consistent attention, patience, and compassion. Recognize where you are in your healing journey and allow yourself the time necessary to process and grow.
> - **Your trauma is part of you, but not all of you:** While trauma can shape aspects of your identity, it doesn't define your entire self. Finding and nurturing parts of yourself beyond your pain allows for a fuller, more balanced life.
> - **Comparison holds you back:** Comparing your journey to others or even to your past self can prevent you from seeing the progress you've made. Every journey is unique; honor your own path by acknowledging your steps forward without judgment.

- **Healing isn't linear:** The road to recovery is rarely a straight line. Allow yourself to experience the ups and downs, and embrace the progress you've made, even if it's messy. Bad days are part of the process, and they don't erase the good ones.
- **Resilience is built over time:** Resilience grows each time you face challenges, even if it doesn't feel that way in the moment. Recognize the strength within you that allows you to endure and rebuild, and see each struggle as a step in building a stronger foundation.
- **Small steps lead to lasting change:** Lasting transformation comes from small, consistent actions rather than quick fixes. Set realistic goals, celebrate each small step, and remember that gradual progress will eventually get you where you want to be.
- **Vulnerability is strength:** Letting down the Mask of Defense takes courage, but it opens the door to real connection, healing, and self-acceptance. Vulnerability may feel risky, but it ultimately allows you to live a life that feels more authentic and connected.
- **Self-compassion is essential:** Being kind to yourself during the healing journey can make all the difference. Self-criticism can reinforce feelings of shame or failure, while self-compassion allows space

for growth, acceptance, and forgiveness of past mistakes.

- **Emotional pain can be a guide, not an enemy:** Avoiding emotional pain often leads to isolation and disconnection. Embracing discomfort, rather than running from it, can reveal valuable insights into your needs, boundaries, and areas for growth.
- **Boundaries can be protective without being isolating:** The Mask of Defense often involves strict boundaries that are harmful in the long run. However, learning to create healthy boundaries allows you to protect your well-being without shutting people out entirely. Healthy boundaries let you build relationships that are safe and supportive.
- **Support systems are vital:** Healing isn't something you have to do alone. Surrounding yourself with supportive friends, family, or professionals can offer relief, perspective, and encouragement when you need it most.

CHAPTER 8

THE MASK OF APPROVAL

HIDING FROM THE
FEAR OF JUDGMENT

The Cycle of Approval

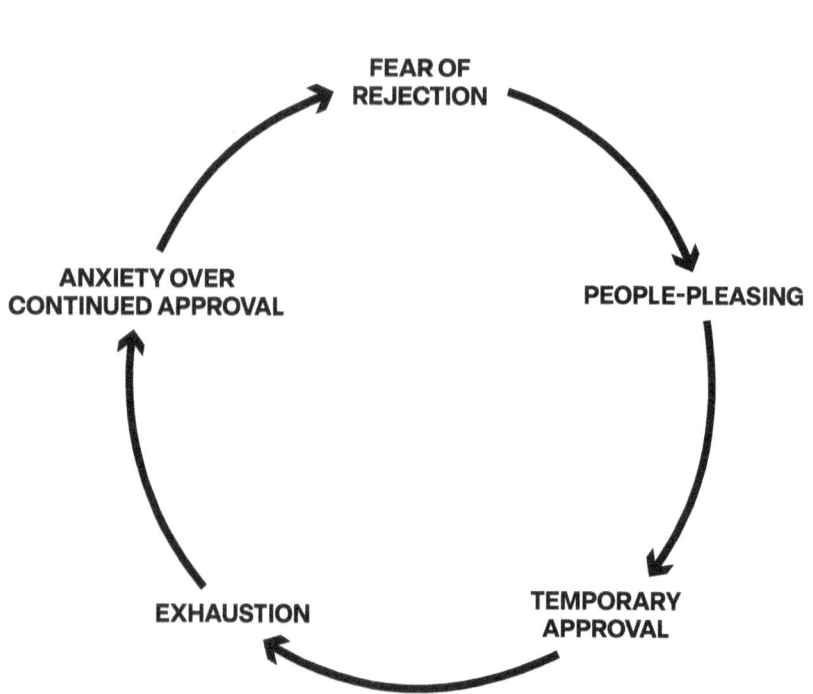

The letter was a back-and-forth battle between anger and the need for approval. On one hand, I needed to express the hurt and anger caused by his actions. I wrote, *You were the only male figure in my life that I had to talk to, and your anger problems ruined that for me.* But even as I poured out the pain, a part of me still yearned for his validation. I wanted him to see me, to acknowledge the strength I'd built in spite of everything. So I added, *I'm glad I went through the things I went through growing up because it made me a strong person and a survivor.*

When we think of those who seek approval, it often aligns with the idea of a "people pleaser." Though these behaviors share similarities, mainly relying on others' opinions to feel valued, they don't always mean the same thing. In excess, both can signal emotional challenges or struggles with self-worth.

While approval-seeking is largely about validation, people-pleasing may go deeper, focusing more on making others happy or feeling responsible for others' needs—a behavior rooted in codependency. People-pleasing often becomes about sacrificing personal boundaries to ensure others are content, whether or not validation is explicitly sought.

But where does it come from? For me, seeking validation became almost like a drug as I moved into the big city.

> **The thrill of acceptance, of being seen in the "right" way by others, was enticing, almost addictive. It drove me to adapt, conform, and often lose sight of who I was beneath the need for approval.**

LIFE AFTER HIGH SCHOOL

After graduating high school, there was still a part of me deeply tied to Mike, my first love, who had recently been found innocent of all charges. I wanted to see him, to be with him without anyone else around. I knew—although I wouldn't admit it—that I needed his validation, one last sense of connection before I moved on.

When I met up with Mike in Ontario, he was different—quieter, understandably affected by everything he'd been through. For my 18th birthday, he took me to a tattoo artist in Oshawa. I didn't know exactly what I wanted, just something tribal that felt bold and transformative. After a long session, I walked out with my first tattoo, my skin still red and raw. It felt powerful, like a rite of passage, a mark that announced I was leaving my old self behind. But as it healed, the imperfections became clear—faded lines, uneven design. I had wanted it to be a symbol of my transformation, and now it felt like a reminder of everything that didn't go to plan.

STEPPING INTO A WHOLE NEW WORLD ... OR SEVERAL

When I moved in with my Uncle Dave and Aunt Kim in Vancouver, I felt like I had stepped into another world entirely. Their home was nestled in a quiet cul-de-sac, a beautiful house with a sprawling backyard and a pool. It felt like an oasis. On some weekends, my uncle would take the family to an island by boat to camp, and there he and I would hike through the forest, following the river that wound its way through, dotted with massive boulders. It was here, amid the wilderness and under his quiet guidance, that I felt truly at ease—a stark contrast to my last few years at home.

I quickly got into a rhythm, getting a job at Boston Pizza and rising to assistant kitchen manager. I made friends—Condessa, Matt, Emily, and Steve. Eventually, I moved in with Steve, and we set up a makeshift bedroom for me in his living room, using wall dividers to carve out a little space. I slept on a tiny mattress with a small shelf at the foot of my bed for my clothes. It wasn't much, but it did the job, and honestly it felt like a step toward independence.

When Steve and Condessa took it upon themselves to break me

into the Vancouver nightlife, they brought me to the Odyssey, my first gay bar. Walking in, it was like stepping into another world. I'd never been around that many gay people—the place was alive.

The music was pumping; people were dancing; everyone was just being themselves, unapologetically embracing who they were. I didn't feel the weight of my mask; for once, I could just be.

We stayed until close before making the 45-minute drive back home, the night still buzzing in my head.

* * *

The third time I went downtown, it was Halloween. Everyone was dressed up, and, being a small-town guy, I decided to go as a punk—not much of a costume, just my usual baggy pants and a white singlet. I was out on the back patio with a drink when I caught the eye of a guy a bit shorter than me, clearly older. He came over, and we started chatting—his name was Wayne. Before I knew it, we were on the dance floor, grinding and making out. The connection was instant and only deepened over the next few months.

Most Fridays, Wayne would come all the way out to Maple Ridge to pick me up, and we'd head downtown for a weekend together—partying, taking drugs, and dancing until the lights came on. On those nights, we'd hit the Odyssey, dance until close, then wander the city, taking in the lights, falling more in love each time.

Despite the 20-year age gap—his 38 years to my 18—we had an amazing connection. The age difference felt natural, comfortable. Maybe it was the lack of older male figures growing up that drew me to someone older, but I'd always been an "old soul," as they say. I felt like 18 going on 35.

In January, I moved in with Wayne, right into his tiny studio in downtown Vancouver. Wayne was a talented interior designer and a brilliant painter, and his clients were some of the wealthiest in the area. Living together was surprisingly easy. We were both Virgos—both neat and organized.

Wayne was a steady first partner, someone with his head on straight who could show me the ropes of "gay life," or at least his version of it.

TIME TO MEET THE FAMILY

When the time felt right, I began to introduce Wayne to my family, starting with my grandparents. They were incredibly accepting, and the connection was immediate. Wayne and my grandma got along like they'd known each other for years. Wayne's Ukrainian background was something my grandma connected with instantly—she adored Ukrainian culture. Her walls were lined with little glass boxes filled with *pysanky*, those beautifully decorated Ukrainian eggs, and she even had how-to videos for making perogies, a Ukrainian delicacy.

It wasn't long before my whole family fell in love with Wayne. He fit right in, and it felt like a missing piece had finally clicked into place. But there was still one person who didn't know about Wayne—my dad. Wayne was well aware of the struggles I had with my father. He saw the anger and resentment I carried, the pain that still lingered from how Dad had treated me growing up. I shared the stories, the memories that still stung, and Wayne listened.

About six months into our relationship, Wayne could see that the weight of my secret was holding me back. He told me gently but firmly that if we were going to move forward together, I needed to face this—to open up to my dad and free myself from the burden I'd been carrying for so long. Wayne knew it was a tough step, but he also knew it was necessary for me to heal and for us to build a future together. It was time to face the truth of who I was and stop letting the need for approval hold me back.

THE LETTER ...

Dear Dad,

I'm writing this letter to you because I'm trying to move on with my life without any stress and the relationship we have needs to change, so I'm going to start by being completely honest with you.

As you may know I am gay and am not going to hide it anymore. In the last year I have been finding more of myself everyday and have been finding myself to be quite a good guy.

Growing up, I know that I didn't have a normal childhood, going through the things that I went through. Apart from the things going on within the family I had a whole lot more going on with myself. I was going through changes that I should have gone through in a much more comfortable environment. I needed someone to talk to about the feelings I had inside of me.

They say that the same sex parent is the child's biggest role model, I never got that from you. My sister didn't get that from you. My sister and I just wanted each other to get along with both you and mom and that was the biggest reason we fought. I guess we found it easier and less stressful being away from you guys.

Besides from living in a small town where being gay was something a lot of people didn't understand, I grew up with a homophobic father who would try to make me afraid of who I really was. You were the only male figure in my life that I had to talk to and your anger problems ruined that for me. Your way of dealing with problems is not what any kid has to go through.

I remember the first incident we had with gay porn on the internet, you and Michelle brought Garrett and I into the computer room and pulled up some files that I had been looking at. You were constantly just yelling at us, asking who it was and all fingers pointed to me. You asked if I was gay, but I was young and didn't know how to answer that.

I then completely lost it and started yelling back. I think that was the first time I yelled back at you. All I was screaming back was "what if I was gay, are you going to kick me out?" I repeatedly screamed this and you know what your answer was "MAYBE." That second I knew you weren't yelling just cause of me looking at porn, but mostly because it was gay porn.

As I got older, more incidents came up with the gay thing. One day you called me into the kitchen and you had a bunch of papers sitting on the kitchen table. You told me to read all of it. So I started reading and it was all about AIDS and how it's a fast spreading disease amongst all gay people. I got up after feeling uncomfortable reading half a page and you made me sit down and finish it. Were you hoping to change my mind and make me afraid of being gay? AIDS can be spread whether you're gay or straight.

Since those events I haven't felt comfortable around you in almost 10 years. I would even feel uncomfortable to be alone with you; cause I was worried about something you would say or I just didn't know how to talk to you.

Last year I came out to all my friends and most of my family and it went pretty good better than I thought it would. I did get bugged all through high school about some rumour that started when I was in grade 9, which stuck with me right until grade 12. I would spend lunch hours by myself in the library cause I would get called out in front of a bunch of people and I just couldn't handle the jokes. It's not easy being gay and having to pretend to be someone you're not. But in grade 12 I came out and people thought it was awesome, I guess I was so afraid of what people thought that I let it get in the way of me living.

When I started coaching gymnastics and staying over with Mike and Brent, you took that and tried to make it look like there was a lot more going on. Not only that but you posted what you thought on Facebook for everyone else to read, and also said that I have been a victim of male predators most of my life. I really couldn't believe that you would do something like that. Put your own son out there to look like a pedophile victim. You may not have meant to make it look this way, but that's something you could have thought about a little more before acting on.

I would rather spend more time with older people mostly

because I feel older than I am, you may not see this but a lot of people do. When I was spending my weekends at Rob the bartender's house yet again you took that and tried to make it look like it was something you feared the most. He was not taking advantage of me or doing anything with me, I stayed with him because we both worked till 2 in the morning on weekends so I would go to his place instead of going out. At the time Rob's place was the most stable place for me to go. You made that into such a big thing that Rob asked me to leave cause he didn't want to be involved.

Moving to Vancouver was the best decision I could have made for myself. Most of my friends are older gay men who are taking great care of me and showing me the ropes. I'm not out partying, doing drugs and having random sex with strangers. I'm doing the gym everyday and eating home cooked meals as much as possible. I have a gay doctor I see so I get all the information I need to keep me healthy and safe.

I've been in a relationship now for 6 months with an amazing guy who is 38. His name is Wayne and he does interior painting. He's smart, good-looking and very talented with what he does. I know you must be shaking your head at this but I've become strong enough not to let you make me feel that what I'm doing or who I am is wrong. Michelle, my sister and my mom have all met Wayne and they think he is a great guy. After 5 months of dating, Wayne and I decided that I would move in with him and start painting with him. Boston Pizza wasn't going where I hoped it would. Wayne and I live in a small apartment up high just a few blocks away from the beach so we have a great view of the water.

Painting is going great with Wayne I'm learning a lot and I'm seeing some amazing houses and condos and am making some pretty good cash. I'm looking at some possible things to do for my future but I'm not sure of what I want to do yet. Photography is something I have always wanted to do and I'm pretty good at it. I am enjoying working with Wayne and painting around Vancouver for the time being. Maybe one day you'll meet him.

I know you blame everyone else for my being gay, but it's no one's fault. I was born this way and I'm happy with who I am. You really have no reason to be embarrassed of me; I'm not like all the gay kids that everyone thinks about. You did raise me better than that and I thank you for that. I'd hate to be a skinny little flamer who sticks out like a sore thumb. I'm masculine, good looking, smart and a good-hearted guy. In a way I'm glad I went through the things I went through growing up because it made me a strong person and a survivor. Writing this letter wasn't the easiest thing for me to do but I did it and I'm glad I did because I had a lot inside that I had to get out. I don't want to live my life with little unsettled pieces floating around; I want a stress free life. So how you want to react to this letter is completely up to you. I just don't want to have that negativity in my life anymore. I'll be coming home in May; maybe I'll see you and we could start fresh. Your call.

Love your son, Rob

Reflecting on this now, it's clear to me how deep the need for approval can go, how much it shapes our interactions, especially with those we love. Writing that letter was my attempt to bridge a gap that had long felt unbridgeable. It was my 18-year-old self's way of saying, "This is me—accept me, or at least understand me."

In the years since, I've come to realize that, while seeking approval from others can feel validating, real peace comes from accepting myself. This letter remains a testament to my growth, a reminder that I was resilient even then and that the journey toward self-acceptance is ongoing.

THE CONTINUAL QUEST FOR DAD'S APPROVAL

The year after Wayne and I got together, we took a road trip to Smithers to celebrate my younger half-brother Garrett's graduation. I took Wayne to all the places that had shaped me—my high school, my elementary school—and I even introduced him to a few of my old teachers. It felt liberating to be able to do that, to just be myself and not feel scared or embarrassed.

The day of Garrett's graduation celebration, Michelle hosted a barbecue. Most of the family had already met Wayne, and he was being his usual charming self, fitting in as if he'd been around forever. But there was an uneasiness in the air, at least for me. The rumor was that Dad would be stopping by with a gift for Garrett. I hadn't spoken to him in almost two years—not since I'd sent that letter—and now, for the first time, I'd be seeing him face-to-face.

Even though I hated to admit it, I still wanted his approval. I wanted him to see that I was happy, that I was with someone who cared about me. But mostly, I just wanted the chance to face him, to see if anything had changed, to see if there was any possibility of something real between us.

When Dad's truck rolled up, there was a buzz in the air. "He's here, he's here." Everyone knew this was a monumental moment for my dad and me; they knew we hadn't spoken in years.

We were all on the back porch when he came in through the front door, making his way into the kitchen. I eventually worked up the courage to go inside, and with my heart racing a million miles a minute, I said, "Hi, Dad" in my deep, steady voice.

He replied with a simple, "Hello" as we shook hands.

Meanwhile, in my head, all I could think was, *Oh fuck, oh fuck, oh fuck*. Finally, I asked if he'd like to meet Wayne.

"Yeah, sure, whatever," he responded.

I headed back to the porch where my sisters were standing, eagerly waiting like kids. Wayne walked in, calm and collected, extended his hand to my dad, and said, "Mr. Goddard, so lovely to finally meet you. I've heard so many great things about you."

As I watched all this unfold, my older sister nudged me, saying, "Breathe." I'd completely stopped breathing and was just standing there, turning pale, as I watched this long-awaited moment play out.

The next thing I knew, we were standing on the front lawn, watching Dad get into his truck and drive away. Then, everything I'd held in for years came rushing out. I broke down, sobbing so hard that my nose bled. I'd anticipated this moment for so long, and now that it had finally happened, it was as if a giant weight had lifted from my shoulders. Was this the approval I was seeking?

EARNING APPROVAL ON THE WORLD STAGE

Over the next few years, Wayne and I continued our journey together. Unfortunately, the painting business wasn't bringing in enough to support us both, so I took a job bartending at the Oasis, a small gay bar located above a Denny's. The place quickly became my second home, with its packed weekly events: karaoke on Wednesdays, strippers on Thursdays, "Fag Fridays," and "Lesbian Saturdays." Sundays were half-price pitchers, and our rooftop patio was the go-to spot. I became deeply immersed in the gay scene, and, in those four years, I felt like my life was a whirlwind of new connections, endless parties, and unexpected opportunities.

Working at the Oasis gave me a taste of popularity I hadn't fully experienced before. I was known on the scene, a familiar face behind the bar, and part of the vibrant community. I soaked up the attention and approval that came with it, feeling a new sense of validation every time someone remembered my name or complimented my work.

The Mask of Approval often takes root in environments where love, acceptance, and validation are conditional. For many, this need for approval forms early in life, especially in households where affection is tied to meeting specific expectations. Growing up, it's easy to internalize the idea that we're only "enough" when we're accomplishing something or meeting a certain standard. As children, we may feel inadequate compared to siblings or peers, sparking a lifelong quest for validation from others. Experiences of rejection or criticism deepen these feelings, making it instinctive to mold ourselves to match what we believe others expect of us. Later, this need for approval often translates into how we navigate adult relationships, workplaces, and social settings, sometimes even leading us to sacrifice authenticity.

In the gay scene, this need for validation became a constant driver, particularly when I began taking on roles in the public eye. Things escalated even further when I entered the "Vancouver's Gay Top Model" competition. The next thing I knew, I was wearing a sash that said "Mr. Gay Canada," prepping to fly halfway across the world to compete in Mr. Gay World in Manila. One minute, I was just a guy working at a bar; the next, I was doing interviews, my face splashed across the front page of newspapers. My confidence felt linked to the positive reactions I received, each piece of praise reinforcing my sense of worth. For many who wear the Mask of Approval, self-worth depends on external validation, and individuals seek to feel valued by meeting others' needs or desires. Although it might bring a temporary sense of belonging, it distances the person from their own values and desires, making true self-expression difficult.

Rob wearing his sash at Mr. Gay World event.

My mentor Dean tried to coach me for the media, but I found myself stumbling through interviews, scrambling to say the right thing. I wanted so badly to impress, to be seen as someone who could represent the community. My go-to line was, "This is a really important competition because there's a lot of work to do in the gay community, and I want to be part of that change." But deep down, I didn't fully know what I was talking about or what change I wanted to make. I was faking it to make it, desperate to maintain the approval I'd gained, hoping that, somewhere along the way, I'd figure out who I was supposed to be.

The constant attention started to feel like a drug. The recognition, the popularity, the way people responded to me—it was intoxicating. Slowly, I found myself depending on these moments for the approval I craved. It was as if the more people noticed me, the more I needed them to notice. I began to rely on the image I was building as a way to feel valued, as though the mask I wore on stage and behind the bar was what defined my worth.

Manila magnified the Mask of Approval, placing me on an international stage where the stakes felt even higher, and my need for validation grew stronger. The competition was a blur of photoshoots, interviews, and the finale show, which aired live. For each category—swimwear, evening wear, casual wear, suit and tie, and national costume—I had to make a

Rob wearing his Mr. Gay World national costume.

statement. I couldn't just show up as a typical Canadian hockey player; I had to stand out. So I went all out: skates, hockey socks, garter belts, red jockstrap, hockey gloves, chest plate, and a massive Canadian rainbow flag cape. I even managed to nearly slip on stage in my skates! South Africa won the title, but for the next year I was proud to represent Canada at events, making appearances in my sash.

THE DARK SIDE OF THE MASK

As I continued my journey, I noticed how much my actions were influenced by a deep desire for approval. It felt empowering to be seen and admired, yet, looking back, I see how much of my energy went into securing that approval.

Each time I wore the Mask of Approval, it chipped away at my sense of self. Constantly molding myself to others' expectations, I started losing sight of my own desires and boundaries. The burnout crept in slowly, like a weight I couldn't shake. I was exhausted from performing for others, pushing aside my needs to meet theirs. It left me with relationships that felt more shallow than real, built on pleasing rather than truly connecting.

Wearing the Mask of Approval creates both advantages and disadvantages. On the one hand, seeking approval can bring a temporary sense of accomplishment, especially in social situations where acceptance feels crucial. It often smooths over conflicts and maintains social harmony, creating a more cohesive group environment. This mask can make someone appear easygoing and agreeable, which helps them fit into diverse social and professional settings. However, these advantages come at a high cost.

For one, constantly seeking validation erodes a person's sense of identity. When all our actions aim to satisfy others, our personal desires and opinions slowly fade, leaving us wondering who we are without that feedback. Emotional burnout is also a frequent consequence, as striving to make everyone happy can be mentally exhausting and leaves little room for self-care. The need for validation can lead to dependency, making it hard to feel secure or valued without external approval. Eventually, this can even breed resentment, as the wearer may feel taken for granted, their efforts going unnoticed or unreciprocated.

The pressure not only pulls us away from our true selves but also creates barriers to forming meaningful relationships. Wearing the Mask of Approval, we share only the parts of ourselves that we think others will accept, hiding anything that might invite judgment or criticism. This guardedness becomes the foundation of our interactions, keeping us from fully connecting with others and embracing who we truly are, as I soon learned.

* * *

While the spotlight was exciting, I could feel the tension building behind the scenes in my relationship with Wayne. Our sex drives were different, and gradually our relationship drifted into a friendship zone.

For a fresh start and to rediscover ourselves, we planned an overseas trip. Dad had promised each of us kids a round-trip ticket anywhere in the world after graduation, with the condition that we stay for at least six months. Wayne and I considered South Africa and Australia, eventually choosing Australia. The move was a mix of excitement and preparation: finding a couple to sublet our apartment, fitting everything into backpacks, getting visas, and lining up a place to stay on arrival. I had this whole image of what Australia would be—hot weather, beaches, and men with those deep Aussie accents. Growing up, I'd had a big crush on Hugh Jackman, so I'd built this idealized vision of what life would be like there. Little did I know, this adventure would bring new challenges and force me to further examine the masks I'd been wearing.

STEPS TO REMOVE THE MASK OF APPROVAL

While the Mask of Approval can help earn the validation we crave, it comes at the cost of authenticity. To remove the mask, we must untether our perceived worth from the opinions of others and develop a healthy level of self-acceptance.

1. **Develop self-acceptance:** Start by cultivating a sense of self-acceptance, acknowledging that your worth doesn't hinge on others' opinions. This can be a gradual process—practice affirming your own value daily, reminding yourself that external validation doesn't define you.
2. **Recognize the triggers:** Become aware of the situations or people that prompt you to seek approval. Is it in social situations, at work, or around family? Noticing these triggers can help you stay mindful and recognize when the Mask of Approval is slipping on.
3. **Practice saying no:** Small acts of boundary-setting, like saying no, can reinforce your own needs and opinions. Start

with situations where saying no feels manageable to build confidence in honoring your own preferences and values.

4. **Shift focus inward:** Reflect on what genuinely fulfills or excites you, independent of others' expectations. Pursue activities and goals that bring you satisfaction, rather than those you think will earn praise. Developing these intrinsic motivations helps break the cycle of needing others' validation.
5. **Challenge belief systems:** Many beliefs about approval and worth stem from past experiences, often built up over years. Challenge the idea that you need others' approval by asking yourself if it's always true. Think back to moments when you were accepted for who you were, without pretenses, to help loosen the grip of these old beliefs.
6. **Allow vulnerability:** Gradually begin sharing your true thoughts, feelings, and needs in relationships where you feel safe. Start small—risking a bit of disapproval by being authentic can lead to more meaningful connections. You may find that showing your true self encourages others to be open with you, creating space for deeper relationships.

Letting go of the Mask of Approval isn't an overnight process, but each small step can bring you closer to a life where you're driven by authenticity, not external validation.

REFLECTIONS AND LEARNINGS: THE MASK OF APPROVAL

Living by Values Rather Than Others' Expectations

My story: Growing up, I came to rely heavily on the validation and approval of others. It became a driving force in many of my decisions and interactions, and I began to equate my worth with how well I could please others or fit their expectations. This need for approval was like an invisible hand guiding me, especially in social and professional circles where validation felt essential. Reflecting on this journey, I now realize how much of myself was sacrificed to fit into others' molds.

Your reflection: Think about moments when you felt compelled to seek approval or validation from others. Was it with family, friends, colleagues, or strangers? Consider how much these external opinions have influenced your choices and behavior. What would change if you were driven more by your values than by others' expectations?

Exercise: Identify two recent situations where you sought approval. Write down why you felt that way and what you could have done differently if you had relied more on your own inner validation.

Stepping Back and Setting Boundaries

My story: Looking back, I can see how deeply my need for approval was woven into my life. At first, I didn't even notice the toll it was taking—meeting everyone's expectations seemed like second nature, part of my daily rhythm. But over time, constantly pushing myself to meet others' standards without pause began to wear me down. Burnout didn't hit until later in life, but when it did, it was overwhelming. The exhaustion came from years of self-neglect, from continually sacrificing my own well-being for the validation of others. It was a cycle that was hard to break; my sense of self-worth felt so deeply tied to others' opinions that stepping back seemed almost impossible.

Your reflection: Are there areas in your life where you're constantly giving without receiving? Take a moment to consider how the need for approval may be leading you to overextend yourself, even if it's at the cost of your own well-being.

Exercise: Identify one boundary you could set with someone close to you, like a friend or colleague. Write down how you might communicate it assertively, and practice implementing it in the coming week. Notice how it feels to prioritize your needs, even if it risks a moment of disapproval.

Reframing Social Media Use and Expectations

My story: Social media became a stage for my search for validation. I found myself frequently checking for likes and comments, and removing posts that didn't perform well. This constant chase for engagement and approval felt exhausting but strangely addictive, and I was left feeling empty despite all the attention.

Your reflection: In what ways has social media or other online platforms affected how you present yourself? Are you editing or curating parts of your life to fit a certain image? Consider how this might be affecting your mental and emotional health.

Exercise: Next time you post online, do it with no expectation of how it should perform. Use it as an opportunity to share something meaningful without checking back constantly. Reflect on how it feels to simply put something out there without focusing on the response.

Diminishing the Need for External Validation

My story: One of the hardest lessons was recognizing that true self-worth comes from within, not from others' opinions. Seeking approval outside myself led to an endless loop, always wanting more validation. I realized that by centering my worth around external factors, I was setting myself up for constant disappointment.

Your reflection: How do you measure your self-worth? Is it based on others' opinions or on your own internal values? Reflect on where your sense of worth comes from and the changes you could make to build a stronger foundation from within.

Exercise: Each morning, write down one thing you appreciate about yourself, regardless of anyone else's opinion. Over time, you may find that self-validation starts to become a habit, helping to lessen the need for external approval.

Embracing Authenticity

My story: Letting go of the Mask of Approval has taught me that authenticity invites real connections. I've realized that those who truly appreciate me don't require me to wear a mask. Although it was scary to show up as myself, I found that being authentic attracted relationships where I could be open and vulnerable without fear.

Your reflection: Are there areas in your life where you feel safe enough to be your true self? Reflect on how those spaces compare to where you feel you have to wear a mask. Consider what it might look like to bring more authenticity into other parts of your life.

Exercise: Identify one relationship where you feel comfortable being yourself. Spend time nurturing that relationship and notice how it feels. Think about small ways to bring that same openness into other relationships over time.

> **MASK OF APPROVAL KEY TAKEAWAYS**
>
> ———
>
> - **Self-worth comes from within:** Relying on external validation can only take you so far. True self-worth is built by accepting yourself as you are, independent of others' opinions or judgments. Seek to nurture self-acceptance, celebrating your unique strengths and imperfections.
> - **Recognize when approval becomes a burden:** Approval-seeking can create a heavy emotional load, especially when it leads to neglecting your own needs. Pay attention to the moments when you find yourself sacrificing your well-being or desires for the sake of validation. Recognizing these moments can be the first step toward reclaiming your time and energy.
> - **Boundaries protect both your time and your energy:** Setting healthy boundaries is essential for maintaining balance. Saying no isn't selfish; it's a

way of respecting yourself and those around you. Practice setting small boundaries to protect your priorities and energy, letting them build into a stronger foundation over time.

- **Authenticity fosters genuine connection:** While approval-seeking may bring temporary acceptance, it often leads to shallow relationships. True intimacy and connection thrive when we show up as our authentic selves. Letting people see the real you may feel risky, but it opens the door to deeper, more meaningful relationships.
- **Growth requires vulnerability:** Shedding the Mask of Approval means leaning into vulnerability and allowing yourself to be seen, imperfections and all. Embracing vulnerability can bring growth, resilience, and an inner strength that can't be found through external validation. Being real with yourself and others isn't a weakness—it's the foundation of a balanced and fulfilling life.

CHAPTER 9

THE MASK OF THE
SEDUCER

USING CHARM TO DEFLECT DEPTH

The Cycle of the Seducer

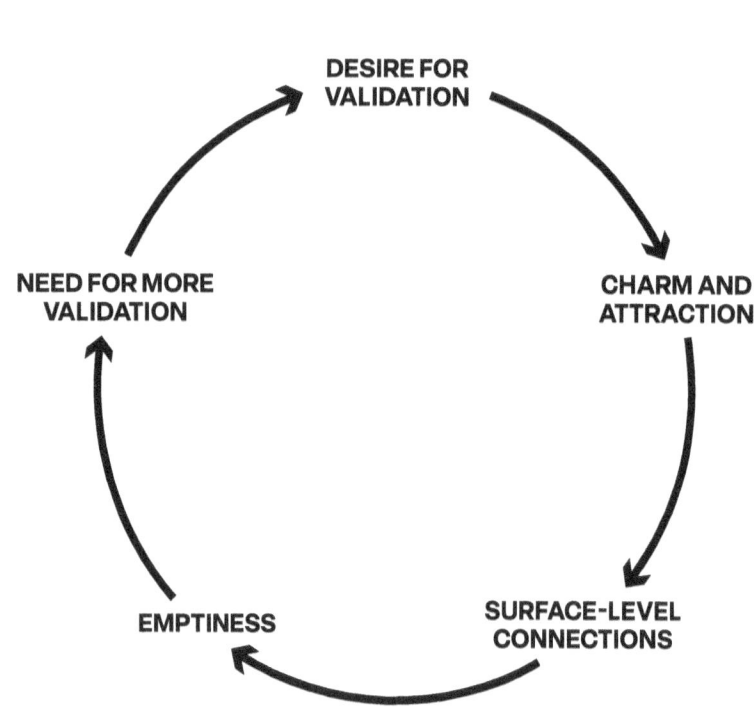

When Liam, a regular at the café where I worked, booked a table one night and brought his husband Chris along, I somehow charmed them both without even meaning to. Their casual flirtations became something more—a mutual attraction that was both liberating and exhilarating. In that moment, my role shifted. It wasn't just about making a good tip or creating a fun experience for customers. It was about the thrill of connection, the possibility of something outside the usual script.

The Mask of the Seducer isn't just about flirtation or attraction—it's about connection, the thrill of interaction, and sometimes the power of intrigue.

I've worn this mask in subtle ways over the years, feeling out the boundaries between charm and intention, the balance of attraction without commitment. I first encountered this in Australia, when I was fresh in a new country, with a clean slate. I was open to new experiences and connections, unbound by past expectations.

NEW COUNTRY, NEW CHAPTER, NEW CHALLENGES

After just two months of our six-month journey, Wayne and I decided to part ways. The split was painful, yet it brought a sense of liberation—a new chapter beginning in a country that felt like an endless playground of opportunity and discovery.

When I started looking for work, a friend recommended a café called Kantine, located in the heart of Sydney's gay village right by Taylor Square. It was a cozy spot owned by a couple, Susan and Chris. Chris was probably the gayest straight man I'd ever met, with charm and flirtation naturally pouring out for his mostly gay clientele. Susan was the equivalent, presenting as a tough, no-nonsense lesbian. They made quite the pair and ran a unique, welcoming spot for the community. They confused a lot of the community though—I can't tell you how many people asked me what the "situation" was with them.

During my interview with Chris, I laid on the charm. I was young, Canadian, and fresh to the scene—elements I knew could work in my favor. Chris saw potential and value in me and gave me a trial shift working the evening with him. Since it was my first shift, the plan was that I'd take orders and he'd help me punch them into the system. Feeling confident from my bartending days, I figured I could rely on memory alone.

It went smoothly at first, until a table of eight older gay men walked in, already warmed up from drinks at their previous stop. Here I was, 21-year-old me, confidently strutting over to take their order. The drink orders were easy—just a few bottles of wine. But when it came to the food, the situation took a turn. Typically, I could remember a few dishes with minor variations, but this group all ordered steaks—each one with a specific doneness and different sides. Standing there, I tried to keep my confident facade as I repeated each order mentally, only to meet Chris at the till and realize I'd lost half the details.

"What's the order?" he asked, glancing over expectantly.

I looked back at the table, mumbling, "One medium rare … um, one medium …"

"You didn't write it down?" Chris's voice cut through my shaky confidence.

"No, I got it. It's just …" I stammered, feeling the pressure mount.

He sighed and slapped a pen and notepad into my hand. "Go back and write it down," he said, pointing back toward the table.

With my tail firmly between my legs, I turned and headed back, feeling every ounce of my ego deflate. Even though I scribbled down the order the second time, nerves must have gotten the best of me—I still managed to mess it up somehow. That night, I had my first taste of failure in the café world, a hard lesson in humility and the value of slowing down.

After close, Chris sat me down out front. He didn't waste any time.

"Look," he said, "I don't think this is going to work out. I can't have mess ups like that. My clientele has come to expect a certain level of service here."

My stomach dropped. His words were blunt, and they cut deep. But I wasn't ready to let go. I needed this job more than I'd let on. Desperation surged, and I found myself practically pleading.

"Please, give me another shot. I know I can do better."

He paused, assessing me for what felt like an eternity. Finally, he nodded, though his expression stayed stern. "Alright. One more chance. But this is it."

I thanked him, trying to keep it together. But the moment I left, the weight of it hit me hard. Walking home, the tears came, a mixture of relief and fear. I couldn't afford to mess this up again, not with everything I had riding on it. This job wasn't just about money—it was my foothold, my way of grounding myself in this new life.

Fortunately, I quickly proved myself at Kantine, becoming a favorite among the regulars. Coming from a place where tipping is the norm, I put in the extra effort to create a memorable experience for everyone who came in. But it wasn't just customer service. The Mask of the Seducer was taking shape, allowing me to navigate the attention, charm my way through interactions, and play into the allure of being the friendly, flirtatious guy on the scene. It became a dance, a careful play of attention and intrigue that kept people coming back for more.

Sometimes, I'd take it further than just banter, sitting on laps and spoon-feeding dessert. It was all part of the mask, allowing me to hold a certain power in those moments—not to lead anyone on, but to enjoy the thrill of connection, the subtle control that comes from captivating others, even briefly.

THE MASK OF THE SEDUCER SOLIDIFIES

Over the next few months, I threw myself into Sydney's social scene, meeting new people and going on dates that would eventually lead to some of my closest friendships. Every new date, every flirtation felt like a thrill, a fresh connection. Playing into the Mask of the Seducer, I was able to pull people in, letting the excitement of a budding connection take hold. But, as things began to feel too serious, I would pull away, reminding myself—and them—that I wasn't ready for anything beyond the moment. I was fresh out of a four-year relationship, and while I enjoyed the thrill of these encounters, I wanted to keep things light and on my own terms.

The Mask of the Seducer gave me control, but it also blurred lines and led to some misunderstandings. Some people got hurt, feeling misled by the intensity of my attention, only to have me retreat. Yet, my connections still brought people together, creating friendships among those I had met, forming a new core group of solid friends. I was no longer one half of "Wayne and Rob." It was just Rob now, and I was finally building my identity as a single gay man.

The Mask of the Seducer often forms in response to a deeper need for validation, love, or acceptance, especially for those who've experienced rejection, neglect, or feelings of inadequacy. For many who wear it, the mask becomes a way to gain admiration without revealing vulnerabilities. To this, I could relate.

THE AMAZING RACE

Back in Vancouver, my friend Ryan—one half of the Ryan and Amy Show—and I had this wild idea to apply for the first season of *The Amazing Race*. We pulled together a hysterical audition video. Ryan's background in video editing and comedy shone through—he's got this way of blending humor with production skill that's hard to beat. Our angle was perfect: I was the "young gun," the athletic one, while Ryan was the jokester. The producers loved it. We were so close to making the cast—if anyone dropped out, we were in. Unfortunately, it didn't happen, but being that close had us buzzing.

Then, out of the blue, the producers reached out before season two, asking if we'd be interested in applying again. We jumped at the chance. This time, they didn't need a full audition tape, just something quick, so we decided to give them a little taste of our sense of humor. In our new video, we told them we'd be willing to "give the producers a second shot" and teased what we could bring to the race. It worked. Next thing I knew, I was flying back to Canada from Australia for the start of an intense, five-week journey.

Season two was especially exciting because, for the first time, the race extended beyond Canada, taking us to places like Hong Kong, Macau, and France. One challenge in particular has stayed with me. We were on Prince Edward Island, and, thanks to a speed bump from the previous leg, we were assigned an extra task. The scene we walked into was like something out of a comedy sketch: a massive, steaming pile of manure, at least 10 feet high and 20 feet wide. Somewhere in that pile were three bottles of moonshine we had to find before we could move on. It was a blazing hot day, the air thick with the smell of the manure, and there we were, putting on our overalls and goggles, knowing we'd be digging through literal crap for who knew how long. We started cracking every joke we could think of, anything to keep us laughing and lighten the situation. We dug like madmen, pushing ourselves to find the bottles no matter what. To this day, I use that challenge as a metaphor with my coaching clients.

Sometimes in life, you've got to dig through a pile of shit to find your "moonshine"—the reward you're after. It's not glamorous, and it's not easy, but those are often the experiences that push you to grow, that show you what you're made of.

Life isn't much different from the race; it throws obstacles in your path, and you either find a way through, or you stop. That day on Prince Edward Island, covered in dirt, shit, and sweat, made me realize that resilience isn't about finding a way out—it's about finding a way through, no matter what it takes.

Rob and Ryan digging through shit on the Amazing Race.

A PERMANENT RETURN ... OR SO I HOPED

Before leaving Australia, I had already decided I wanted to return for good. However, a part of me struggled deeply with the thought of leaving my mom behind. She was still battling her addiction, and the need to be there for her—to somehow keep her grounded—tugged at me. Yet, I knew I couldn't put my life on hold anymore; I had to take this step for myself. She understood, and though I could sense her own inner conflict, she supported me.

When I returned to Australia, I moved in with my good friend Damien, who had been a steady anchor during my previous trip, and his husband Simon. The plan for my return to Australia was straightforward: arrive on a tourist visa, then transition to a student visa. Given my active lifestyle, personal training seemed like the perfect fit, so I enrolled at the Australian College of Sport & Fitness (ACSF). Damien, ever the supportive friend, helped me navigate those first few terms, making sure I had what I needed to settle into my studies and my new life in Australia.

AN UNDENIABLE CONNECTION

In Australia, I got into a rhythm of work and study. Two Kantine customers, in particular, became a part of this rhythm. One was a handsome Irish dad who came in regularly with a friend and their young sons. They'd arrive as soon as we opened, a predinner outing for the kids, ages two and three. The Irishman's son would ride his scooter through the café, leaving a joyful mess. It took a while for me to realize they weren't two straight dads escaping their wives, as I'd initially assumed. His friendly demeanor, paired with an accent and a clean-shaven face, pulled me in, but the mask held my own interest just out of reach, allowing the attention to be a game.

The second, Liam, was a tall, muscular man who often strolled by with his cocker spaniel, Molly. He had a chiseled face and an easy confidence, with flirtations that left a charge in the air. We shared occasional hellos, brief conversations out the front of the café that left a tingle. There was a mutual attraction, but with the mask firmly in place, I could enjoy the excitement without inviting anything deeper. With both Liam and the Irishman, it was about creating a moment of connection—a thrill that kept the interaction alive without requiring full authenticity.

Even though our connections remained within the walls of the café, or just outside of them, there was an underlying desire to take things further. With Liam, there was a mutual dance of attraction—a silent understanding that went beyond friendly conversation. Each interaction felt like a game where we were both leaning into the Mask of the Seducer, testing boundaries with flirtation and playful glances, without actually committing to anything. The thrill of that connection, mixed with the safety of knowing neither of us would push for more, allowed me to bask in the attention without risking intimacy. It was exhilarating, knowing that if we ever crossed that line, it would be on our terms, feeding the seductive energy that kept us both drawn in, yet still at a safe distance.

One night, I saw a familiar name on the reservation list—*Liam*. I felt a rush of excitement. So far, our interactions had been quick, fleeting moments, but now he'd be sitting at my table, giving us a couple of hours to interact. As he walked in, a big smile spread across his face, and I met it with one of my own. There was no denying it:

the energy between us was magnetic. The booking was for four, and with him were two of his mates. Liam casually mentioned they were waiting on his husband, Chris. That name sounded familiar, but I hadn't quite put a face to it.

Then, walking through the door, was his husband, and to my surprise it was the Irishman I had been serving most early evenings. How did I get so lucky? Not only had I been flirting with both Liam and Chris individually, creating a spark with each, but it turned out they were together. This made things a lot more interesting—and, honestly, a bit easier than trying to navigate two separate connections.

As the night carried on, I leaned into my usual charm, and Liam played along—a mutual game of intrigue that neither of us could resist. His charm was magnetic. We tested boundaries in that playful, teasing, *thrilling* way, without giving too much away. I was working to hold his attention, keeping the dance going, while he mirrored it right back. This wasn't just another friendly exchange; the Mask of the Seducer was fully at play, creating a layered connection that kept everything light and captivating without dipping into vulnerability.

We exchanged playful, bold remarks, and Chris, though a bit shy, was clearly entertained by our banter. This wasn't like the typical flirting I did with customers to create a fun atmosphere and score a good tip. This was different. There was a deeper attraction, a genuine desire to see where things could go beyond the walls of the restaurant. Chris added another dimension, blending seamlessly into our dynamic. It became this flirtatious triangle that amplified the tension, an experience where the thrill of attraction was fully mutual.

For me, the Mask of the Seducer wasn't just a tool—it was the thrill of the chase, the allure of seeing how far my charm could take me without letting any real vulnerability slip through. This game, this dance, was familiar yet electrifying, reminding me of the ways I'd learned to connect without exposing too much of myself. That night, I fully embraced the mask, crafting a memorable experience that was equal parts connection and mystery.

When Liam's and Chris's dining experience came to an end, I couldn't let the opportunity slip away. I suggested we exchange numbers and catch up outside of work. They were all for it. Just like that, after a quick exchange, we started a conversation through text immediately.

The next day, we locked in plans for the coming Friday, which also happened to be my last shift at the restaurant. I couldn't think of a better way to end the night and my final shift than by winding down with two charming men, enjoying a drink and their company.

When Friday arrived, I wasn't subtle about the fact that I was eager to close early. Luckily, it was a quiet night, so by 8 p.m. I was on my way to their place just around the corner in the St. Margaret's building. The 11-storey complex housed a mix of cafés and shops below, with residential apartments above. As I reached their door, Liam greeted me with a kiss that seemed like it had been building up for ages—a long, anticipated kiss that made every nerve spark. He led me upstairs, where Chris was putting their son, Tim, to bed.

Have you ever been in the presence of someone where the sexual energy was so intense that it practically buzzed in the air? The kind of chemistry where, despite holding a conversation, 90 percent of your mind is occupied with thoughts of tearing each other's clothes off? That was exactly how it felt between us. We chatted, but the electricity flowing between us was undeniable. For the first 30 minutes, we managed to keep things tame. They showed me around the apartment, and we took our time getting to know each other. But then Liam walked over and gave me a long, deep kiss, and Chris followed suit. Suddenly, I found myself in the middle of an exhilarating three-way kiss with both of these incredibly attractive men.

We didn't waste any time stripping down and making our way downstairs to their bedroom. Weeks of built-up anticipation and chemistry were finally being released, and it felt incredible. I wasn't new to the three-way or group experience, but this was different. Between us, it felt natural and comfortable. The energy flowed effortlessly, and everything about that night felt mutual, balanced, and right.

I ended up spending the night with them, nestled between them in their big king-sized bed. It was surprisingly easy to relax, taking turns snuggling up with each of them, feeling fully at ease. I'd never experienced this level of attraction to two men simultaneously, especially two men who were together in a committed relationship. By morning, we all agreed that the connection was as comfortable as it was exciting and that we wanted to see more of each other.

* * *

Over the coming weeks, we developed a deeper connection. I found myself slowly starting to shed the Mask of the Seducer, letting my guard down and allowing myself to be more vulnerable with them. I started spending weekends at their property out in Berrima, and with each encounter, I opened up a little more. We were undoubtedly dating one another, and it couldn't have felt more right. Of course, with them having a three-year-old, there were some unique challenges—public displays of affection were naturally limited whenever he was around.

One morning in the country, we woke up snuggled together under a giant duvet, and as we were slowly coming to, the bedroom door suddenly burst open, and in walked Tim. I don't think I've ever flown under the covers so fast in my life. He ran in, all smiles and energy, and jumped onto the bed. The guys were doing their best to divert him from landing right on top of me, discreetly guiding his attention away. Meanwhile, I was suffocating under the thick blanket, barely able to breathe as I listened to them chat with him about how he slept. All I could think about was getting a breath of fresh air!

The boys and I eventually had the more serious conversation about what we were and where this was heading. We all agreed that we loved the chemistry and connection we'd developed, and we made it official—we were in a relationship. Let me tell you, if you want information to spread quickly, just tell one person in the gay community. Word traveled fast, and, before we knew it, we were the new hot throuple in town. We made our first big appearance together at a New Year's party, where we were definitely the talk of the night.

AS THE SEASON CHANGES, SO DO THE LEAVES

In the early days of our relationship, I was still deep into my personal training studies, working through my diploma. Liam held a senior role at a big corporation, and Chris was running his own business, which he had built over the past year and a half. Seeing how my teacher worked with corporate clients, I felt inspired to start my own business. Chris offered to help me set it up, and soon I was training his team. We arranged a trade: I'd train their staff twice a week, and they'd handle my website and social media. Just like that, my first business, TEAMFIT, was born.

At first, I was training Chris's team and the social media company's staff, but my client base quickly grew. I soon had contracts with four companies I was training weekly, along with individual clients and couples. My sessions took place in various parks around Sydney, though I was strategic about which ones. Parks like the Domain and Bondi Beach charged fees for running a business on their grounds, so I set up in spots like Frog Hollow, Glebe Park, and Observatory Hill.

Every morning at Observatory Hill, I'd arrive early enough to catch the sunrise right next to the Harbour Bridge. That quiet, tranquil start before my clients arrived became a cherished moment in my day. I was thrilled to work outdoors, riding my bike all over the city with a large duffle bag stuffed with gear: mats, resistance bands, push-up bars, rope ladders, and occasionally 8 and 12 kg kettlebells hanging off my handlebars. The city parks allowed me to be creative, turning park benches, trees, walls, and landmarks into workout equipment.

I'm forever grateful for the support Liam and Chris gave me as I embarked on my entrepreneurial journey. They were there, encouraging and guiding me as I grew my business from a budding idea into something substantial. Our relationship deepened as well. We took trips together to places like New York City, and eventually we had the conversation about moving in together. But as much as I loved being with them, a part of me always held back. Deep down, I struggled with fully committing, feeling like an outsider in the life they had built together before I entered the picture. Over time, subtle feelings of exclusion crept in. The need to keep me hidden from their son was always there, along with the reality that I couldn't join them on family trips, as their families didn't know about us. They'd refer to me as the "family friend" to certain people, which stung every time I heard it.

Being labeled that way, felt like a quiet reminder of my place on the periphery. Their corporate positions meant I wasn't invited to attend any events, leaving me at home, often watching their son instead. Though I cherished my relationship with them, the invisible boundaries left me feeling like a part of me was always on the outside, yearning for something just out of reach.

Over the next two and a half years, we dated on and off, and, during that time, it became harder to ignore the underlying issues within their relationship. It was like the honeymoon phase had ended, and they were back to their reality. Gradually, I realized I had been a kind of "band-aid" for their relationship—a shared interest that had brought them closer together.

And yet, I kept holding on. Even as the cracks deepened, even as I felt myself becoming an afterthought, I stayed. Because walking away meant facing something even harder—the truth that maybe I had never truly belonged in the first place. My self-worth was challenged in ways I never expected. The emotional highs were intoxicating, but the lows cut deep. I spent nights alone, crying, questioning if I was enough, if I was worth more than being someone's temporary fix.

As time went on, I noticed that my presence was sometimes a way to deflect their focus from the cracks in their own partnership. Even so, I kept going. Where was my self-worth in all of this? I started noticing a pattern of people-pleasing across other areas of my life. Certain friendships mirrored this cycle—I was always the one making the effort, bending to accommodate others' schedules and receiving little in return.

The turning point for me was watching a video by Jay Shetty on true friends and true love. It went like this.

> There are two things we should never have to chase: true friends and true love. People make time for who they want to make time for. People text and reply to people they want to talk to. When someone tells you that they're too busy continuously, believe them. Don't try to convince them otherwise. Don't try to force them to make time for you. If they want to, they will. It hurts, but you can't force someone to have feelings for you. Remember, the genie in Aladdin could do everything apart from that.[9]

That video was a wake-up call—one that echoed everything I had been feeling but hadn't yet allowed myself to fully accept. In chasing approval and affection, I had sidelined my own needs, mistaking sacrifice and persistence for true connection. It was time to take a new path and finally start prioritizing me.

But I had to ask myself: What was I really chasing? Connection? Love? Validation?

Looking back, I realized that connection was what I sought most. Growing up without a close-knit family and navigating a strained relationship with my dad meant I was always chasing his approval—approval that never quite came in the way I needed as a young, closeted boy. I found comfort in the support and affection I received from Liam and Chris, but was that all it was?

I was allowing the pattern to repeat because I was chasing *connection* so much. We loved each other; we cared for each other; I didn't doubt that—but it was complicated. Was I holding on to this relationship, setting myself up for repeated hurt, just to grasp at those fleeting moments of closeness?

As difficult as it was to admit—I was.

The Unconscious Needs Driving the Mask

The truth is, everything we do is driven by a set of fundamental human needs. Whether we recognize it or not, we're constantly seeking **certainty**, **variety**, **significance**, **love and connection**, **growth**, and **contribution**. These needs shape our behaviors, our choices, and—if we're not careful—the masks we wear to meet them.

For me, wearing the Mask of the Seducer was never just about attraction or intimacy. It was about fulfilling these core needs in ways I didn't even realize at the time.

Core Need	Met Unresourcefully	Met Resourcefully
Certainty	Knowing I could attract or keep someone interested gave me a sense of control, a buffer against rejection.	Build self-trust and emotional stability.

Core Need	Met Unresourcefully	Met Resourcefully
Variety	The excitement of flirtation and romance offered escape from deeper emotional wounds.	Explore new experiences and hobbies.
Significance	Attention, desire, and validation made me feel seen, valued, and important.	Develop self-worth and personal purpose.
Connection	At its core, this was what I craved most. I longed for closeness, for someone to choose me, even if it meant compromising myself in the process.	Cultivate genuine, reciprocal relationships.
Growth	In some ways, every relationship taught me something, but was I truly growing? Or was I repeating the same lessons, hoping for a different outcome?	Pursue personal challenges and self-reflection.
Contribution	I told myself that being there for others, giving them affection, was a way of caring—but was I really giving, or was I just trying o fill my own emptiness?	Give from abundance, not self-sacrifice.

The problem wasn't the needs themselves—*they're universal, part of being human.* The problem was how I'd been trying to meet them. I had mistaken seduction for connection, attention for love, and persistence for belonging. I had convinced myself that if I played the role well enough, if I gave enough, if I endured enough, I would eventually be chosen in the way I so desperately wanted.

But the truth was, **I needed to choose myself first.**

I began to categorize those around me as parts of a tree: leaves, branches, or roots.

The Mask of the Seducer often played a subtle but significant role here, shaping how I connected with others. The seducer in me loved the thrill of connection, the chase of validation, and the intrigue of drawing others in without fully showing my true self. It allowed me to lean into charm and attraction, creating temporary bonds that, at times, felt like they could be something deeper. It led me to connect with people who were leaves in my life—those who brought short-term lessons or excitement but eventually fell away with the changing of the season.

Then there are the branches—people who seem strong and dependable until the weight of true commitment tests them, and they snap. With the Mask of the Seducer, I could maintain a certain allure, a magnetic pull that made people feel like we had a strong connection. But because I kept the relationship on a superficial level, the trust wasn't deep enough to handle real emotional weight. My relationship with Liam and Chris had elements of both branches and roots. They were branches because, despite the incredible chemistry, the structure of our relationship wasn't solid enough to sustain our deeper needs. Their lives were complex, balancing family, careers, and their own issues. When I came along, I was like a breath of fresh air—a fun distraction from their struggles. But as our time together unfolded, it became evident that I was just a temporary bond on a branch that could break under pressure.

Finally, there are the roots—those rare, enduring connections that survive the storms and nourish us deeply. A tree may have countless leaves and branches, but only a few roots. I learned that while the Mask of the Seducer could help me attract people, it couldn't turn a leaf or branch into a root.

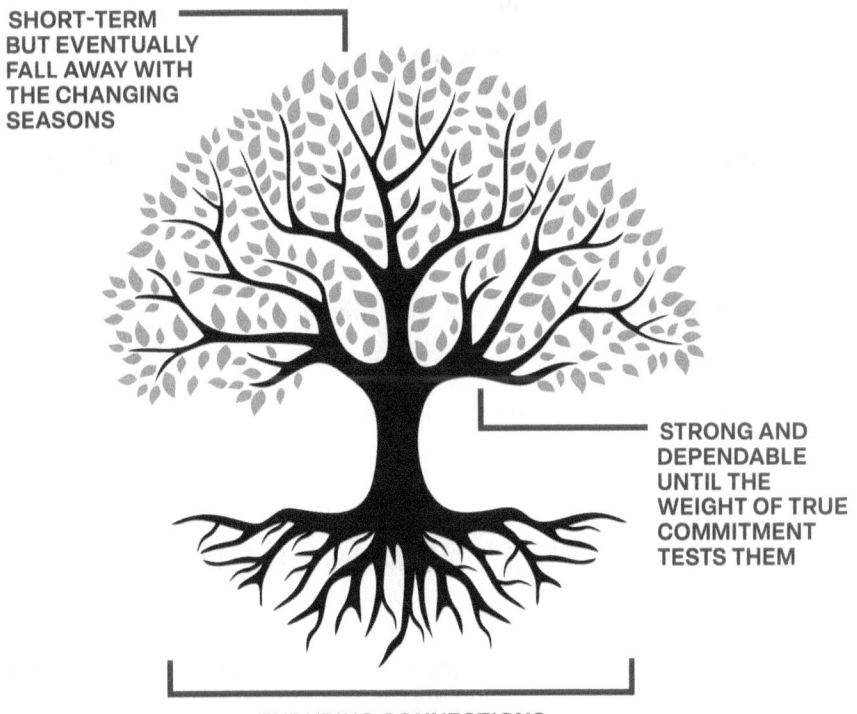

The roots are the people I can connect with without the need for charm or allure. They're those who see beyond the mask, who don't need me to play any role but my true self. They're the people who remain strong, who give as much as they take, who have a genuine foundation of trust and mutual respect.

One of the most valuable lessons I took from this experience was realizing that self-worth can't be sustained by shallow connections. While the Mask of the Seducer had helped me draw people in, it also kept me from forming the roots I truly needed. The people pleaser in me was prioritizing connection over authenticity, making me seek approval in ways that ultimately left me feeling hollow.

The Mask of the Seducer taught me the allure of connection without commitment, but it also taught me the importance of moving beyond the mask. I needed to connect with people who could see me for who I really was, not just the captivating surface I projected. Looking back, I don't dismiss the potential for a throuple or deeper relationship, but I've learned that the foundation needs to be strong—rooted in mutual understanding, open communication, and genuine commitment.

STEPS TO REMOVE THE MASK OF THE SEDUCER

As thrilling as the Mask of the Seducer can be, ask yourself: have you ever felt lonely in a room full of people? Despite the admiration and excitement, the connections I formed while wearing the mask often lacked emotional depth, leaving a persistent sense of loneliness. And the constant need to captivate others? It was draining, both emotionally and mentally. When we remove the Mask of the Seducer, we open ourselves up to deeper, genuine connection—the type of connection many of us truly need, even if we don't see it at first.

1. **Acknowledge the insecurity behind the mask:** Start by recognizing that the Mask of the Seducer often stems from insecurity and a desire for external validation. Ask yourself: why do I seek attention or approval in this way? Understanding the origins of this mask can be the first step toward healthier, more authentic connections.
2. **Shift focus from external validation to self-worth:** Begin to cultivate a sense of self-worth that doesn't rely on others' approval or admiration. What would it look like to validate yourself without needing someone else to do it for you? Practice self-compassion, recognize your strengths, and work on embracing who you are—no applause required.
3. **Practice vulnerability in relationships:** Allow yourself to be emotionally open with others, even if it feels uncomfortable at first. Vulnerability doesn't mean sharing everything at once, but rather letting others see the real you. As you open up, you create space for deeper, more meaningful connections that move beyond charm and surface-level appeal.
4. **Develop genuine emotional connections:** Focus on building relationships rooted in mutual respect, shared interests, and emotional depth, rather than relying on seduction or superficial charm. Ask yourself: who in my life do I truly connect with? Let those connections become a foundation for real intimacy and lasting bonds.

5. **Challenge the fear of rejection:** The fear of rejection often fuels the need to seduce or charm others. Remind yourself that rejection is a natural part of life and doesn't diminish your worth. Not everyone's approval or attention is necessary for you to feel valued. Accepting this truth can help you break free from the cycle of seduction and find a deeper sense of peace within yourself.

REFLECTIONS AND LEARNINGS: THE MASK OF THE SEDUCER

Forming Genuine Connections

My story: I often sought validation through charm or superficial connections, a dynamic that initially felt rewarding but ultimately led to a lack of emotional depth and a lingering sense of loneliness. In interactions, I'd use flirtation or humor to engage people, creating a momentary thrill but finding myself longing for something deeper once the spark faded.

Your reflection: Consider moments in your life when you may have leaned on flirtation, humor, or attraction to gain attention or affirmation. What were you hoping to feel in those interactions? Reflect on whether any of these moments left you feeling unfulfilled or misunderstood afterward.

Exercise: For your next interaction, focus on connecting through shared interests or open, honest conversation, rather than relying on charm or wit. Reflect on how it feels to engage in a way that prioritizes depth over validation.

Presenting a More Authentic Self

My story: The Mask of the Seducer showed up in many of my relationships, almost like second nature. I was so accustomed to charming my way through interactions that I often kept people at a comfortable distance, allowing only the parts of me I thought they'd admire.

Your reflection: Have you ever kept people at arm's length, allowing them to see only the curated or "ideal" version of yourself? Reflect on what it has cost you to maintain that distance. Are there people in your life you'd like to be more open with, inviting them to see more of who you truly are?

Exercise: Choose one person with whom you feel ready to share a deeper part of yourself. In your next interaction, let go of the need to impress, and focus on simply being present. Observe how it feels to offer a more genuine version of yourself.

Leaning into Openness and Vulnerability

My story: Wearing the Mask of the Seducer allowed me to control my relationships without letting anyone in too deeply. Keeping things light and playful shielded me from rejection and pain but also kept true intimacy at bay. This approach felt safe, but, in truth, it was isolating.

Your reflection: Are there underlying fears of rejection, judgment, or inadequacy that drive you to seek external validation? Consider what it might feel like to release these fears, even slightly. What kind of connections could open up if you allowed yourself to be more vulnerable?

Exercise: Identify a relationship where you can begin to be more open.

Start by sharing a personal story or thought you usually keep private. Reflect on how it feels to allow vulnerability and how the other person responds to this openness.

Reflecting on Authenticity

My story: Entering a throuple with Liam and Chris allowed me to let down my guard and experience vulnerability. For the first time, I felt safe enough to dive deeper emotionally, feeling accepted as I was and loving the chance to be truly open with them.

Your reflection: Think about the relationships in your life where you feel free to be your authentic self. What might it look like to prioritize emotional depth over surface-level charm in other relationships? Are there connections in your life that encourage you to show up fully as yourself?

Exercise: Identify a close relationship where you feel supported. Spend time nurturing that connection, focusing on meaningful conversations. Reflect on how it feels to be your genuine self and how you might bring this level of authenticity into other relationships.

Stepping Back and Letting Relationships Develop Naturally

My story: The turning point for me came after watching Jay Shetty's video on true love and friendship. His message made me realize I had been giving more than I was receiving in my relationships, constantly chasing approval, love, and connection. Letting go and prioritizing self-respect became a powerful act of self-worth.

Your reflection: Reflect on the relationships where you may be chasing approval or love. What would it look like to step back and allow these people to make an effort instead? How might it feel to stop prioritizing those who don't prioritize you?

Exercise: For one week, practice what I call "open-door" interactions. Instead of initiating contact or plans, let others come to you. Observe how it feels to let relationships unfold naturally without extra effort on your part. Reflect on what this teaches you about reciprocity in your relationships.

MASK OF THE SEDUCER KEY TAKEAWAYS

- **Authenticity creates genuine connection:** Wearing the Mask of the Seducer may attract attention and temporary validation, but it ultimately keeps true intimacy at a distance. Real connection comes from letting people see the unfiltered version of you. When you're authentic, you draw people who appreciate you for who you truly are, not just for the persona you project.
- **Vulnerability is a path to deeper relationships:** The Mask of the Seducer often stems from a fear of rejection or being seen as "not enough." Learning to open up and allow others to see the real you—even if it feels risky—can lead to fulfilling, deep

connections that aren't dependent on charm or attraction.

- **The importance of boundaries and self-worth:** Overreliance on external validation can be exhausting, creating cycles of emotional burnout. Recognizing your worth outside of others' opinions and setting boundaries in relationships protect your energy and make room for authentic connections, not ones based on superficial attention.

- **Letting go of control for true intimacy:** The need to control relationships by keeping them surface-level prevents genuine closeness. Releasing this control—embracing both the highs and lows of being fully known by someone—builds trust and opens up more meaningful, reciprocal relationships.

- **Self-reflection uncovers root causes:** Understanding why you wear the Mask of the Seducer can be a powerful step toward change. Reflecting on past experiences, feelings of inadequacy, or unmet needs can reveal how you came to rely on charm or attraction. This awareness empowers you to make conscious choices that prioritize emotional depth over validation.

CHAPTER 10

THE MASK OF INDEPENDENCE

SHIELDING FROM DEPENDENCY

The Cycle of Independence

When I first came to Australia, I threw myself into my independence like it was my lifeline. After all, I'd moved out at 16, supporting myself through high school while navigating a world of relationships and responsibilities most teenagers couldn't imagine. But Australia was different. Here, I was building a life as an adult, trying to figure out who I was outside of any relationship, building a business from the ground up, and carving out a space just for me. I was independent, and it felt empowering.

But even as I thrived, something nagged at me. Despite the support I received over the years from friends, there was a part of me that felt uncomfortable accepting it. The more success I found, the more I realized that this independence came at a cost. Yes, I felt strong, and yes, I'd created a life I was proud of. But that constant push to stand alone kept me at arm's length from everyone around me, no matter how much they cared.

OCTOBER 5, 2015—A NIGHT ETCHED IN MY MEMORY

On October 5, 2015, I was working the night shift at Kantine, following my usual evening routine. I always worked alone, with the owner lingering to help if needed. Regulars had come in, ordering their usual meals, chatting away and filling the room with a fun, inviting energy. Around 7:30 p.m., as I was at a table taking an order, I turned and saw two gentlemen at the door. One of them I'd seen before, but the other stopped me in my tracks.

Standing there was a beautiful man, with short dark hair, lean build, and captivating blue eyes. Suddenly, I was nervous. This gorgeous man was standing right in front of me, and I felt my usual confidence waver. Flustered, I managed to put on a big smile and asked if they wanted a table for two, inside or outside. They chose a table inside, by the window.

With this guy at my table, everything felt different. I assumed he was on a date, and, for the first time, I felt intimidated. Nervous to flirt with him directly, I turned my attention to his date, who was a good sport and had a great sense of humor. I learned they were celebrating the beautiful man's birthday—October 5. Locked that in.

Something about this man was different. Have you ever met

someone who just takes your breath away? That's what it felt like with him. He was exactly my type, but it was more than his looks. There was a kindness in his presence that felt magnetic.

As the night came to an end, the guys asked for their bill, and I said goodbye. There he went—the perfect guy. Someone with whom I'd exchanged only a few words, but there was something undeniably real in those moments. I wondered if I'd ever see him again, if he'd return. It felt impossible to ask for his number, especially since he seemed to be on a date. All I could do was hope he'd come back. He left me with a hunger for more.

A TWIST OF FATE

On January 2, 2017, I was at the gym in my building, a shared space for residents from six nearby buildings, fully equipped and perfect for my usual workout. It was chest day, and I was in the zone, music pulsing through my earbuds as I powered through my sets. Then, as I finished a set and looked up, there he was—the guy from the café, the beautiful man.

In that instant, everything else faded away. Seeing him there, in my gym, felt surreal. My mind went blank, and all focus on my workout vanished, replaced by a steady stream of glances in his direction. I noticed every detail: the ankle-high socks, black sweat shorts, the gray singlet clinging to his shoulders, the way beads of sweat ran down his forehead. I couldn't stop taking him in, my gaze tracing every line and curve of his body as I tried to play it cool, pretending to focus on my workout.

Eventually, I made my way across the gym, purposefully walking past him. He looked up, and, for a split second, our eyes met. That same electricity from two years ago at the café hit me all over again, leaving me flustered and breathless. My heart raced as I made my way to the exit, my mind spinning with questions: *Why was he in my gym? Does he live here now? How long is he visiting? Which building is he in?* All the way home, I couldn't stop replaying that moment, each question intensifying the feeling of excitement and anticipation.

Later that day, I was at the café with my friend Andy, describing this "hot daddy" I'd seen at the gym. Andy casually suggested he might have spotted him on Scruff, the gay dating app.

The very next day, I headed back to the gym at the same time, hoping to see him again. And there he was. My workout took on a whole new level of intensity as I tried to make a good impression, sneaking glances whenever I could, hoping for a bit of eye contact. Soon, he finished his workout and left. But I was determined to make the most of the moment, so I watched him through the gym's floor-to-ceiling windows, following his path as he walked down the street and entered a building just a few doors down from mine. Success—I now knew where he lived. Cue the creepy stalker vibes.

I hadn't logged into Scruff since moving to Australia, but the moment called for it. After dusting off my old account, I found the man's profile under the username Andy had given me—and sent him a "woof" (a Scruff version of a Facebook "poke"), plus a quick message: *Hello.*

What followed was a torturous wait. I was glued to my phone, checking constantly, picking it up, putting it down, checking again. Then, finally—*ding, ding*. It was him! My heart raced as I read his reply. We began a bit of small talk, each reply sparking a little more excitement. I couldn't resist adding some light flirtation, and he flirted right back. I mentioned wanting to meet him, and he invited me over. I suggested coffee first, wanting to slow things down a bit. We set a date for a couple of days later at my local café, Hale & Hearty. I sent him my number, logged off the app, and counted down the hours until our date.

THE FIRST DATE

The day finally arrived—the day I was meeting the man from the gym. I was sitting at the café, nerves bubbling, while my friend who owned the shop was giving me encouraging winks and nods. I was nervous, excited, barely able to sit still as I waited. Then I see him—walking toward me, looking as handsome as ever. He spotted me sitting outside, and a smile spread across his face. He approached, and I stood to shake his hand. "Hi, I'm Rob."

He responded with, "Nice to meet you, I'm Pete."

I couldn't wipe the smile off my face—the energy I felt just being near this man was unreal. To think that, two years ago, I had seen him briefly at the café, and now here we were, having coffee together.

We sat and chatted, sharing stories about what we did, slipping in the odd flirty comment here and there. It was impossible to stop smiling—both of us were grinning from ear to ear. *Could he be the guy I've been waiting for?* Throughout the date, all I could think was how I'd love to introduce him to my family. He had everything—great smile, great energy, beautiful eyes, and he was even in the arts. And did I mention he spoke both Italian and French? Tick, tick, tick. *How did I get this lucky?*

Eventually, we said our goodbyes, as Pete had to head into work. But we kept texting, and soon he messaged saying his work plans had changed. Being cheeky me, I responded, *Oh no! That's terrible. Whatever should we do?* Without hesitation, he invited me over. My heart was racing, adrenaline pumping through my body. I jumped in the shower, brushed my teeth, and made my way to his apartment. Up to the ninth floor I went, knocked on the door, and he answered with a big smile. As I closed the door behind me, he started walking toward his bedroom, then stopped, turned around, walked right up to me, grabbed my face, and started kissing me. The tension we'd both felt all morning and afternoon finally erupted.

I'll spare you the details, but after we shared that first moment, we lay there holding each other. It was perfect. We couldn't let go, and I didn't want to leave. I ended up spending the night, and I found myself staying over again the next night, and the next. We were completely wrapped up in each other. I was crazy about this guy. He made me feel things I'd never felt before, and, for the first time, I could envision a future I hadn't allowed myself to consider.

OVER BEFORE IT BEGAN

Pete and I found our little rituals—one of our favorites was going to the park, sitting on a bench, and eating Magnum bars together. It became our thing, just talking, connecting over the simplest moments. Whenever we agreed on something, I'd say, "Okie dokie." This soon became me saying, "Okie," and him answering, "Dokie." It was silly, but it was ours, and it felt like the start of something special.

The honeymoon phase was everything I'd hoped it would be—filled with laughter, late nights at the movies, dressing up for shows, dinners out, and endless conversations. We were nearly inseparable, wrapped up in each other and building memories together. Every day felt like an adventure, and I was falling for him fast and hard. It was like this whole new world had opened up, and, with every moment, I found myself drawn closer to him, wanting our connection to deepen, to last.

But there was something I was still wrestling with, something unresolved. My previous relationship—one that wasn't just with a single person, but with two people and a child—was still heavy on my heart. For over two years, Liam, Chris, and their son had been my world, and those memories, emotions, and connections weren't something I could simply set aside. I wanted to give myself to Pete fully, but I knew I couldn't until I sorted through the lingering feelings. Despite how strongly I felt for him, I realized I needed to clear the air and find closure with my past before diving into something new.

Ending things with Pete was one of the hardest choices I'd made. I could see the heartbreak in his eyes as I explained my need for space. I tried to reassure him that it wasn't goodbye forever, just for now—but anyone being broken up with knows that's cold comfort. It was brutal because we had been on such a high, and yet I knew I wasn't ready to give him all of me.

THE PERFECT PLAN

A couple of weeks passed, and, in that time, the void Pete left became undeniable. I missed him, missed us. Every day, he was on my mind—his laugh, his smile, our talks, everything. I wanted him back, and the longer we were apart, the clearer that became.

One day, as I walked past our favorite pizza spot, Angelino Pizza, I realized I had to do something to get him back. I came up with a plan to get Pete back in a way that would make him feel as special as he was to me.

I went to the stationery store and picked up a small blank book—about 50 pages, just enough for what I had in mind. I filled the pages with messages to him, expressing everything I hadn't said before, pouring out how much I missed him and how deeply I cared. But instead of writing it all out plainly, I spread it across the pages in snippets, a puzzle he'd have to flip through to piece together. The last page presented him with a choice: he could either drink the bottle of pinot grigio waiting at the table by himself or meet me at our park, where I'd be waiting with two Magnum ice cream bars. This wasn't just a grand gesture—it was me showing him that I was ready to open up, to let him back into my life and start anew.

Pete accepted my invitation to meet at the restaurant, so I made my way to Angelino a bit early. I left the book with Anna, one of the owners, explaining that it was part of a surprise, and headed over to the park, hiding in the bushes so I could see Pete as he arrived at the restaurant. My heart was pounding with excitement and nerves. Once Pete arrived, I made my way to our favorite bench and waited. Would he think it was a silly idea? Would he laugh and just take the wine? Or would he choose me and the Magnums waiting in the park?

My heart raced as I waited, eyes glued to the path I hoped he'd take. Then, just as I'd imagined, he appeared around the corner, that unmistakable grin on his face. My relief and joy were instant, and I felt a little silly but also so thrilled that my plan had worked. As he approached, that grin only grew wider, and I could tell he was both amused and a little charmed by the whole setup.

He sat beside me, and we hugged as I explained myself, apologizing and sharing everything I hadn't said before. When we kissed, I felt that familiar warmth and ease. I was right back in my happy place.

"I guess we better make our way to our dinner reservation, huh?" I teased. He smiled, grabbed my hand, and together we headed to the restaurant, back where we belonged.

TOO GOOD TO LAST

While Pete and I kicked our honeymoon phase back into high gear, I was studying massage therapy, building my personal training business, and starting to develop my massage practice. I had been growing my personal training business, TEAMFIT, for the last couple of years, working toward a 457 visa and aiming for sponsorship through my own company. I was ticking all the necessary boxes—appointing my accountant as CFO, hiring another personal trainer to work under me, setting everything up to look like a fully functioning business. There was a part of me that thrived on the independence—proving to myself that I could build this on my own, without relying on anyone.

Meanwhile, Pete was preparing to spend a month overseas, seeing Athens, Santorini, Zagreb, Venice, and Berlin. The night before he left, we held each other, made love, and just savored every moment. In the morning, I helped him bring his bags down to the Uber waiting out front, gave him the biggest hug and kiss goodbye, and watched him drive away. The ache of him leaving stuck with me, but I told myself I could hold down the fort alone. After all, I was used to being independent.

Then I received the news: the government had abolished the 457 visa program back in April. Suddenly, the plan I'd invested years into, my strategy to secure a future in Australia, was stripped away.

I was floored—defeated, angry, all of it. My mind raced with thoughts of leaving. *Fuck Australia, stupid government.* With Pete overseas, I was stressing about how to tell him. But instead of opening up, I went inward, trapped by the Mask of Independence that told me I had to fix this on my own, that I couldn't let him see me panicked or without a backup plan.

The anxiety was overwhelming, to the point that I couldn't go to class or see my clients. I was waking up stressed and going to bed stressed. I kept telling myself I had to handle this alone and needing support was a weakness I couldn't afford to show.

I withdrew from Pete over text, my responses growing minimal and more spaced out. How was I supposed to tell him I was thinking of leaving? One night, he messaged me, trying to understand my sudden coldness. *You've seemed a bit cold and distant (pardon the pun) since I left. And I'm not sure why. Is something the matter? Has something happened? I spent most of yesterday just worrying about you, wondering why you hadn't written me back, thinking something's wrong. I know it's difficult being apart, and I'm sorry if I'm incessant with sending you photos from my holiday, but I was hoping you could still be there for me nevertheless. It's not easy traveling by myself, a little stressful, to be honest. I just want you to know that I'm here for you, if you're struggling and need to chat. I'm always here for you. I love you.*

His message broke me. Here he was, opening up, showing his

vulnerability, and I was hiding behind my Mask of Independence, refusing to lean on him or let him in. I felt terrible, but my instinct was still to handle it all myself.

* * *

Pete and I planned to talk the following night, and just the thought of that conversation sent my anxiety spiraling. The Mask of Independence kept me locked in my thoughts, urging me to keep everything under control, but deep down I knew I couldn't keep it up much longer. The more I avoided, the more trapped I felt. My mind was a constant storm of what-ifs and fears about how Pete would take the news.

When we jumped on FaceTime, I was already emotional. He could see right away that I wasn't alright—there was no more hiding. I just had to tell him. I tried my best to explain the reasons behind my choice to leave, assuring him it wasn't about him and I just didn't have any fight left in me. But the words were hard to get out; every part of me felt the weight of what this meant for us.

"You can't leave!" he said. "I want to marry you. We can go the partner visa route." As lovely as that sounded and as much as I wanted a future with him, the thought of relying on a partnership visa terrified me. I couldn't bear the idea of a visa dictating the terms of our relationship. I wanted an organic, genuine connection with Pete, not one shaped by the pressures of immigration requirements. I needed to know we were together out of pure love, not because of a piece of paper binding us.

We were both crying, hearts breaking through the screen. I hated myself for putting him through this, especially while he was overseas and alone. As the call wound down, we sat in silence for a moment, each of us struggling with the reality we were facing. It was late for him, and he needed to get some rest, so we said our tearful goodbyes and ended the call.

Over the next week, I found myself turning to music to make sense of things, knowing Pete would understand. One song I couldn't stop listening to was "Don't Let Go"—not the original by En Vogue, but a cover by my good friend Greg Gould. There was something haunting about the acoustic version; it captured everything I felt but hadn't been able to say. That song became a way for me to sink into my feelings for Pete, giving me a bit of hope amid the uncertainty.

Pete, in turn, shared a piece of music that reflected his feelings for me: "Symphony No. 5 in C-sharp Minor" by Gustav Mahler. He suggested I listen to it in bed, headphones on, with the volume up. When I did, it was beautiful, almost transporting, as if his emotions were woven into the notes.

THE POWER OF INDEPENDENCE

For many, independence is more than just a value; it's an aspiration, something we tell ourselves we should embody because society praises self-reliance.

Often, people adopt independence as a core value, but in reality it's an aspirational value—a way of projecting an idealized version of strength. Beneath this so-called independence lies fear, loneliness, and a reluctance to trust others.

When Pete returned home, we met up for coffee to talk things over. He asked me again about my plans, and I couldn't give him a clear answer. My insistence on independence felt less about self-reliance and more about keeping control, about safeguarding myself from the fear of abandonment or the fear of being let down by someone close to me.

On the outside, I probably looked like I had it together, like someone who didn't need others. But inside I was wrestling with the fear of letting anyone get close enough to disappoint me. What if I trusted Pete, let go of the mask, and it didn't work out? Or worse, what if I lost myself in the relationship, tangled up in something where a visa became the only thing holding us together?

The visa dilemma became symbolic, embodying the connection I wanted with Pete but also the freedom I feared I'd lose. My desire for control, my Mask of Independence, was keeping me at a distance from the one person I wanted most. This inner battle tore at me, turning a simple choice about staying or leaving into a test of my willingness to trust, to be vulnerable, and to truly let someone else in. If I was going to move forward, I knew I'd have to confront my fears and take off the mask, exposing myself and allowing Pete to see me fully—doubts, insecurities, and all.

I practically thought myself into a second wind and started researching how I could possibly stay. My temper tantrum was over; I cleared my head and refocused. A friend suggested the skilled visa points option. Massage was on the list, though just barely. Finally, here was my way to stay without relying on Pete. Once I made that decision, I messaged him to meet up and share the news. I asked if he'd consider getting back together, but it didn't go as smoothly as I'd hoped.

I just spent the last few weeks of my trip mentally disconnecting from you and moving on, and now you want to work on it? He was understandably angry and confused. I'd put him on an emotional roller coaster, breaking his heart for a second time. It was a *no*. He asked me to respect his decision and give him space.

But I knew how I felt about him. I knew what I wanted, and I knew he felt it too. I spent the next few months working hard to prove my commitment—to show him I was here to stay and that I wanted to be with him. Letters, photos of us, messages—I even reached out to his friends for advice. Pete became a constant in my thoughts, and every corner of my neighborhood felt like it was laced with memories of him. I'd be training in my local park, scanning for him, hoping to catch a glimpse. I'd picture him walking by, so vividly that it felt real.

One day, I received a message from Pete, asking if I'd like to come over for a chat. Without hesitation, I said yes. He invited me for dinner, and I could barely contain my excitement. It felt like a good sign. My mind raced with possibilities, filled with optimism and hope that I might finally get the answer I'd been waiting for.

Have you ever felt those butterflies when you're about to see someone you really like? This was that, times 10. My excitement was in overdrive. I made my way to his apartment building, only a five-minute walk from mine, and buzzed the intercom. He answered, letting me onto the ninth floor.

Standing in front of his door, my nerves and excitement peaked. Would I get the answer I wanted? Finally, he opened the door, and I couldn't help but smile when I saw him.

"It's a yes," he said.

Those words were music to my ears. I was elated, so happy to hear them. I wrapped him in a big hug. A second chance—well, technically a third. Everything was finally aligning. I'd found a way to stay in the country on my own, without having to depend on anyone else, and I had the man of my dreams back. I was also able to hold on to the Mask of Independence and prove, not only to myself but to everyone else, that I could stay in the country and make it on my own terms.

Looking back, I can see how the Mask of Independence can be particularly damaging in relationships. This mask kept true intimacy at a distance because it prevented me from leaning on others or letting them see my vulnerability. By insisting on handling everything myself, I unknowingly denied Pete the chance to show up for me, to be a part of my support system.

The Mask of Independence also crept into my professional life. I was addicted to the entrepreneurial lifestyle. Life on my terms, flexibility, time—but in reality I was working a lot between my two businesses. While I did have some flexibility, my time was limited.

I once had a coaching client who was deeply established in his business, managing a successful team. Despite this, his need to remain entirely self-reliant had him handling most tasks on his own, which ultimately led him down the path of exhaustion and burnout. The thought of delegating or asking for help felt foreign to him. When we explored the pros and cons of his strategy, he realized how his version of independence was costing him time, energy, and even his health.

Like with all masks, recognizing when the Mask of Independence is holding us back is the first step to shedding it. It's not about abandoning independence altogether but about understanding that true strength comes from balance. It's about knowing when to stand on your own and when to let others in.

> **Vulnerability isn't a weakness; it's the very foundation of meaningful connection and support. Allowing others to see our real selves, even when it feels uncomfortable, is an essential step toward living more authentically.**

Even though I can now see the truth in how these realizations would have served me, I didn't always see so clearly.

PROTECTION ... OR SABOTAGE?

The next few months were magical, and Pete and I grew closer with every date. The holidays came upon us quickly, and Pete and I made plans to head to Melbourne to meet his family. Being the youngest of seven, he had a big family, and I spent time trying to remember everyone's names. We'd have our little rehearsals, and I'd come up with creative ways to memorize his siblings in order, noting unique things about each of them. The family gathering took place at a golf club, and the whole family was there—parents, siblings, cousins, nieces, nephews. It was a large, close-knit family. They handed out presents with Pete's dad playing Santa. Pete's elderly parents, who must have been in their mid- to late-70s, still had a sharp wit and a great sense of humor. After gifts, Pete's dad took out his violin and played for everyone, an act that felt woven into the family's musical tradition.

Watching Pete's dad play, I found myself imagining Pete with my family. My younger sisters both play piano, and my dad loves his small-town music sessions. In my mind, I could see Pete and my sisters bonding over a piano, creating music together. And with his love for history, I imagined him and my dad engrossed in deep conversations about topics that didn't necessarily interest me, but that might build a bond between them. The entire scene made me picture a future where our families were connected, where Pete fit perfectly into the world I came from.

However, bad news was on the horizon. After speaking with an immigration lawyer, I learned that massage therapy was only eligible for state sponsorship in Tasmania, which meant I'd have to move there for two years to secure the visa. The only other option was to move to a rural area and find a business willing to sponsor me for two years. Another obstacle, another roadblock—I was gutted. I paid my taxes; I contributed to society, yet staying in the country felt like an uphill battle. It felt like an ultimatum, almost as if the universe were pushing me toward the path I dreaded: a de facto visa through Pete.

As I sat in Pete's family room one night, surrounded by his loved ones, it felt like I was experiencing an out-of-body moment, watching myself from the outside. I started to analyze everything, assessing our relationship through the lens of an immigration officer. Would they see our commonalities? Would they see how much we loved each other despite our differences? Suddenly, I felt like an outsider in his family's world. I listened to their conversations about music, history, and family stories, feeling as though I had nothing to contribute. Pete's passion for music and history made him part of the family's inner circle, while I began to feel like a spectator, aware of every little difference. I worried how these differences might be perceived, wondering if immigration would judge us as incompatible.

I felt compelled to examine everything, questioning not only how Pete and I fit together but also how much of myself I was losing to this constant need to prove my worth and my right to stay in the country. Was it really about independence? Or was my fear of abandonment driving this need to do everything on my own? Or was it simply the uncertainty of trusting in something so fragile, where so much was at stake?

I began pulling away from Pete, even acting disrespectful and inconsiderate. Christmas was a clear example. I invited Pete to a big gathering at my ex's place, insisting that it was just a friendly get-together with a bunch of mutual friends. Looking back, I realize how unfair it was to ask him to spend such an intimate holiday there—it was a giant red flag.

* * *

For New Year's, I suggested we stay at my ex's apartment to look after their cat while they were away. I knew Pete was uncomfortable with the idea, but I pushed for it, determined to maintain this tie with my past while dragging him along.

During New Year's Eve, we had drinks with my friend Axel and one of Pete's close friends, making a fun night of it as we watched the fireworks. But later, as Pete and I became intimate, I did something completely selfish, getting myself off and then rolling over to go to sleep without thinking about him. It was disrespectful, and Pete rightly called me out. The argument that followed wasn't just about that one night—it was about everything. He confronted me about the way I'd been treating him, the way I'd been acting distant and dismissive. I had an excuse ready for everything, but deep down I knew the truth. I was terrified of what the visa would mean for us, and instead of being open about it, I was clinging to my independence, convinced it would somehow keep us safe from the strain I feared would tear us apart. However, in trying to protect our relationship, I was actually sabotaging it.

Over the next week, I did a lot of reflecting. I loved Pete more than he'd ever know, and I wanted a future with him, even marriage—but not with a visa looming over us, turning every moment into an obligation. My own mind had become my worst enemy. I was anywhere but the present, spinning fears in my head and creating walls of resistance. I felt like I had to jump ship before we got in too deep.

I organized a meetup with Pete. We hadn't spoken much since our New Year's blowup, and I was feeling the weight of everything unsaid between us. I decided to get one of his favorite whiskeys and invited him for a walk to the park. We strolled until we found a quiet bench, and, as we sat, I pulled out the bottle. The moment had come to start that dreaded conversation, and I could feel my heart sinking with every word.

I rambled, trying to form a story about our relationship, fumbling to explain why I couldn't be with him and tossing out one excuse after another. I told him I didn't feel we had enough in common and I couldn't see longevity for us. But that wasn't the truth. That was the visa talking. In reality, I loved him with every ounce of my soul, and I was madly in love with the vision of what we could be together. I wanted a beautiful, authentic relationship, free from legal pressures and obligations. But here I was, throwing it all away.

Tears filled both our eyes as we took turns sipping from the bottle. He was understandably confused, hurt, and struggling to make sense of it all. "Where is this coming from?" he asked, his voice laced with frustration and sadness. We both agreed we didn't want to end our relationship with bitterness; we wanted to remain in each other's lives, however complicated that might be.

As soon as he wasn't with me, I wanted him back, confusing him to no end. I invited him over for dinner and a movie, and we ordered some Thai food before nestling into the couch to watch *The Mountain Between Us*, which seemed fitting considering the situation. Except in our case, I had placed the mountain between us with all the drama.

As the movie ended, Pete and I kissed. I instigated it, and he was a little resistant until finally saying no. He called me a bastard and got up, angry and confused, and made his way to the door. "What's your MO?" he asked.

"There's no MO, I'm just confused. I'm sorry." As he walked out the door, I told him I loved him.

"Doesn't feel that way," he said, and then the door closed behind him.

The next day, he came over to talk. He put his foot down, making it clear he needed space. He was right. I had to own my shit. The damage had been done, and I had no choice but to leave him in peace.

I made a promise to myself that day that I was going to get him back. All I needed was to make it over, around, through the mountain of securing a visa, and I wouldn't have this problem anymore. Easier said than done.

WHY WE WEAR THE MASK

Reflecting back on this time, I can see how firmly the Mask of Independence was in place. My stubbornness in handling everything on my own was unshakable—a trait passed down from my parents to my sisters and me. Stubborn and independent. I realize now that this mask is often rooted in early experiences of betrayal or abandonment. From the lack of emotional support as a young gay boy to navigating the complexities of my mother's early struggles with alcoholism, these layers of my past had built a foundation that taught me, subtly but powerfully, that I had to be self-reliant.

Somewhere along the line, my independence became hyper-independence—a form of self-protection. The Newport Institute's article on hyper-independence trauma captures this struggle perfectly, explaining how people with a history of trauma may develop an excessive reliance on themselves. We avoid vulnerability and the potential hurt that comes from depending on others. This hyper-independence is more than self-reliance; it's an insistence on autonomy, often to the extreme.[10] We're unwilling or unable to depend on others, even when in dire need, as I was with Pete. Even simple things like asking my dad for money felt impossible.

Although independence sounds noble, it can sometimes be unhealthy, leading to burnout, loneliness, and physical strain. For those who carry hyper-independence as a response to trauma, self-reliance is a mask—one that keeps us isolated. We convince ourselves that if we can be strong enough on our own, we won't need anyone and, therefore, can't be hurt or let down. In my case, that meant blocking Pete from seeing my vulnerability, even though I was struggling. I didn't trust him with my fears about the visa. Deeper down,

I didn't trust anyone—not even myself or the government process.

Crafted from my fears, the Mask of Independence became both a guiding force and a shield. It offered protection, but it also held me back, making me question every choice, every moment of vulnerability. Ultimately, it kept me from seeing how I was preventing the very connection I craved.

STEPS TO REMOVE THE MASK OF INDEPENDENCE

Removing the Mask of Independence isn't a one-time decision. It's an ongoing journey that starts with understanding why we wear it in the first place.

1. **Recognize the fear beneath the mask:** Acknowledge the fear of vulnerability and disappointment that fuels it. Realize that this fear often stems from past experiences where you felt unsupported or let down. Remember, relying on others doesn't equate to weakness—it's part of what makes us human. For me, facing this fear meant looking at my relationships and understanding why I felt the need to keep everyone at arm's length.
2. **Gradually open up:** You don't need to bare everything all at once. Start by sharing small vulnerabilities with trusted individuals. For example, you could let a friend know when you're feeling stressed or ask for advice on something that's been weighing on you. This gradual process of opening up lets you experience the trust and understanding that others

are willing to offer without feeling exposed. When I allowed myself to do this, I found that even small gestures brought a sense of relief.

3. **Accept help:** Practice allowing others to help you, whether it's with small tasks or larger emotional support. This step can feel uncomfortable at first; after all, accepting help when you're used to relying on only yourself feels like foreign territory. But as you start letting people support you, you'll see that it actually strengthens your relationships and doesn't diminish your independence. In fact, it was through learning to accept support that I found a deeper sense of connection and respect in my relationships.

4. **Reframe self-worth:** Challenge the belief that your value is tied to how self-sufficient you are. For years, I believed that being strong meant handling everything alone, and I tied my self-worth to my independence. But over time, I learned that self-worth can coexist with relying on others. Asking for support is a natural part of life—it doesn't diminish your strength or worth.

5. **Create connections:** Building deeper, more genuine relationships based on mutual trust can help you balance independence with emotional connection. By forming these meaningful connections, you create a support network that can help you let go of hyper-independence. As you experience the positive effects of collaboration and emotional support, you'll find it easier to peel back the mask. Through connection, I found that I could be both strong and supported, independent yet connected.

Letting go of the Mask of Independence isn't about giving up your self-reliance. It's about finding balance and learning that strength can coexist with vulnerability and independence doesn't mean facing life alone.

REFLECTIONS AND LEARNINGS: THE MASK OF INDEPENDENCE

Choosing Connection over Independence

My story: The Mask of Independence made it very difficult and very uncomfortable for me to ask for help. Fueled by fear, my instinct to handle everything alone prevented me from sharing my burdens. Even though I wanted to have that deep connection with Pete, I still wasn't allowing him in.

Your reflection: Are there situations where you've chosen independence over connection? What past fears or experiences do you think may have driven you to make this choice? What do you think might happen if you allow others to support you?

Exercise: Next time you're in a position of needing some help or wanting to share a personal thought, take the opportunity to ask or confide in someone you trust. Notice how it feels to take that step.

Learning to Rely on Others

My story: Growing up, I didn't have much emotional support, especially from my father. This lack of support shaped my belief that I had to handle everything myself, but there was also a dilemma of me having to prove myself. When it came to the situation with Pete and the visa, I feared and felt I couldn't rely on him and it would only add pressure and undermine our relationship.

Your reflection: Think about how your past may have shaped your independence. Are there aspects of your history that make it hard to depend on others? How might your life change if you allow yourself to lean on those close to you?

Exercise: Write a letter to your younger self, acknowledging how your independence served you then. Then list three ways, even if small, you might allow yourself to rely on others now.

Practicing Vulnerability

My Story: When Pete suggested we consider the partner visa, it terrified me. I loved him deeply but couldn't bring myself to relinquish control over my own path. The visa felt like it would put me under his power, even if he didn't see it that way. My Mask of Independence kept me from fully embracing our relationship and trusting in what we could build together.

Your reflection: Think about the ways you prioritize control over connection. Is there someone in your life who could benefit from seeing more of your authentic self?

Exercise: Make a list of three personal things you haven't shared with anyone. Choose one and, in a safe setting, share it with someone you trust to start practicing vulnerability.

Balancing Independence and Closeness

My story: As I grappled with visa challenges, I realized I was fighting the idea of leaning on Pete, even though he wanted to support me. I felt stuck, unsure how to balance my need for independence with my love for him.

Your reflection: Is there a relationship in your life where you struggle with balancing independence and closeness? What keeps you from leaning in and sharing your burdens?

Exercise: Spend time journaling about what independence means to you and how it relates to relationships. Then, reach out to a close friend or loved one and discuss what you've written, inviting them into your process.

Learning to Accept Support

My story: After Pete and I broke up, I felt the impact of my Mask of Independence more deeply than ever. I loved him, but my fear of depending on him had stopped me from fully committing, leaving me with lingering regret.

Your reflection: Are there regrets in your life related to times you held back instead of trusting others? How could acknowledging this help you in future relationships?

Exercise: Take time to write about someone in your life who has been supportive. Write down moments where they showed up for you. Reflect on ways you might let others support you more freely, and share these thoughts with that person, if possible.

MASK OF INDEPENDENCE
KEY TAKEAWAYS

- **True independence balances self-reliance with connection:** Throughout my journey, I realized that real independence isn't about distancing myself from others, but about finding harmony between self-reliance and meaningful relationships. True strength lies in knowing when to stand alone and when to lean into connection, allowing others to support me along the way.
- **Fear of vulnerability often fuels hyper-independence:** My need to handle everything on my own often came from a fear of vulnerability, which I struggled to confront. Recognizing this fear allowed me to start opening up, especially after the breakup with Pete, and to begin building trust without feeling like I was sacrificing my autonomy.
- **Accepting help isn't a sign of weakness:** I had to learn that letting people in doesn't diminish my strength or independence. When Pete offered his support, it didn't mean I was weak; rather, it showed me that true independence can coexist with letting others help, building trust and connection along the way.

- **Masks can protect, but they can also impact relationships and connection:** The Mask of Independence protected me in ways, but it also put distance between me and the people I loved, often limiting my growth and ability to connect meaningfully with others.
- **Self-worth isn't dependent on independence alone:** A part of my self-worth was tied to my ability to stand on my own, but I came to see that true worth isn't dependent on how independent I am. Valuing myself means recognizing that allowing connection and support is part of a fuller, richer life.

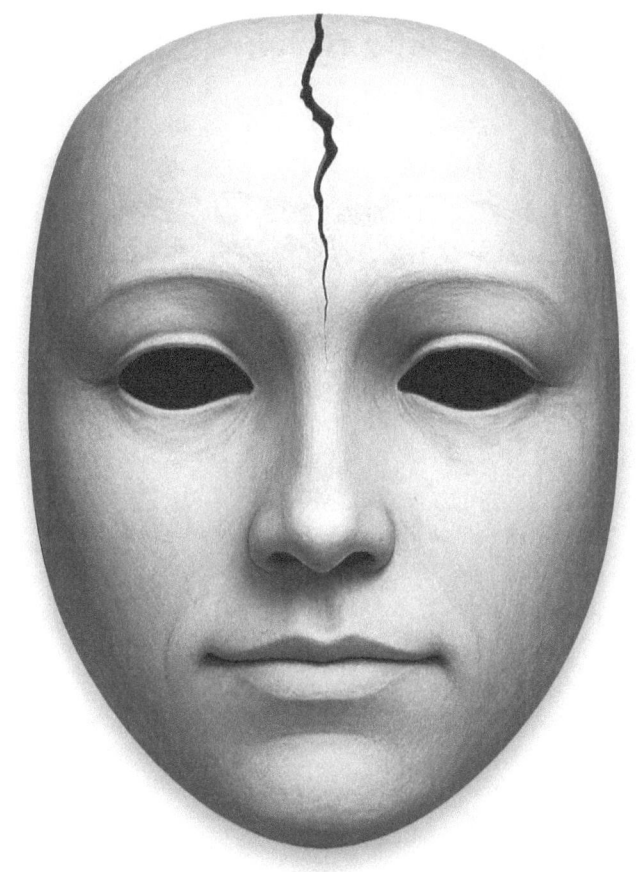

CHAPTER 11

THE MASK OF NORMALCY

COPING WITH LIFE'S CHALLENGES

The Cycle of Normalcy

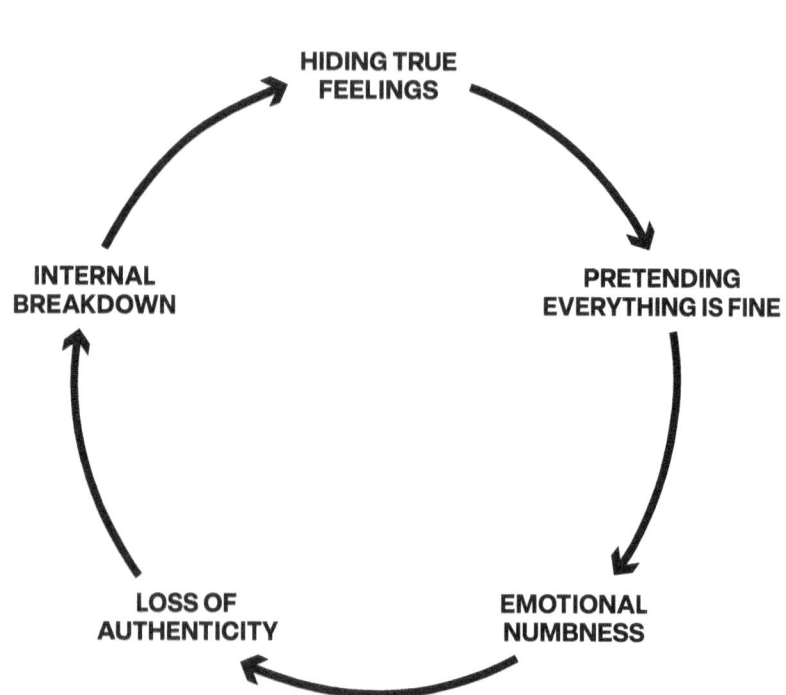

Let me ask you this ... have you ever felt like the world is crumbling around you or you've got too much on your plate but when people ask, you respond with, "I'm fine"? Of course, you have. We all do it. In the realm of social media, life often appears as a constant party—life is good, things are great, everything is *fine*! This is what I like to call the "FHF"—the "fucking happy face"—or what some may call the "happy mask." Often, it's the chosen mask for those of us dealing with depression, using it to conceal real struggles under a guise of happiness and "normalcy." But behind the scenes, we grapple with inner turmoil or feel the weight of external pressures.

Too proud, not wanting to burden others, or fearing judgment—I get it! This was the mask I wore for years, and part of the inspiration behind this book.

On social media, life looked grand. I'd done some cool things, traveled, and lived an adventurous life. But, as you know, I've had my share of struggles. God forbid I let anyone see it. I was wearing my own "FHF," hoping the world would buy it, and maybe, in some way, hoping I would buy it too.

THROWING MYSELF INTO MY BUSINESS

After ending things with Pete, I poured all my energy into my massage business to make it thrive. My days quickly shifted from a handful of clients to an exhausting schedule—seven days a week, 14-hour days. I'd start my mornings at 5 am, heading across the city to meet my first client for a boxing session, then bike to the opposite side of town for a corporate group training, only to head back again for massage clients in my makeshift setup at home. My life had turned into a relentless cycle of work, sleep, and eat. I was on the hamster wheel of routine, grinding day in and day out.

The bright side? I was making good money. My debts were all paid off, and my bank account was steadily filling up. Around this time, I moved into a two-bedroom apartment with my friend Michael, who worked for Qantas. With his flight schedule, he was in and out, so I transformed my room into a mini massage studio. I had just enough space in my room—barely—to set up my massage table at the foot of my bed. It became a daily ritual: setting up and taking down the table, arranging the candles, and putting on some calming music to create that perfect atmosphere. Each time, the process got smoother and quicker.

In the beginning, my skills were basic at best. However, with every client, I refined my technique a little more, learning what worked and what didn't, and building up my confidence in the process. Little by little, this simple setup and basic routine transformed into something real, something sustainable.

The Mask of Normalcy was still firmly in place for the world to see—everything seemed fine on the surface, a life filled with purpose and stability. But behind it, I was on a path of self-discovery, figuring out my identity and direction one massage at a time.

ONE OF MY MOST CHALLENGING MOMENTS

During one of my most challenging experiences, the Mask of Normalcy was both a shield and a wall, hiding a personal struggle that few knew about. Even as I navigated relationships with Liam and Chris, went through the visa ordeal with Pete, and worked tirelessly to stay in Australia, there was another battle I was facing back home—my mother's addiction to alcohol. Every trip home was like opening Pandora's box. I never knew what state I would find her in. Would she be sober? Would she be lost in her struggles, lying in bed, drunk and withdrawn, leaving me to manage yet another crisis? The constant worry followed me, always dreading that phone call that could bring the worst news.

Over time, I'd learned to pick up on her drinking cues. When she was drunk, she spoke in a distinct, childlike voice—a sound that was all too familiar. Also, the anger I felt toward Gary intensified when she was drinking. I resented his lack of support.

One trip home stands out as the most painful. Mom had recently broken her ankle, requiring surgery that left her mostly bedbound with screws in her ankle and a portable potty by her bed. Her drinking already confined her to her room for days at a time, but now, with her injury, she had even more reason to stay in bed.

When I arrived, I called out to her, but there was no response. The house was eerily quiet. I made my way into the kitchen first and was met with the sight of dirty dishes piled high, moldy food caked onto plates—a mess that hadn't been cleaned in days, maybe weeks. The place looked neglected, abandoned. I braced myself and went to her bedroom.

As I opened the door, a wall of thick, musty air hit me, reeking of stale urine and neglect. Her room was dark; broken curtains hung askew; cobwebs stretched across the ceiling, and dust coated every surface. No windows were open. There she was, lying in bed, barely conscious, engulfed in a suffocating atmosphere. The portable potty sat unused beside her, while stains covered the carpet—a grim mixture of alcohol, milk, urine, and Pepto-Bismol. It looked like a halfway house, the room of someone truly struggling with life, shackled by the chains of trauma and addiction that had haunted her for years.

Seeing her like this, I felt the crushing weight of her pain—a pain that had become a part of our family story, one we all carried silently, each of us wearing our own version of the Mask of Normalcy.

Seeing my mother, once a strong, vibrant woman, lying in her own filth broke something inside me. I couldn't believe the state she was in, and my anger surged—not toward her, but toward her partner. Where was he? How could he leave her in this condition?

I sprang into action, calling my aunt, who came over with her daughter to help. She brought cleaning supplies, and together we scrubbed the kitchen, tidied up the living room, doing whatever we could to make the house livable again. It took my mother nearly two days to get out of bed. When she finally did, I helped her to her favorite chair in the living room, gently placing her there to give her some sense of comfort.

Then I returned to tackle her bedroom. I opened the windows, trying to clear the thick, stale air that clung to everything. Her bed linens were soaked and soiled, so I stripped them off, only to find that the mattress itself was covered in black mold, as if she hadn't moved in days. I tried washing the sheets repeatedly, hoping to get rid of the smell of urine, but no matter how many cycles they went through, the stench remained. Eventually, I gave in and bought her a new set of sheets, pillowcases, and a mattress protector, hoping it might bring her a small sense of comfort and dignity amid the struggle.

In an effort to clear out her space, I gathered her clothes into a giant pile in the living room and turned it into a bit of a game, "Keep, donate, or throw away." She resisted at first, wanting to hold on to every piece, every memory, but I encouraged her to let go of things she didn't need, explaining that it would give her a fresh start.

When I opened her second closet, I found something heartbreaking: five large garbage bags filled with empty wine and vodka bottles—her hidden stash. The depth of her addiction was laid bare right there in those bags, as if hiding them would somehow keep her secret safe.

Finally, the house felt somewhat refreshed—new sheets, a cleaner kitchen, a tidied living room.

Despite it all, she was always grateful for the help. And still, I felt the weight of resentment building toward Gary, who, in my eyes, had let her down over and over again.

Through all of this, the Mask of Normalcy became my lifeline. When people asked how I was doing, I'd smile and say, "I'm fine. Life's good." Few people knew the truth. I didn't want them to know this side of my life, to see my mother as someone who struggled with addiction. I wanted them to see the strong, loving, beautiful woman she was. So, I kept it hidden, portraying a life that seemed normal and fine.

My mother was a master of the Mask of Normalcy. Whenever we spoke on the phone, she would tell me stories of how she had cleaned the kitchen, gone for walks, made lunches for her partner—painting a picture-perfect life, as if everything was normal, like she was managing just fine. To this, I could relate.

HIDING BEHIND "I'M FINE"

It's easy to say "I'm fine" to mask everything. But looking back, I see the cost of that facade. For both my mother and me, hiding behind the mask only made the struggles more isolating, more painful, and sometimes more unbearable.

This mask, while it gave me a sense of control and protection, prevented me from seeking the help I needed. I wanted to figure it all out on my own, and this mindset affected my relationships, my mental health, and led to me feeling misunderstood and alone in my struggles.

For me, "I'm fine" became a ritual response—and let's be honest, it's an acceptable answer in today's world. It takes the pressure off both parties. You can almost sense the sigh of relief on both sides when "I'm fine" is said. The person giving it is thinking, *Thank God, I don't have to explain what's actually going on physically or emotionally for me right now.*

The person hearing it might be thinking, *Oh, thank goodness, they aren't going to go into detail.* It's a small white lie that spares everyone involved from uncomfortable truths and the weight of emotional depth.

However, "I'm fine" and the Mask of Normalcy paint over what we really want to say. They don't reflect how we truly feel or what life is actually like. Often, the truth of what we want to share feels too complex, too painful, or too burdensome to reveal. So, as I learned, we put on the mask, say "I'm fine" with a smile, and carry on with our day.

I once read an article that perfectly captured this experience, reinforcing how each time we say "I'm fine" when we're not, we deny ourselves the chance to confront our real feelings. This self-denial holds us back, keeping us in a loop of superficial interactions and missed growth, as we sacrifice potential for personal transformation and meaningful relationships to maintain appearances. To reverse these effects, we must learn to acknowledge our reality, accept that it's OK to not be OK, and express our true thoughts and feelings. Life truly begins when we stop pretending everything's fine. Only then can we move past the mask and experience a life lived authentically.

ORIGINS OF THE MASK OF NORMALCY

The Mask of Normalcy often originates from a need to shield ourselves from vulnerability, especially when life feels overwhelming. It's a defense mechanism—an automatic response, where "I'm fine" becomes a mantra, allowing us to keep up the facade of calm and control, even when we're drowning in stress, anxiety, or despair.

> **Growing up, I learned to reflect back that strong, unbreakable image my father projected—a symbol of masculinity and resilience, leaving little room for weakness or vulnerability.**

The mask serves as a way to cope with personal and professional challenges, to hide the emotional turmoil and daily transitions that weigh heavily on us. It even keeps us from facing our own pain, or shields others from the truth of it. I saw this so clearly in my mother. She would isolate herself, tucked away in her darkened room, a prisoner to her own shame and unresolved trauma. Her reality was uncontrollable, but over the phone, she could paint the picture of a good life. She was an expert at putting up a front and saying "I'm fine" to preserve a sense of normalcy, even as her life unraveled.

This mask is particularly common during crises—financial stress, relationship breakdowns, or health issues—where holding on to some semblance of "normal" becomes a way to cope. It can feel safer to keep things surface-level, to focus on maintaining appearances, even when the effort required to keep up that front wears us down.

WHEN THE MASK BECOMES HARMFUL

I once worked with a client who came to me seeking guidance to transition out of a toxic relationship. He was 65 years old and had been dating a younger man. This relationship had left him bruised—not just emotionally, but mentally and even physically. He experienced emotional abuse, mental manipulation, and occasional physical harm that left him feeling lost, angry, and deeply frustrated. Yet, even during some of the relationship's darkest moments, he wore the Mask of Normalcy. To the outside world, everything seemed fine. He maintained the appearance of composure, hiding his true struggles from family and friends, never revealing the emotional torment he was experiencing.

Our sessions became a rare space where he could take off the mask and express his pain. For years, he'd been bottling up anger, frustration, and sadness, emotions that were becoming harder to contain. The downside of maintaining this mask was the toll it took on his mental and physical health. Suppressing his true feelings led to exhaustion, anxiety, and even breakdowns, creating an emotional distance in his closest relationships. He struggled to communicate with those he loved, and he felt isolated, trapped by the need to appear fine.

In our sessions, we delved into the beliefs he held about maintaining that mask, and we discovered its roots in his childhood. Growing up with a strong, macho father, he had learned early on to hide anything that might be seen as weak or "sissy." The Mask of Normalcy had protected him for years, shielding him from judgment. But it was also a barrier to healing. As we worked together, he began to take down that mask, one layer at a time, to look honestly at the pain and damage caused by his relationship. This process gave him space to breathe and, finally, to recognize that what he was enduring wasn't fine—it was harmful, and he deserved better.

In acknowledging this, he found a new sense of clarity and self-worth. Removing the mask allowed him to see himself and his situation more clearly. For the first time, he could say, "I'm not fine, and that's OK." He no longer had to pretend, and, in this newfound honesty, he found the courage to seek the life he truly deserved.

REALITY BENEATH THE MASK

Over time, my social media presence grew, and my online life painted a picture of healthy optimism and success. My body looked great, business was booming, and I was traveling across the globe to network marketing events, having recently stepped into that world. On the surface, I seemed to be thriving, projecting a life of normality and perfection for all to see. However, beneath it all, I was struggling. I was constantly battling visa challenges, dealing with the stress of my mom's alcoholism, and starting to feel the weight of having to show up every day for people—a pressure I had placed entirely on myself.

It didn't help that my future was still uncertain. Both my original visa options had fallen through, leaving me in a tough spot. It was as if I was living in limbo, no closer to finding a way to stay. I knew I had to find another solution. But unless you've been through something like this, you'll never understand how messed up your head can get when your whole life is riding on a visa. It was this constant, underlying tension guiding every decision I made.

What I Actually Mean When I Say "I'm Fine"

*Some days, when I say, "I'm fine," I'm
putting on the Mask of Normalcy.
I'm up, washed, and dressed, and now I'm
fighting to manage the day as best I can.
This mask helps me seem OK, like I'm keeping pace, but
inside I'm screaming, feeling a weight of pain and anguish.
All I want is to crawl away, curl up, and
wait for things to settle down.
But instead, I keep this mask in place—because life is
already hard enough, and staying focused, holding it
together, feels like an uphill battle I'd rather not share.
I'm not actually fine, but saying it is easier; it requires
less energy than explaining how I really feel.
I'm too tired to respond any other way.*

*Behind the mask, I'm falling apart—my
mind overloaded and overwhelmed.
Yet here I am, looking at you, talking to
you, so I must be fine, right?
I keep this Mask of Normalcy in place to stay positive, to keep
things steady because, after all, nothing else has changed.
Rather than pulling you into my world and
bringing us both down, "I'm fine" works.*

*Right now doesn't feel like the time or place for my true feelings.
I don't need more judgment or pity because I've learned
that it often leads to attempts to "fix" me.
I've shared these feelings before, and it didn't go well.
But in this moment, as I wear the mask, I'm fine—my mood is
balanced, my thoughts slower, and the overwhelm fades a little.
I'm not truly OK, but for now I've got this small bit of calm,
enough to smile, to keep up appearances, and to manage my day.
Maybe, if I keep saying it, the Mask of
Normalcy will make "I'm fine" feel real.*

STEPS TO REMOVE THE MASK OF NORMALCY

While the Mask of Normalcy provides protection in times of crisis, it also acts as a barrier to vulnerability. Learning to be vulnerable is an important step toward removing the mask and accepting support.

1. **Acknowledge the facade:** Admit to yourself that you've been pretending everything's fine. Take a moment to recognize the pain, struggles, or discomfort you've been hiding beneath the surface. This self-awareness is the beginning of an authentic path forward.
2. **Create a safe space for vulnerability:** Find trusted individuals in your life and start by opening up to them. You don't have to share everything at once—begin with small, honest details about what you're going through. Vulnerability allows you to shed the need to appear "fine" and connect authentically with others.

3. **Accept that it's OK to not be OK:** Life has ups and downs, and it's perfectly normal not to have it all together. Embracing this reality helps break the cycle of perfectionism and the constant need to project that everything's OK. Acceptance of your true feelings allows space for healing and growth.
4. **Seek support:** You don't have to go through this alone. Reach out to a therapist, support group, or close friends who can offer understanding and guidance. When you have people to lean on, it's easier to release the Mask of Normalcy and process the emotions you've been keeping inside.
5. **Practice self-compassion:** Be kind to yourself as you navigate showing your true emotions. Remember, it's human to face struggles, to feel vulnerable, and to be imperfect. Allow yourself grace in the process, knowing that each step brings you closer to living authentically without the mask.

Removing the Mask of Normalcy is a journey, and with each step, you'll find relief in allowing yourself to be seen as you are, embracing both the highs and the lows of life.

REFLECTIONS AND LEARNINGS: THE MASK OF NORMALCY

Opening Up to Others

My story: Hiding behind the Mask of Normalcy, I showed the world a version of success—thriving in business, traveling, and looking great. Yet behind the scenes, I was struggling with visa issues, my mom's alcoholism, and mounting pressure to keep up appearances.

Your reflection: Where in your life are you projecting "everything is fine" when it's not? What might it feel like to show even a small part of the truth?

Exercise: Identify one person you trust. Share a specific moment or feeling you've been hiding. Notice how it feels to drop the mask, even briefly.

Stepping Away from Social Media and Public Persona

My story: Social media amplified the mask. I felt the pressure to be inspiring, to share success, and to motivate others. But this came at a cost—I ignored my own struggles for fear of letting people down.

Your reflection: Do you ever feel pressure to be a role model or source of inspiration? How has that affected your ability to share your true self?

Exercise: Take a break from social media or your public persona for one day. Use that time to connect with your feelings or a trusted friend, being fully honest about where you're at.

Reflecting on the Opinions of Others

My story: Rejection, especially from family, made the mask harder to remove. I wanted to prove myself, but it came at the cost of my mental health. I didn't realize I was isolating myself further by pretending to be OK.

Your reflection: Have you ever worked hard to prove yourself to someone, only to feel more alone in the process? How did that affect your relationships and mental health?

Exercise: Write a letter to someone (you don't have to send it) about what you've been trying to prove. Reflect on whether their opinion still matters as much as it once did.

Practicing Vulnerability and Authenticity

My story: The mask allowed me to avoid difficult conversations and emotions, but it also cut me off from genuine connection. I was surrounded by people yet felt incredibly alone.

Your reflection: What would it take to let go of the need to appear "fine" all the time? How might it change your relationships if you allowed yourself to be seen?

Exercise: Practice letting your guard down in one small interaction today. It could be as simple as admitting, "I'm having a tough day," instead of saying, "I'm fine."

Considering the Burden of Concealed Struggle

My story: When the Mask of Normalcy was still firmly in place, I didn't want to burden others with my problems or risk exposing my mother to judgment. My priority was maintaining the image of a thriving, put-together life, even if it meant struggling in silence.

Your reflection: Have you ever avoided sharing your struggles to protect someone else, even at your own expense? How did it feel to carry that weight alone?

Exercise: Reflect on one challenge you've been hiding. Write down how you think sharing it might affect both you and the person you're protecting. Consider how much of that weight you can continue to carry by yourself.

MASK OF NORMALCY
KEY TAKEAWAYS

- **Hiding pain doesn't make it disappear:** Wearing the Mask of Normalcy may keep up appearances, but it doesn't resolve the struggles underneath. True healing begins when we acknowledge what's really happening.
- **The mask protects, but it also isolates:** While the mask can shield us from judgment or rejection, it often creates a barrier between us and those who care about us, leading to feelings of loneliness and disconnection.
- **Vulnerability is not weakness:** Sharing your struggles doesn't make you weak; it allows for deeper, more meaningful connections and invites support from others.
- **Pressure to appear perfect is exhausting:** Constantly maintaining the appearance of having it all together takes an emotional toll. Recognizing this pressure is the first step to letting it go.
- **True connection comes from authenticity:** Allowing others to see your struggles can create a sense of relief and foster genuine relationships. You don't have to carry everything alone.

CHAPTER 12

THE MASK OF
PERFECTION

HIDING BEHIND FLAWLESSNESS

The Cycle of Perfection

Have you ever had a moment where everything looks picture-perfect on the outside, but inside you're barely holding it together? For me, it wasn't just a moment; it was a way of life. From running a business to navigating relationships dictated by visas, I had perfected the art of looking like I had it all figured out—even when my world felt like it was crumbling.

THE START OF SOMETHING REAL

Since living in my apartment and training outside in the park, I frequently noticed a guy, David, walking his little shih tzu named Bentley. David was clean-shaven, with pasty white skin, about my height, and usually wearing a similar outfit—pants, a T-shirt, and sunglasses. I thought he was handsome. Once in a blue moon, we would cross paths in the lobby of our building and exchange a polite "hi." Now that I was single, I decided I was going to make more of an effort.

One particular day, as I was in the park making my way to the gym, we crossed paths and both stopped to say hello. The usual small talk—"Hi, how are you?"—but through my questions, I was very intentional about what I asked. "What floor are you on? And what apartment?"

A few days later, I decided to act. I took one of my new business cards and attached it to a note saying, *You, me, drinks?* I made my way up to the 11th floor, slipped the note under his door, and rushed back home, heart racing. That evening, I eagerly awaited David's text. But nothing came. Then a day passed, two days, three days, and still nothing. I was confused and awkward, not sure how to navigate the situation. I even saw him in the park, and we waved at each other, which only made the situation more confusing.

Something wasn't adding up. Maybe his flatmate had thought it was garbage and chucked it. Maybe he had a boyfriend. Maybe Bentley ate it. Whatever the case, I wasn't about to let it slide. So I tried again. This time, I wasn't wasting another business card. I wrote on a simple piece of paper: *Hey, Rob from 903. Wanna have drinks?* I added my number at the bottom and slipped it under his door.

That evening, my phone buzzed with a text message. Sure enough, it was David. Thank God!

We arranged to have drinks Friday night at my place. He'd be finishing his shift around 8 p.m., and I was trying to stay calm—easier said than done. Adding to the chaos, I was in the middle of a 48-hour deep cleanse. No food, just water and supplements. Cleansing is great for the body, but let's be honest, it's terrible for socializing. Nervous and dangerously sober, I decided to cheat a little with a quick shot of tequila. When David arrived, so did the bottle of vodka he brought along. Cleansing plan: officially derailed.

We both must have been a little jittery because the cocktails went down way too fast. Before we knew it, we were halfway through the vodka, and the conversation was flowing. Fun, flirty, and a little messy—just how I like it. At some point, I had to address the elephant in the room (or should I say the note under the door).

"So … did you ever get that first note I left?" I asked, my buzz giving me just the right amount of boldness.

David smirked. "Of course I did! I texted you right away."

Cue the record scratch in my brain. "Wait, what? I never got anything."

He looked genuinely confused. "I texted the number on your business card…"

I pulled out one of my brand-new cards, and there it was, clear as day: the wrong phone number. I'd been handing out these cards like Oprah giving out cars, thinking I was networking up a storm, and, the whole time, people were contacting some poor stranger.

We burst out laughing. He'd been messaging a random person, probably confusing the hell out of them, while I was sitting at home, drowning in rejection. Another drink was poured to toast my epic business card fail.

As the drinks kept coming, David's dog Bentley eventually came up in conversation. In our drunken wisdom, we thought it would be a fantastic idea to go upstairs and visit him.

As we stepped into the elevator, I could feel the moment building. Fueled by vodka and bad decisions, I leaned in and kissed him. He paused, looking a bit thrown off, and asked, "Wait, don't you have a boyfriend?"

"Nope," I said without missing a beat. "We broke up months ago." And then I kissed him again, thinking I was smooth as hell.

Back at my apartment, the cocktails continued to flow, and the words started to slur. Nerves were long gone, replaced by drunken confidence. I leaned in again, and we started kissing on the couch. Subtlety? Long gone. Restraint? Thrown out the window. I was drunk, horny, and very into this guy. Things escalated, and we stumbled our way to the bedroom.

That's when it hit me. The spins. The *oh-no-I've-had-too-much* spins. I pushed myself off David and bolted to the bathroom, where I was promptly punished by the detox gods. Round one of puking: complete. I rinsed my mouth, regrouped, and—because clearly I don't know when to quit—returned to the bedroom, leaning in for more kisses.

Big mistake.

Seconds later, the spins came back with a vengeance. Round two. Back to the bathroom I went, this time with less dignity and more despair. From the hallway, I heard David's voice, steady but tinged with pity: "I'll speak to you tomorrow." I glanced up just in time to see him walking out of my apartment, dog in tow, leaving me to contemplate my life choices. What a way to make a first impression.

The next morning, the hangover was as brutal as the embarrassment.

I replayed the night in my head, cringing with every detail. A 48-hour detox followed by copious amounts of alcohol was clearly not the power move I'd imagined. At lunch with friends, I recounted the disaster, turning it into a cautionary tale about drinking responsibly. They laughed, of course, but I couldn't shake the shame.

STRENGTHENED CONNECTIONS AND TOUGH CONVERSATIONS

Over the next few months, David and I built a connection. We genuinely enjoyed each other's company—we shared a taste for nice home design and both loved to cook, spending hours in the kitchen experimenting. He even taught me how to make pasta from scratch, a skill he'd mastered as a trained chef. But as I got to know him better, it became clear that he lived in a very small, comfortable bubble. His dog was his world, and his routine revolved around work, sleep, and walking Bentley. He had never traveled overseas, never been to the gym, never been to a concert, and never wore shorts or singlets.

During one of our usual morning walks, my mind was consumed with the question I knew I had to ask: would he sponsor me? My time was running out, and I couldn't keep pushing it aside. But how do you ask a question like that? How do you bring up something so big without making it seem transactional? My mind raced, trying to determine the best approach.

I could feel the tension in the air. David wasn't oblivious—he knew my situation, and I think he sensed what was coming. Still, I couldn't escape the feeling that this moment would define everything.

I had to ask. I didn't just blurt it out; I started by discussing my situation, where I was with my visa, and how I was running out of options. Finally, I worked up the courage to ask, "Would you be open to sponsoring me?"

His response caught me off guard. "You're not just dating me for a visa, are you?"

"No, not at all," I replied, trying to keep my tone steady. "I actually really like you and enjoy spending time with you." And it was true—at least partially. I genuinely liked David, but the visa situation was undeniably playing a role in how fast things were progressing between us.

After what felt like an eternity, he responded. "Yes. Yes, I'll sponsor you." A wave of relief rushed over me—finally, a solution, and one that could actually work. Or at least I hoped it would.

I dived into researching everything we needed to make it happen. There was a long list: living together, opening a joint bank account, registering the relationship since we'd only been together for a few months, collecting photos, letters, witnesses—the works. We still had a long journey ahead of us. The real work was just beginning.

THE DAY EVERYTHING CHANGED

Over the next couple of weeks, the preparations began. It was a strange mix of excitement and anxiety. On one hand, we were taking this step together; on the other hand, the pressure of knowing it was partly driven by a looming deadline hung heavily in the air.

The day came to head to the office and register our relationship—a necessary step in the de facto visa process since we hadn't been living together for the required time. On paper, it was just a formality, but the emotional weight it carried meant it was anything but. For me, it felt like freedom was finally within reach, a huge step forward in my journey to secure a future in Australia. For David, well … let's just say it felt more like a jail sentence. Still, he showed up and signed the papers, but something shifted that day. Suddenly, our relationship felt different—unnatural. The process made everything real in a way that was heavy, calculated, and suffocating. What should have been the organic growth of a relationship turned into a task list, a job we both had to clock into every day. Every moment was tied to the visa.

"Let's take a photo for the visa."

"Let's meet your parents—and don't forget the photos for the visa."

"Let's move in together for the visa."

I hated every second of it. This was exactly why I'd pushed Pete away. I didn't want a relationship dictated by a visa. I didn't want it to feel like work. But here I was, doing exactly what I'd feared most—letting the visa overshadow what should have been an intimate and meaningful connection.

In the middle of all this chaos, there was an added layer of pressure I couldn't ignore: everything had to be perfect—or at least appear perfect—for the immigration officers. The de facto visa process wasn't just about love; it was about proving love, showcasing it, documenting it, and packaging it neatly for strangers to dissect and evaluate. Every photo we took, every joint decision we made, and every interaction we had was filtered through that lens. Were there enough pictures of us smiling together? Did our timeline make sense? Did it look like a legitimate relationship?

I felt like we were building a portfolio, not a life. Every moment had to be calculated to create the perfect image, the perfect story. And that kind of pressure seeped into every interaction. It was exhausting.

PERFECTION—A FAMILIAR MASK FOR MANY

The Mask of Perfection is probably one of the most common masks we wear—and also one of the sneakiest. It's the mask that says, "Don't worry, I've got this. Everything's great, no cracks here." It's about projecting a flawless image, ensuring all parts of our lives look like they're running smoothly, even when they're not.

In my case, the Mask of Perfection wasn't just for the visa officers. I was also trying to convince myself that I had everything under control. But I didn't. The truth was, the more I tried to create this picture-perfect relationship, the more artificial it felt. And the more artificial it felt, the more it chipped away at the real connection David and I were trying to build.

While perfectionism often begins as a personal pursuit, its grip extends well beyond the individual, infiltrating professional spaces and shaping entire work cultures.

> **The workplace becomes an arena where the Mask of Perfection thrives—where the pressure to project an image of flawlessness becomes both a defense mechanism and a performance strategy.**

One of my clients embodied this struggle. He came to me after reaching breaking point—burnout had consumed him, and his health was slipping. A once high-performing executive, he was no stranger to perfectionism. But as the weight of always "having it together" took its toll, the cracks began to show. His self-esteem plummeted; his relationships became strained, and even his physical health suffered as stress compounded over time.

While workplace perfectionism often begins with good intentions—wanting to excel, impress, and achieve—as those goals morph into unattainable expectations, the cost becomes evident. In my client's case, perfectionism was not only eroding his well-being but also his connection to others. The mask he wore at work made it difficult to form authentic relationships, both in and outside of the office. The fear of showing vulnerability kept him isolated, and the need to meet ever-increasing demands left him questioning his own worth.

The turning point came when he realized that striving for an unattainable ideal wasn't sustainable. Our work together focused on peeling back the layers of his perfectionism, helping him recognize that vulnerability wasn't a weakness but a strength. By challenging his internal beliefs and embracing imperfection, he began to find a balance—one where success didn't come at the cost of his well-being.

The roots of this mask run deep. Many of us pick it up early on—maybe due to the praise we got for being the "good kid" who always followed the rules or for being the straight A student who made the family proud. Or maybe it was the criticism we faced when we weren't enough, a subtle reminder that anything less than perfect was unacceptable. Over time, we learned that imperfection wasn't safe, and hiding it became second nature.

However, the pressure to look perfect, act perfect, and be perfect takes a toll—not just on us, but on our relationships too. Because here's the kicker: when we wear this mask, we keep people at arm's length. We think hiding our flaws will make us more lovable, but it just makes us harder to connect with.

> **People don't fall in love with perfection—
> they fall in love with humanity.**

At its core, the Mask of Perfection is all about control. We try to control how people see us, thinking that if we can make everything look perfect, we'll be safe from rejection, failure, or disappointment. But the truth is, we can't control how others see us. No matter how flawless we try to appear, we can't avoid the things that make us human. And in trying, we miss out on so much. Growth, learning, real connection—it all comes from embracing our imperfections, not hiding them.

THE WAR INSIDE MY HEAD

The day finally came for David to move in. His dad drove down from Newcastle to help, and I got to meet him for the first time. Meeting his dad should have been a big step in solidifying our bond, but instead I was in full survival mode. My subconscious mind was working overtime, strategizing every move to protect the visa.

Just days after he moved in, I felt the weight of everything come crashing down. It was clear we were pulling away from each other, and I knew we couldn't continue like this. So, in possibly the worst-timed conversation of my life, I suggested we take a step back and rebuild as friends.

"Are you serious?" David was livid—and understandably so. He'd just packed up his life, moved in with me, and now I was telling him I thought we should start over as friends. "You used me! This is all fake!"

The words cut deep, and our argument escalated. I tried to justify my reasoning, explaining that I wasn't trying to hurt him. I wanted us to salvage what we had before it disintegrated completely under the pressure. But for him, it was impossible to see it as anything other than betrayal.

THE CRUSHING WEIGHT OF THE MASK

For some, the Mask of Perfection stems from a need for outside validation. We crave that constant feedback from our external environment, affirming that we're good enough. For us perfectionists, achievements often go hand in hand with self-worth. Without external validation and recognition, we're left with a gnawing sense of emptiness.

The Mask of Perfection doesn't just crave praise—it's also haunted by a relentless, harsh inner critic. You know, the voice that insists no matter how well you do, you're still not good enough. This voice often originates from significant figures in our lives—parents, teachers, or caregivers—who held us to impossible standards.

Personally, the weight of trying to control and perfect everything was crushing. The fear of failure, rejection, or losing the life I was trying to build kept me in survival mode, wearing the Mask of Perfection like armor—armor that was slowly suffocating me.

Looking back, I see how much of my energy was consumed by trying to keep everything in balance. The Mask of Perfection wasn't just something I wore for others—it became the lens through which I viewed myself. I needed David to believe I was the perfect partner.

I needed the immigration system to see us as the perfect couple. I needed the outside world to think my life was thriving. But behind the scenes, I was drowning in doubt and fear, questioning whether I was even capable of pulling it all off.

The hardest part was knowing I wasn't living authentically. I wasn't showing up fully for David because I was stuck in survival mode. Every decision I made was tied to the desperate need to stay in the country, and that pressure bled into every aspect of our relationship. While we had plenty of genuine moments, the weight of the visa process was always present.

Not only was I trying to do this balancing act with David and the visa, but I was also trying to manage my unresolved feelings for Pete. Still working in my massage business, every session became a time to replay the battles raging in my mind. Most of those thoughts revolved around Pete. I was mentally crafting the perfect letter to give to him when I finally reconnected after the visa was done. But the truth was, I was consumed by guilt and regret over how I had left things with him. I wanted this visa to work, but I also couldn't let go of the fantasy future I had created with Pete—a future that felt more like a movie than reality.

I was doing everything to move past my feelings for Pete and be fully present for David, but I was stuck. There were times when Pete was a distant memory and I was fully embraced in what I was creating with David. But every time I was doing massage, the thought would come back. It became an obsession. Every stroke, every knead of a client's muscles gave me space to spiral deeper into the world of what-ifs. What if I'd handled things differently? What if Pete and I had stayed together? Was I chasing a fantasy, or had I truly let something real slip away? Meanwhile, there was David—a kind, genuine guy who had moved mountains to help me, but I couldn't fully be present in our relationship. I was stuck in the past with Pete, dreaming of the future, chasing a visa, and ignoring the reality in front of me.

David knew about Pete, and Pete knew about David, but neither of them knew the extent of the chaos in my head. Pete had to distance himself to protect his heart, but I kept holding on to this cinematic idea of us, as if I were a soldier leaving for war, not knowing if I'd return or if he'd still be there. It was irrational, but I couldn't help it. Songs became my solace, their lyrics a reflection of the emotions I couldn't express. They made me sadder, hungrier for something I couldn't have, and more deeply entrenched in a fantasy that was taking up way too much headspace.

The truth is, I was torturing myself. Instead of focusing on David and the relationship we were building, I was living in the past and chasing an uncertain future. I allowed myself to dwell in the world of what-ifs and should-haves, making me my own worst enemy.

BUILDING A RELATIONSHIP, BUILDING A LIFE

Despite the suffocating visa process and my fears around our relationship, over time, David and I managed to build something special. We worked well together, laughed a lot, and created a little sanctuary of peace in our lives. We even added a new member to our family: Brodie, a blue-eyed, cross-eyed, seal point Tonkinese cat. Brodie and Bentley became inseparable. As a kitten, Brodie would chase Bentley's fluffy tail, and, as he grew, they became snuggle buddies and wrestling partners. It was a chaotic but beautiful little family, and during the moments when the visa wasn't front and center, it felt like our own slice of normalcy.

I also focused on bringing David out of his comfort zone, helping him experience new things. For starters, I introduced him to the gym. David had always been self-conscious and didn't want to be seen in shorts or a singlet, so we started by going at 3 a.m. when no one else was around. It was like training someone from scratch—squat technique, push-ups, lunges, the basics. Over time, he fell in love with it and turned into a full-blown gym junkie.

It didn't stop there. I also organized David's first concert. And not just any concert—Celine Dion. That's right, my homegirl Celine. Now, being a guy who hadn't seen her live, he was resistant at first. But I knew better. As soon as she came on and he heard that incredible voice, he turned to me and said, "OK, she's pretty fucking good." Success! Not long after, I took him to see another icon—Pink. I mean, how's that for a solid introduction to live music?

After meeting David's family, it wasn't long before his mom and dad became like a second set of parents to me. His mom—a big, tough Maori woman—didn't take any crap but loved good banter. She and I would go back and forth, teasing each other relentlessly, but it was all in good fun. Their family dynamic was so different from mine. They talked every day, checked in with each other, and supported us in everything we did. They represented what I had always imagined a family should be.

A WEDDING, A MASK, A WORLD APART

While David had met my mom over FaceTime, he hadn't experienced my world back home. He knew bits and pieces about my family dynamics, but meeting everyone in person would be a whole other story. Finally, my sister's wedding provided the perfect opportunity to head home.

For me, planning a trip home was always a mix of emotions. On one hand, it was a chance to reconnect with family. On the other hand, it meant stepping back into an environment that often triggered feelings I'd worked so hard to manage—or at least hide. David and I would be showing up as a couple, with me not only navigating the pressure of our visa story but also the complicated dynamics of my family. For this trip, the Mask of Perfection was dialed up to the maximum.

David and I decided to turn the trip into a four-week adventure, starting in LA and ending up at Yosemite National Park. Yosemite was stunning—massive waterfalls, breathtaking views, and … the moment David decided to stand directly under a waterfall and get drenched.

It was beautiful, yes, but it was also his ticket to catching a cold. By the time we reached San Francisco, he was sniffling and coughing. Cue the Canadian solution: DayQuil, my trusty go-to remedy. Back home, it was the miracle cure for colds. What I didn't anticipate was how David, unfamiliar with Canadian cold meds and feeling pretty miserable, would take matters into his own hands.

Roughly two hours into sightseeing in San Francisco, I glanced at him in the car. Something wasn't right. His eyes were wide, his movements a little too relaxed. Then I saw it: the empty bottle of DayQuil. Panic mode.

"David, what the hell? You're only supposed to take thirty mil every six to eight hours!"

"Oh," he said casually, like he hadn't just chugged over 300 ml in two hours. "I thought you just drank it until you felt better." He'd drunk it like it was a cocktail at the beach!

The cold medicine in the United States is much stronger than it is in Australia, with all its restrictions. So, there I was, panicking, yelling at David, frantically googling the side effects of consuming too much DayQuil. Meanwhile, he was vibing, entirely unaware of the chaos he'd just unleashed.

Back at the hotel, I left him to rest while I went to do laundry, explicitly telling him to *stay put*. But of course, David had other plans. When I returned, he was gone. Cue more panic. I called him, trying to figure out where he had wandered off to.

"Where are you?"

"I don't know. I'm very high, but I'm in a park, and I think I'm petting a really cute dog," he replied.

Eventually, I got him back to the bar below our hotel. He sauntered in, still very much *out of it*. But, to his credit, he was having the time of his life, marveling at the world around him as if he'd discovered a new dimension. I sat there, half-concerned, half-laughing at the absurdity of it all. He was truly high, but at least he was enjoying himself.

I had to admit it was a little funny watching him embrace the world with this childlike wonder. He had no idea what was going on, and somehow he was just fine with it.

The moral of the story? Don't drink an entire bottle of DayQuil in under two hours, especially if you're in a strange city, prone to wandering, and not entirely sure how strong the meds are.

* * *

Finally, we arrived in Smithers. As we pulled into the driveway of my dad's place, my nerves began to bubble beneath the surface. Meeting David's parents had been easy—they were warm, welcoming, and had an openness about them. With Dad, things were … different.

As we stepped out of the car and David took in his surroundings, I steeled myself. I had prepared him to meet my dad, painting a picture of a hard-ass country bloke, the kind of guy who lived for guns, hunting, and small-town life, with a tough exterior to match. Let's just say I didn't soften the edges when describing him, and David had built up this whole image in his head of a gruff, mean, manly man. So, you can imagine his surprise—and mine—when we were greeted at the front doorstep with a big bear hug. It was the last thing either of us expected.

The next few days were about giving David the full Canadian experience—campfires, s'mores, canoeing on my dad's lake, and, of course, shooting guns. David had never even held a gun, let alone fired one, so this was a brand-new adventure for him. My dad, of course, had plenty to choose from: handguns, a .22, a shotgun, you name it. To make it even better, he'd gone out and bought one of those big zombie targets. He wanted David to have some fun with it, and, honestly, so did I.

We walked down to the end of the driveway and into the woods, finding a clearing to set up. Dad went into full-on instructor mode, going through his usual training spiel about how each gun worked. He started with the handgun, firing off a demonstration shot. Now,

David had only ever heard guns on TV, so the loudness of that first shot made him literally jump sideways, letting out a big scream. I was pissing myself laughing; he was so caught off guard.

When it was David's turn to shoot, he was visibly nervous. The first round startled him just as much as the demonstration. The kickback didn't help. But as we moved through the different guns, I could see his confidence growing. By the end, the look on his face said it all—he was loving it. I admired his sense of adventure. For someone so introverted and with little experience in the world of "firsts," David was always willing to give anything a go, even if he needed a bit of a push—and the reward was always worth it.

Later that night, we brought David back to his comfort zone—the kitchen. David and I showed my dad and his girlfriend how to make pasta from scratch. We whipped up a beautiful pappardelle with a rich ragu, which was a slight upgrade from the bear stew Dad had served David on our first night. Cooking together was fun, a little bonding moment.

For a while, everything felt normal—whatever that means. Dad and his partner, David and me, all in the kitchen, laughing, cooking, and enjoying each other's company. It was one of those rare moments where the weight of unresolved issues between my dad and me seemed to slip away. A band-aid over the cracks, sure, but in that moment, it felt like enough.

* * *

As the wedding drew closer, my sister asked me to be the MC for her big day. Of course, I couldn't say no, but it came with its own challenges—like making sure my dad's speech didn't go completely off the rails. Dad has this unique talent for starting a story about one thing and somehow blending it into something completely unrelated. One moment he's talking about grocery shopping, and the next he's describing a bear climbing a tree. It's like trying to piece together a puzzle with half the pieces missing. I couldn't let that happen at my sister's wedding.

So, I took it upon myself to prepare him. I researched the usual MC duties and the structure of a father-of-the-bride speech, then sat him down at dinner to recall his favorite memories of my sister. From there, I pieced together a speech that would keep him on track—hopefully.

The next day, we went to visit my mom. This was another experience I had to prepare David for. I'd told him about her struggles with drinking and the complicated dynamic we shared. Visiting her always stressed her out—not because she didn't want to see me, but because she was embarrassed. You never knew what you were walking into when you showed up at her door.

When we arrived, she was still in bed in the middle of the day, sleeping off whatever she'd had to drink the night before. When she finally emerged, her face was bloated, and her steps were slow, but her excitement to meet David was genuine.

The house though—it was a disaster. The kitchen was a mess, and the bathroom was filthy, with black mold growing beneath the shower mat. David and I sprang into action. We rolled up our sleeves, threw on some hot pink cleaning gloves, and did what we could to make her space livable.

Every time I came home, the scene was the same: a messy house, my mom drunk, and Gary using her home as a free place to crash. But no matter how I felt about the situation, I didn't let it get in the way of making the most of my time with her.

* * *

Finally, the day of the wedding arrived, and David and I showed up looking sharp in our carefully coordinated outfits. We played our roles perfectly—partners, a couple who fit together seamlessly. And honestly, at times, it felt real. When we were out and about, laughing and enjoying each other's company, it was easy to forget the elephant in the room: the visa. But no matter how good we were at putting on a show, the truth cast a shadow over our relationship.

Despite the emotional tug-of-war, the wedding itself was beautiful. Watching my baby sister walk down the aisle to marry the love of her life was such a gift. She got married in a quaint little church, and as I watched the ceremony, I could barely hold back my tears of happiness. It felt like just yesterday that my sister and I were kids, growing up in our small town. And now, here she was, a bride, embarking on this new chapter of her life.

CHOOSE AUTHENTICITY OVER PERFECTION

The Mask of Perfection, like most masks, serves a purpose. It provides a sense of control and security in a world where vulnerability often feels like a risk too great to take. For me, it gave me the confidence to move forward during one of the most uncertain times of my life. It helped me navigate the visa process, maintain a facade of stability in my relationship with David, and present an image of myself that felt necessary for survival.

For all its benefits, the Mask of Perfection comes at a steep cost. Maintaining perfection is exhausting. Every action, word, and decision felt magnified, scrutinized not just by David or the immigration process, but also by my own relentless inner critic. I found myself constantly questioning whether I was truly enough. The mask also created disconnection, forming barriers between me and the people I cared about most. My relationship with David, though filled with moments of joy and intimacy, was clouded by the constant pressure to make everything look picture-perfect. When I was constantly strategizing, it was difficult to be present. Perhaps the most insidious cost of all was self-deception. The mask tricked me into believing the very facade I created—that I could juggle it all flawlessly: the visa, my relationship with David, my unresolved feelings for Pete, and the future I was trying so desperately to build. Deep down, I knew that perfection was a mirage I could never sustain.

While the Mask of Perfection served its purpose during those challenging times, it ultimately left me drained and disconnected, showing me that striving for authenticity, not perfection, was the only path to true peace and connection.

It's in our imperfections, our struggles, and our vulnerabilities that we find true connection and growth. And while the mask may have helped me survive, it's only by removing it that I've been able to start truly living.

STEPS TO REMOVE THE MASK OF PERFECTION

Ultimately, removing the Mask of Perfection means giving yourself permission to be flawed—that is, to be *human*—and practicing self-compassion.

1. **Acknowledge the fear of imperfection:** Recognize that the need for perfection is driven by a fear of being seen as inadequate or unworthy. It's essential to understand that everyone has flaws, and true self-worth doesn't come from being flawless but from embracing imperfections.
2. **Challenge unrealistic expectations:** Reflect on whether the standards you set for yourself are realistic or if they're driven by external pressures. Begin to question why you feel the need to meet these expectations and consider whether they're truly aligned with your values.
3. **Allow yourself to make mistakes:** Give yourself permission to fail, make mistakes, and be imperfect. By taking small risks and allowing for imperfection, you gradually become more comfortable with vulnerability. Mistakes are an essential part of learning and growth, not a reflection of your worth.
4. **Practice self-compassion:** Develop a practice of self-compassion by being kind to yourself, especially when you fall short of your expectations. Instead of being critical, offer yourself the same understanding and forgiveness you would extend to a friend. Self-compassion allows you to accept yourself as you are, flaws and all.

REFLECTIONS AND LEARNINGS: THE MASK OF NORMALCY

Embracing Vulnerability and Imperfection

My story: Hiding behind the Mask of Perfection, I showed David, his family, and the immigration officers a version of myself that looked flawless. I meticulously crafted an image of the perfect partner, the perfect applicant, and the perfect life. But underneath, I was struggling—juggling my past with Pete, my present with David, and the relentless pressure of securing my future in Australia.

Your reflection: Where in your life are you striving for perfection to gain approval or avoid rejection? What would happen if you allowed someone to see the imperfect, vulnerable side of you instead?

Exercise: Take a moment to identify one area of your life where you feel pressure to be perfect. Share one small imperfection or struggle with someone you trust and observe their reaction. Notice how it feels to let go of the need to be flawless.

Examining the Motives Behind Certain Actions

My story: Perfectionism consumed every aspect of my life. Even in my relationship with David, I found myself questioning every move. Was I holding his hand because I wanted to or because it looked good for the visa? Was I truly present, or was I performing for the immigration officers in my head? This constant need to control and curate every detail left me emotionally drained and disconnected.

Your reflection: Have you ever found yourself performing in your relationships or daily life instead of being present? What would it look like to let go of that performance and just be yourself?

Exercise: Spend one day observing your actions. Ask yourself, *Am I doing this because I genuinely want to, or because I feel I should?* Challenge yourself to make one decision based on your authentic feelings rather than external expectations.

Aligning with Your Authentic Self

My story: I wanted to appear the ideal partner, the perfect fit for David and his family. I tried to mold myself into what I thought the visa required, what his family expected, and what society deemed acceptable. But in the process, I lost sight of who I really was. I was no longer living authentically; I was living for appearances.

Your reflection: In what areas of your life do you feel the need to meet others' expectations at the expense of your authenticity? How might that be impacting your sense of self?

Exercise: Write down three ways you feel pressured to meet others' expectations. Then write down one way you can challenge or reframe those expectations to align more closely with your authentic self.

Accepting Imperfection

My story: The highs with David were incredible, but the lows hit even harder. Every argument, every moment of doubt, sent me spiraling into fear—not just fear of losing him but fear of losing my visa and my future. The Mask of Perfection demanded that I keep it all together, even when my emotions were unraveling.

Your reflection: How do you react when things start to fall apart? Do you feel the need to hold it all together for others, even when you're struggling inside?

Exercise: The next time you feel overwhelmed, pause and acknowledge your emotions. Share what you're feeling with someone close to you, even if it's just, "I'm having a hard time today." Practice embracing imperfection in small, manageable ways.

Overcoming Fear of Judgment

My story: Living with the Mask of Perfection meant constantly questioning myself. Was I acting out of love or obligation? Was I making decisions for David and me, or for the visa? This endless overanalyzing left me exhausted, disconnected, and unable to fully enjoy the present.

Your reflection: Do you find yourself overthinking your actions, wondering if they're "good enough" or if you'll be judged? How might it feel to give yourself permission to simply be?

Exercise: Write down one situation where you often overthink or feel pressure to be perfect. Then, imagine how you might approach it differently if you weren't worried about judgment or expectations. Try putting that into practice the next time you encounter a similar situation.

MASK OF PERFECTION KEY TAKEAWAYS

- **Perfectionism isn't sustainable:** The Mask of Perfection may provide temporary protection, but

it's exhausting to maintain. It creates a disconnect from ourselves and others, robbing us of authentic joy and connection.
- **Vulnerability is the antidote:** True strength comes from embracing imperfection and allowing others to see us as we are. Letting go of the need to control everything opens the door to deeper relationships and personal growth.
- **The cost of control:** Trying to control how others perceive us often leads to losing sight of our authentic selves. In my pursuit of perfection for the visa and my relationship, I lost my sense of identity and my ability to enjoy the present.
- **Authenticity builds connection:** People connect with our humanity, not our perfection. Removing the mask allows for genuine connections built on trust, acceptance, and shared vulnerability.
- **Perfection doesn't define worth:** Our worth isn't tied to how flawless we appear or how perfectly we perform. True worth comes from our ability to show up authentically and embrace the messy, imperfect parts of life.

CHAPTER 13

THE MASK OF SURVIVAL

PERSEVERING THROUGH LIFE'S CHALLENGES

The Cycle of Survival

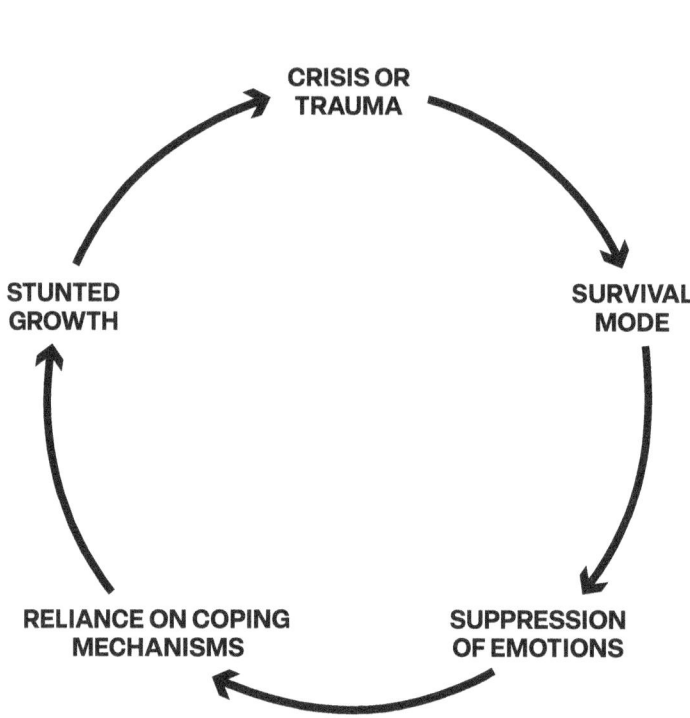

No planes in the sky, no cars on the road, no boats in the rivers or oceans, and no trains on the tracks. Suddenly, the world was on pause, and everyone was scrambling to adapt and survive. Confined to our own spaces in lockdown, we fought over toilet paper, hoarded supplies, and clung to anything that might get us through. Social gatherings disappeared; human connection was reduced to pixels on a screen, and the value of touch—a handshake, a hug—became painfully clear.

But I had already been living in survival mode long before the pandemic hit.

For months—years, even—I'd been walking a tightrope, trying to maintain relationships, build businesses that would secure my future, and navigate the unrelenting complications of my visa process. And now, with the weight of a global pandemic pressing down, survival took on a whole new meaning. This wasn't just about adjusting—it was about enduring. Another layer of difficulty added to an already overwhelming situation.

And then, as if the weight of the world wasn't enough, a letter arrived—a letter that completely shattered me.

THE CRACKS WIDEN

When David and I returned to Australia, the cracks in our relationship were difficult to ignore. Our fights would get so intense that David repeatedly threatened to move out. Each time, I'd beg him not to leave. I couldn't shake the thought that immigration might come knocking one day, asking to see proof of us living together. What would I do if they found us separated? The fear was overwhelming, and I clung to the idea of us staying together, even when it was tearing us apart.

While David and I loved each other, we wanted our own lives. Trapped in this complex, suffocating situation, we had no room to move.

We eventually moved into a new apartment—a brand-new building called the Waterfall by Crown. It was a luxury complex, complete with an infinity pool overlooking the city, a rooftop gym, and even a rooftop theater. The heart of the property was a stunning garden and fountain, creating a tranquil oasis. Stepping onto the pool deck felt like being transported to a tropical resort, far removed from the chaos of our daily lives. The poolside hot tub quickly became our go-to spot for unwinding with a glass of wine, watching the sunset paint the city in hues of orange and pink. Being among the first residents in the building, we often had the place to ourselves, making it feel like our personal escape.

Our apartment was on the top floor, a gorgeous two-bedroom, two-bathroom unit with soaring ceilings and a breathtaking view of the city skyline. Situated at the end of a long hallway, it felt private and secluded, a little haven amid the luxury. It quickly became home for us, and for Bentley and Brodie too. The two of them had this adorable routine—they always knew when David was coming home from work. Like clockwork, they'd sit by the door, ears perked and tails wagging, waiting for the sound of his footsteps. As soon as he appeared at the other end of the hallway, they'd bolt down to greet him, tails wagging in excitement. It was one of those simple moments that brought so much joy to our day-to-day lives.

As great as the apartment was, offering us a fresh space and a new start, the wedge between David and me still remained. I found myself traveling more with my massage table, taking it to other cities for work. Part of it was to make more money, but another part was just to get away—to create space between us. David hated having clients at the apartment, having to constantly be quiet in his own home. I don't blame him. It wasn't ideal. Not only was our relationship feeling like a job, but our home was a workspace, with people coming and going.

Massage wasn't my only source of income. David and I had started working in the CBD oil space, launching a business together. We also got into crypto, and it quickly became a major part of our lives. The CBD business was exciting—we built a solid customer base, and it felt good to be working together on something that aligned with both of our interests. Crypto, on the other hand, was a whirlwind. We joined a recruiting platform and began seeing some serious payouts. The buzz and excitement it created between us were obvious. There were days when payments would hit our accounts, and we'd just stare at the numbers in disbelief. It gave us something to bond over, something to focus on together.

For a time, it felt like we were on the same team again, sharing wins and dreaming big. The potential for financial freedom was exhilarating, and it brought a spark to our relationship that we hadn't felt in a while. But even with these successes, the underlying cracks in our foundation were still there. The unresolved issues, the mistrust, and the strain of our circumstances didn't just disappear because the money was rolling in.

If anything, the highs of these ventures highlighted the lows in our relationship even more. The pressure to succeed in business, coupled with the personal tension at home, was a lot to juggle. We were thriving professionally but struggling personally—a bittersweet contrast that was hard to reconcile. The apartment, as beautiful as it was, became a space filled with both triumphs and unspoken tension. It was a home, but it wasn't the sanctuary it should have been.

A MASK FORGED BY FEAR AND UNCERTAINTY

During the pandemic, the Mask of Survival wasn't just a personal experience—it became a global phenomenon. Fear and uncertainty turned the world into a pressure cooker, forcing the fractures in society to split open into vast, unbridgeable gulfs.

The world was no longer just fighting a virus; it was fighting itself. Conspiracy theories about the origins of COVID-19 ran rampant, dividing communities and sparking heated debates about everything from masks to vaccines. Misinformation spread like wildfire, pitting neighbors, friends, and even family members against each other. Social media became a battlefield of opinions, turning once-strong connections into fractured relationships.

Racism and xenophobia bubbled to the surface, fueled by political rhetoric and fear. Blame was cast far and wide—on governments, on specific nations, on ethnic groups. The world was grappling with more than just a pandemic; it was reckoning with its own deep-seated prejudices. As the streets emptied due to lockdowns, they filled again with protests, voices demanding justice for the marginalized and oppressed. The pandemic became a mirror, reflecting the ugliest parts of humanity back at us.

While fear and desperation created division, it also spurred resilience, innovation, and a sense of solidarity in some pockets of society. For many, the Mask of Survival became more than a metaphor—it was a daily necessity. Life as we knew it changed overnight, and survival—financially, emotionally, and physically—became the only goal.

During the pandemic, the Mask of Survival allowed me to push through, but it also meant suppressing the fear, frustration, and sadness that came with witnessing the world unraveling. Maintaining the facade of strength was exhausting when, deep down, I was grappling with the same uncertainties and anxieties as everyone else.

The world's division mirrored the divisions in my own life—between David and me, between my aspirations and my reality, between the image I projected and the truth of what I was experiencing.

For me, the Mask of Survival wasn't new. I had been wearing it for years, navigating the relentless challenges of my visa struggles, financial instability, and my turbulent relationship with David. But the pandemic amplified everything. Suddenly, my personal challenges were compounded by the external chaos of a world in lockdown. The financial pressure was suffocating. Due to restrictions, my massage business came to a grinding halt, and David had to take on the burden of supporting me. For someone who had fought so hard to maintain independence, relying on someone else was a bitter pill to swallow.

DON'T MAKE PLANS DURING A PANDEMIC

As Christmas approached, I planned a trip to Adelaide for work. My goal was to earn some money before heading back to Sydney for Christmas and then continuing to Surfers Paradise for more work. But fate had other plans. During my time in Adelaide, the borders between Queensland and New South Wales abruptly closed, throwing a wrench into my carefully laid plans.

With no immediate way to return to Sydney, I flew to Brisbane with a mate to spend a few days there before heading to Surfers Paradise to work. Those days were filled with moments that felt like a reprieve—beach outings, leisurely lunches, and catching some sun. As always, I documented the highlights on my social media, sharing snapshots of my life in a way that made it appear carefree and full of adventure. Little did I know that those posts would come back to haunt me.

* * *

Before heading back to Sydney, I made the decision to leave the massage business behind. It wasn't an easy choice, but it felt necessary. The toxic environment that had taken root before I left for Adelaide had been weighing on me, and I couldn't bring myself to return to it. I sold and gave away all my equipment to one of my last clients in Brisbane. It was like shedding an old skin, letting go of a chapter that had brought more stress than joy in its final days.

When I told David about my decision, he was relieved—though, in typical David fashion, he didn't believe me at first. He thought I was joking or that something was wrong. But for once, I wasn't playing games. I was ready to turn the page.

THE LETTER THAT SHATTERED MY WORLD

Coming home was different this time. It felt like a weight had been lifted, like a thorn had been pulled from our relationship. With the massage business no longer a source of conflict, we found ourselves in a better rhythm. We had settled into a routine with the visa process, and it was no longer the constant source of stress it once was. For the first time in a long time, we started to genuinely enjoy each other's company.

Yet, even as things improved between us, a new source of tension loomed. My visa approval, which had been due in January, still hadn't arrived. Days turned into weeks, and weeks into months. By the time March rolled around, I was starting to feel the familiar sting of uncertainty. I kept telling myself that immigration was just backed up and my approval was right around the corner. But as the weeks dragged on with no word, my confidence began to waver. The waiting game became a quiet, gnawing presence in the background of my life.

* * *

March 18, 2021, began as a regular day. I was sitting at home, doing my usual routine, while David was out at the shops. It was quiet, unassuming. That is until I opened my laptop and saw an email from immigration sitting in my inbox.

This was the email I had been waiting for—the culmination of 10 years of struggle, sacrifice, and perseverance. My heart raced with excitement as I clicked it open, expecting to finally see the words I had longed for. But as I read, my stomach dropped.

> Dear Rob Goddard,
>
> We have received information that your sponsor does not wish to proceed with his sponsorship.
>
> It is essential for the finalisation and grant of a partner visa application to have an approved sponsorship.

Ten years of waiting, planning, and working tirelessly toward this moment, and this was the outcome. My dreams of permanent residency were shattered in an instant.

A million thoughts raced through my head. *Who had caused this?* It couldn't have been David—he promised he'd never do this. Maybe one of his friends. After all, many people knew about our visa process and the struggles we were facing as a couple. Which one of them could have sabotaged me? I couldn't make sense of it, and the uncertainty only fueled my panic.

I grabbed my phone and called David immediately.

"Hey, I've just received this email from immigration saying my sponsor no longer wants to continue sponsorship. What's going on?" My voice trembled with panic.

"Oh shit," he responded. "I'll be right home."

I couldn't sit still. I paced the apartment, running through every possible scenario in my head, trying to piece together what had happened. It couldn't have been him. It just couldn't. I knew we had our problems—but this? No way. He wouldn't do this to me.

When David walked in, he avoided my gaze, scanning the floor like it held the answers. His usual confident stride was gone, replaced by something hesitant, almost fearful. He stood frozen in the doorway as I demanded, "Was it you or one of your friends?" His lips parted slightly, but no words came out. Finally, he gathered his courage and, in a low voice, admitted … "It was me."

His confession hit me like a freight train. My heart shattered into a million pieces, the weight of betrayal crushing me. All the emotions I had been holding in—the fear, the frustration, the hope—came pouring out. I screamed at him, punched doors, and let out all the anger and devastation that had been building inside me.

"Why? Why would you do this? I've spent the last ten years working toward this. This is my home. How could you do this to me?"

"I'm sorry," he said quietly, his voice filled with guilt.

But sorry wasn't enough. Sorry couldn't fix the years of effort that were now slipping through my fingers. Sorry couldn't undo the betrayal that left me feeling broken and defeated.

I sobbed uncontrollably, my mind racing to find a solution.

Once I had gathered my thoughts, I reached out to a friend, an immigration lawyer who had been guiding me throughout this journey. I explained the situation, the email, David's confession.

He offered a glimmer of hope. "You need to respond with a statutory declaration from David, explaining that it was a mistake—that you had a disagreement and it was resolved quickly. Have him sign it and send it back immediately."

David revealed that he had sent an email to immigration in December but hadn't received a response until now. The fact that he had done this months ago and kept it from me only deepened the wound.

It turned out, while I was away, one of David's mates had been keeping a close eye on my social media posts. According to them, I was off gallivanting across Australia with another man who was a close friend of mine, posting as if I was dating him, and completely disrespecting David in the process.

To David, it must have felt like a slap in the face—a complete betrayal of everything we'd been through. I can see why he reacted the way he did. To him, it was as if I was mocking all the sacrifices and struggles we'd faced together. In his eyes, I was treating it as a joke, taking the piss, as the Aussies say.

We eventually sat on the couch to talk. With his hand resting on my leg, his voice soft, he said, "I'm so sorry. We'll figure this out."

But I couldn't let it go. The anger, sadness, confusion, and sheer panic overwhelmed me. "Do *not* touch me right now," I snapped, pulling away. I wasn't ready to accept his apology, not while I was still processing everything that had just happened.

It felt like a sucker punch. For the first time in a long time, we'd been rebuilding our relationship, finding joy in each other's company again. We were laughing, spending more time together, and even beginning to feel like a team. And then this—this misunderstanding, this assumption, this intrusion—brought it all crashing down.

It wasn't just the argument or the accusation that hurt. It was the fact that someone else's meddling had pulled us back into the toxic cycle we'd worked so hard to escape. It was a stark reminder that no matter how far we thought we'd come, we were still navigating a fragile situation that could shatter at any moment.

We organized our statement of declaration, explaining the situation, and promptly emailed it to the immigration office. The next day, we received a follow-up email requesting one final piece of information: my health examination. Initially, I was confused—I had already completed two of these. But after digging deeper, I realized I had made a rookie error. There were specific clinics authorized to conduct health examinations for visa purposes, and instead of following those instructions, I had gone to a generic doctor and manually uploaded the results myself. Apparently, the approved clinics automatically upload the results directly to the visa application system. Whoops! Lesson learned: read the instructions carefully.

THE MOMENT OF TRUTH—WOULD I STAY? OR WOULD I GO?

With everything finally submitted, it became a waiting game. The visa process had consumed my life, especially in the last six months. I felt like a broken record, constantly talking about it, thinking about it, and obsessing over every little detail. Whenever someone asked how I was, my answer would inevitably circle back to the visa.

In my desperation to stay, I had lost myself. The Mask of Survival had taken over, driving every decision, action, and conversation. I became a version of myself I barely recognized, someone willing to lie, bend rules, and push boundaries—all in the name of survival. The hunger to stay in this country overshadowed everything else. I had let this process, this need to survive, define me.

But then came the haunting question: who was I, outside of all this? For the last 10 years, I'd been "Rob, the visa guy," always pivoting, maneuvering, and strategizing to keep one foot in the door. This wasn't my true character—it was a product of the bureaucracy, the endless rules, and the uncertainty of my future. I had lived so long in survival mode that I didn't even know who I was outside of it. Was my inability to commit to people a reflection of my circumstances? Or was it something deeper? Was it fear—fear of getting too attached to a country, a person, or a life that could be ripped away at any moment?

No more than two weeks later, the email arrived. My permanent visa had been granted. I had made it. I was at my friend Quinton's house when the news came, and I couldn't hold back the tears. Relief, joy, and happiness poured out of me as I cried. The moment I had been waiting for, fighting for, dreaming of for so long had finally come. I could now officially call Australia home.

Imagine carrying a burden every single day for 10 years—thinking about it nonstop, feeling it in every breath—and then, suddenly, it's gone. The relentless pressure disappeared like it had never been there, replaced by an overwhelming sense of freedom. It was a breath of fresh air, a clean slate.

When David came home that night, I gave him the biggest hug and thanked him with all my heart. This wasn't just a victory for me; it was a relief for both of us. That weight, which had hung over us for the past three years, was finally lifted. The highs, the lows, the constant struggles—it was all behind us.

We had been tested in ways we never imagined, but I'll always be grateful for David. He taught me so much about myself, just as I hope I did for him. Despite the challenges, I wouldn't have made it through this journey without him. By the time we reached the end, what we had built wasn't just a partnership—it was a deep and lasting friendship. We had supported each other through every twist and turn, and neither of us wanted to let that go.

Yet, even as I celebrated this milestone, part of me was still stuck in the past. I couldn't shake the thought of Pete. Winning him back remained an obsession, a constant hum in the back of my mind. The idea of finally being with him, free from the constraints of the visa, consumed me. It was a dream I couldn't let go of, even as I moved into this new chapter of my life.

For the first time in a decade, I felt truly free. I could finally drop the mask.

THERE'S ALWAYS A COST

For some, wearing the Mask of Survival means avoiding deeper emotional or psychological issues that feel too daunting to face. It means focusing solely on immediate needs or clinging to any semblance of control in an increasingly unpredictable and chaotic time.

For some, it becomes a source of strength and resilience, allowing them to endure when everything else feels like it's falling apart. But the cost of wearing the Mask of Survival is immense. Beneath the surface, there's emotional disconnection, profound loneliness, and the quiet depression of losing touch with our true selves and the people around us.

STEPS TO REMOVE THE MASK OF SURVIVAL

Often, when we wear the Mask of Survival, we don't realize we're in survival mode. We're simply doing what's necessary to get through the day. However, survival mode shouldn't be a permanent state, and only by acknowledging when the mask no longer serves us can we begin to remove it.

1. **Acknowledge survival mode:** Recognize that you've been operating in survival mode. Understand that this mask was necessary to navigate difficult circumstances, whether it was visa struggles, financial pressures, or navigating the global pandemic. It served its purpose, but survival mode is only meant to be temporary. It's time to identify where it's no longer serving you and start releasing its grip.
2. **Allow yourself to feel:** When survival becomes your focus, emotions often get pushed aside to prioritize "getting through." Reconnecting with those buried feelings is essential for healing. Start with small steps—journal, speak

with a therapist, or confide in someone you trust. For me, this process started when I finally began to admit just how overwhelmed and defeated I felt during my visa struggles. Giving space to those emotions helps you process what you've endured.

3. **Ask for help:** The Mask of Survival often isolates us, making us believe we must bear every burden alone. One of the hardest lessons for me was learning to ask for help. Whether it was leaning on a friend, speaking with an immigration lawyer, or just having David sit with me during my breakdown, I discovered the power of connection. Asking for support doesn't mean you're weak—it means you're human.

4. **Shift from surviving to thriving:** The mask keeps us focused on making it through the day, but life is about more than just surviving. Once the immediate crisis passes, allow yourself to dream again. For me, it was thinking about what I wanted my life in Australia to look like beyond the visa battle. I began to rediscover what brought me joy, even in small ways, like moments of laughter with friends or the satisfaction of helping others.

5. **Prioritize self-care and healing:** Survival mode doesn't leave much room for self-care, but it's a critical part of moving forward. This can look like practicing mindfulness, enjoying physical activities that make you feel good, or simply allowing yourself moments of rest without guilt. After all the chaos and strain of survival, taking care of yourself is the first step toward rebuilding.

By removing the Mask of Survival, you can begin to shift from merely existing to fully living—embracing the parts of life that survival mode often puts on hold. It's a journey that takes time, but it's one that leads to growth, healing, and true freedom.

REFLECTIONS AND LEARNINGS: THE MASK OF SURVIVAL

Appreciating the Present

My story: Living in survival mode kept me trapped between two worlds—the past I couldn't release with Pete and the fantasy future I imagined with him, while also trying to navigate my relationship with David. At times, it felt real, but more often it felt like a mission we were both trying to complete. I clung to memories of Pete, analyzing what went wrong, while simultaneously shaping a future with David, not out of love, but necessity. In the end, I was nowhere—lost between longing for the past, chasing an illusion, and simply trying to survive the present.

Your reflection: Do you find yourself caught between reliving the past or fantasizing about an ideal future? How might this be preventing you from fully experiencing the present and the people in your life right now?

Exercise: Take a few moments to write about one area of your life where you feel stuck in the past or caught up in future fantasies. Then, write down three things you appreciate about your present circumstances or relationships. Reflect on how you might bring more presence and gratitude to these areas moving forward.

Facing Your Fears

My story: When I finally let go of the Mask of Survival, I realized how much of my life had been shaped by fear—fear of failure, rejection, or losing everything I had worked so hard to build. But fear isn't meant to be a permanent state. It's a signal, not a destination. As I started to confront those fears, I discovered a strength within me that I never knew existed: the strength to trust myself and my journey, no matter how uncertain it might feel.

Your reflection: Are fears driving your decisions or keeping you in survival mode? What might happen if you face those fears instead of letting them control you?

Exercise: Write down one fear that has been holding you back. Then, write a short response to that fear as if you were comforting a friend. What would you say to encourage them to take a step forward, despite their worries?

Prioritizing Your Own Needs

My story: Every decision I made was calculated. Do I speak up or stay quiet? Do I go out or stay home to avoid confrontation? I wasn't just living for myself—I was living to meet expectations, avoid rejection, and keep everything from falling apart. Survival wasn't just a phase; it was a way of life, and it left me exhausted and emotionally disconnected from both myself and the people I loved.

Your reflection: Have you ever felt like you're living for others' expectations rather than your own? How might that be holding you back from feeling connected and true to yourself?

Exercise: Reflect on one area where you feel trapped by expectations. What would it look like to make decisions based on your own needs instead of catering to others? Write down one small decision you can make this week that prioritizes your needs or desires over external pressures.

Approaching Each Challenge with Intention

My story: The financial pressures, the visa uncertainties, and the tension with David kept me locked in survival mode for years. I was constantly reacting—never proactive, never present. The Mask of Survival helped me endure those moments, but it also kept me from experiencing the joy and connection I desperately craved. Even as I fought to hold everything together, I could feel the cracks growing deeper.

Your reflection: When life feels overwhelming, do you find yourself reacting to everything around you without taking time to process or plan? What would happen if you allowed yourself to step back and reflect instead of always pushing forward?

Exercise: Choose one challenge in your life right now that feels overwhelming. Take 10 minutes to sit with it—write about it, talk it out, or simply reflect. Instead of reacting immediately, think about what you truly need in this situation and how you can approach it with intention.

Shifting from Surviving to Thriving

My story: Wearing the Mask of Survival, I became an expert at doing whatever it took to endure. I adapted, compromised, and even sacrificed parts of myself to stay afloat—whether it was appeasing David, maintaining the illusion of stability, or suppressing my feelings to avoid conflict. But in the process, I lost sight of who I truly was. Survival became my identity, and I forgot what it felt like to live freely and authentically.

Your reflection: Where in your life are you in survival mode, pushing through challenges without pausing to reflect on how it's impacting you? How might it feel to give yourself permission to stop surviving and start living?

Exercise: Take a moment to identify one area of your life where you feel like you're just "getting through." Write down one small step you could take to move from surviving to thriving—whether it's asking for help, taking a break, or exploring something that brings you joy.

MASK OF SURVIVAL KEY TAKEAWAYS

- **The mask of survival is both a shield and a barrier:** While it helps us navigate challenging situations and endure hardships, it also isolates us, suppresses emotions, and keeps us from living authentically.
- **Survival mode often comes at a personal cost:** Constantly focusing on survival can lead to emotional exhaustion, disconnection from loved ones, and a loss of self. It keeps us reactive rather

than proactive, limiting our ability to dream and grow.
- **The mask of survival can stem from fear:** Whether it's fear of failure, rejection, or losing control, this mask is often rooted in the desire to protect ourselves from perceived threats, real or imagined.
- **Living in survival mode distracts from the present:** Dwelling on past pain or fantasizing about a perfect future prevents us from being fully present and appreciating what we have in the here and now.
- **Recognizing the mask is the first step to removing it:** Awareness of how and why you wear the Mask of Survival is key to releasing its grip. It served a purpose, but it doesn't have to define your life.
- **Reclaiming joy and authenticity is possible:** Shifting from surviving to thriving involves small, intentional steps: embracing vulnerability, asking for support, practicing self-care, and focusing on the present.

CHAPTER 14

THE MASK OF CYNICISM

DEFENDING AGAINST DISAPPOINTMENT

The Cycle of Cynicism

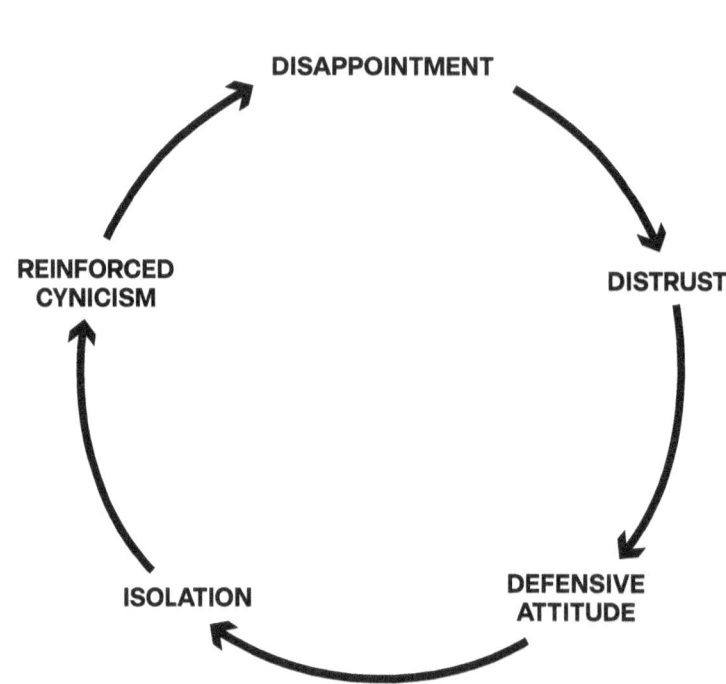

If you've grown up with an alcoholic parent or had a loved one suffer from addiction, it's easy to fall into a place of cynicism. Constantly being let down, having your trust broken time and time again can condition you to expect the worst. This happened with my mother. The trust was broken. We were let down one too many times. Relationships fractured to the point where we told ourselves, *What's the point?*

The idea of cynicism isn't new. In fact, it dates back to ancient Greece, where the philosophy of Cynicism was founded by Antisthenes, a disciple of Socrates. The ancient Cynics, like Diogenes of Sinope, believed that happiness came from living a simple life, free from societal expectations, wealth, or status. They rejected superficiality and focused on living in accordance with nature, often describing what they saw as the corruption of human desires. Diogenes famously lived in a barrel, carrying a lantern in search of an honest man—his way of critiquing the hypocrisy of society.

At its core, ancient Cynicism was a philosophy of liberation. It sought to strip away illusions and encourage people to focus on what truly mattered. But over time, the word "cynicism" has taken on a different tone. What began as a pursuit of authenticity and freedom has morphed into a defense mechanism, rooted in mistrust and skepticism.

Modern cynicism isn't about seeking truth or rejecting materialism; it's about shielding ourselves from disappointment. Unlike the Greek Cynics, who used their worldview to challenge society and grow, we often use cynicism to protect ourselves from vulnerability and hurt.

WHAT CREATES A CYNIC?

Cynicism isn't something we're born with—it's learned over time. Interestingly, research has shown that the seeds of cynicism start to form in childhood. A study by Candice Mills and Frank Keil explored how kids develop the ability to question what people say, especially when those statements seem to benefit the speaker.

Here's what they found:

Younger children, like kindergarteners, tend to take people at their word. They don't yet recognize when someone might be twisting the truth to serve their own interests. But as kids get older—around second or fourth grade—they begin to notice patterns. If a character in a story says something that conveniently benefits them, older kids are more likely to think, *Wait a minute, is that really true?*

By the time kids reach sixth grade, they've developed a much sharper eye for spotting bias. Not only can they identify an outright lie, but they also start to understand that people might unintentionally skew the truth because of their own biases or perspectives.[11]

This progression shows how, as we grow, we learn to question the world around us. If we're let down too many times, what starts as a healthy sense of skepticism can evolve into cynicism. When people repeatedly break our trust or we see self-interest driving people's behavior, it's easy to think, *Everyone's just out for themselves.*

For some, cynicism develops in childhood. For others, it occurs later in life after a string of disappointments. Either way, the pattern is clear: cynicism often grows when we begin to expect that people's words and actions are always motivated by their own self-interest.

As children, certain experiences can become the seeds that eventually sprout into full-blown cynicism:

- **Broken promises:** A parent repeatedly says, "We'll go to the park tomorrow," but they never go. Over time, the child learns to doubt what people say.
- **Witnessing hypocrisy:** A child hears an adult preach honesty but then watches them lie to a neighbor or friend. This inconsistency creates confusion and mistrust.
- **Social rejection:** Being left out of birthday parties or playground games teaches the child that people might not always have their best interests at heart.
- **Family conflict:** Living in a home marked by arguments,

broken relationships, or divorce can erode a child's belief in connection and love.
- **Unfair treatment:** Seeing others rewarded despite putting in less effort fosters the belief that life is inherently unfair.

Not all children respond to these experiences the same. Some might develop resilience, while others put up walls. But for those who begin to see the world through a lens of skepticism, the Mask of Cynicism starts to form.

> **The Mask of Cynicism isn't something we put on intentionally—it's a reaction, a shield, a way of saying,** *I won't let myself be hurt again.*

As adults, these early experiences can influence how we approach relationships, opportunities, and even ourselves. We tell ourselves we're just being "realistic," but in truth we're guarding wounds that have never fully healed.

MY VERSION OF THE MASK

As a child, I was shielded from much of my mom's drinking, thanks to my sister. She bore the brunt of it, experiencing the full weight of what was happening long before I began to notice. For my sister, the door to trust slammed shut early. She learned to expect the worst because, in her experience, hoping for something better only led to more pain.

For me, it was different. I didn't fully give in to the Mask of Cynicism, but there were certainly days when it felt firmly in place. I had to learn to protect myself by setting boundaries—emotional walls that kept me from being consumed by my mom's struggles. And yet, through it all, there was still this flickering hope within me. I wanted to believe she could change, even when everything—and everyone—around me was telling me otherwise.

But even with that hope, cynicism left its mark. It's hard not to feel jaded when the people you're supposed to trust the most let you down time and time again. My sister and I carried those lessons into adulthood in different ways. For her, it showed up as a hardened exterior, a refusal to let some people in. For me, it came in quieter moments of doubt, wondering if the effort I put into relationships was worth it when the outcome so often felt the same.

When you grow up in an environment where trust is repeatedly broken, it's easy to start seeing the world through a lens of mistrust. You expect people to fail you because that's the pattern you know. And the more you expect it, the more you unconsciously push people away, reinforcing the cycle of disappointment.

The Mask of Cynicism becomes our way of coping. We think we're protecting ourselves, but, in reality, we're closing ourselves off—from others, from joy, and even from ourselves. While cynicism might feel like strength, it often comes at the cost of connection.

THE MANY VOICES OF CYNICISM

With the Mask of Cynicism come the voices—you know, the voices that are dismissive, scrutinizing, or, in some cases, sarcastic. If you've been hurt or let down, these voices may be familiar to you. They manifest in different forms.

The Dismissive Voice

"Sure, like that's ever going to happen."

This voice shuts down possibilities before they even begin. It's the one that rolls its eyes at a friend's ambitious new business idea or scoffs at the thought of trying something new.

Example: If a coworker suggests a creative solution during a meeting, this voice might creep in: *Yeah, like the boss would ever approve that.*

Impact: Sure, this dismissive voice protects us from disappointment, but it also keeps us from seeing opportunities that might actually succeed.

The Overly Critical Voice

"That plan has too many flaws to succeed."

This is the voice that picks apart ideas, people, and situations, finding every reason why something won't work. It masquerades as being realistic, but it often leaves no room for optimism or growth.

Example: Imagine a big-picture person, full of excitement, sharing their plans for a cross-country road trip. Then, the small-picture person—guided by this voice—starts pointing out all the potential pitfalls: "What if the car breaks down? What about bad weather? What if you get lost?"

Impact: I sometimes call this the "candle blower" voice—it blows out the light of excitement before it even gets a chance to shine. Yes, it can feel like it's keeping us safe, but it often discourages others and limits our ability to embrace possibilities.

The Sarcastic Voice

"Oh, sure, because everything always works out perfectly."

Sarcasm adds a layer of humor to cynicism, but, more often than not, it's a shield for deeper disappointment or mistrust. This voice deflects vulnerability with sharp remarks, creating distance between us and others.

Example: When someone shares their dream of running a marathon, you respond with, "Guess you'll start running once Netflix stops making shows."

Impact: While this voice can seem playful, sarcasm often hurts relationships. It can feel discouraging to others and lead to the avoidance of real connection.

The Jaded Voice

"People never change."

This voice comes from a place of exhaustion and repeated disappointment. It assumes the worst about people, making it hard to trust or give anyone a second chance.

Example: A former friend reaches out to apologize and reconnect, but this voice kicks in, saying, *They're just going to hurt me again.*

Impact: In my coaching, I often listen for absolutes like "never" or "always." When clients use language like this, I challenge them to explore whether it's truly accurate. This voice may feel safe, but it isolates us from opportunities for reconciliation and deeper connection.

The Defensive Voice
"It's better to expect the worst and not get hurt."
This voice often emerges in people who have been through a lot. It can seem like wisdom, as it frames itself as practical, convincing us that staying guarded will protect us from pain.

Example: Imagine your partner suggests planning a trip together. Instead of joining in on their excitement, you say, "Let's not get ahead of ourselves; something will probably come up to ruin it."

Impact: While this voice might feel practical, it often robs us of joy and stops us from fully engaging with life.

The Pessimistic Voice
"What's the point? It's not going to work anyway."
This voice is formed by those who have been through many failures and constant disappointments. It convinces us that failure is inevitable, so there's no use in trying.

Example: You're thinking about applying for a new job, and the voice says, *What's the point? They won't hire me anyway.* Or you're about to jump on a call with a potential client, and the voice warns, *Don't get too excited; they're probably not going to sign up.*

Impact: The pessimistic voice stops us from taking risks and can lead to missed opportunities and regret.

The Judgmental Voice
"How naive can you be to believe that?"
This voice dismisses others' optimism or ambition as foolish, masking insecurity with superiority. It criticizes hopefulness and enthusiasm, often pushing people away.

Example: A friend shares their big vision for a new company and the positive change they hope to bring to the world. This voice thinks, *They clearly don't know how things actually work in that industry.*

Impact: I've been on the receiving end of this voice many times, and it's taught me how isolating it can feel to have your hopefulness dismissed. For those who hear this voice within themselves, it can limit collaboration and connection while keeping you stuck in negativity.

While these voices can feel protective, shielding us from vulnerability, they also close us off—from others, from opportunities, and from joy.

Take a moment to reflect:
- Which of these voices do you recognize in yourself?
- How have they shaped the way you approach relationships, opportunities, or even yourself?

Understanding these voices is the first step to loosening the grip of the Mask of Cynicism.

THE ROLE OF THE LIZARD BRAIN IN CYNICISM

Cynicism isn't just an emotional response; it's rooted in our biology. At the heart of it is what's often called the *lizard brain*, the primal part of our mind responsible for survival instincts. This part of the brain is designed to protect us from danger, triggering the fight-or-flight response whenever it senses a threat.

When we've been hurt in the past—whether by broken trust, disappointment, or rejection—the lizard brain steps in, interpreting these emotional experiences as dangers to avoid in the future. It convinces us that vulnerability is risky and trust is dangerous, urging us to put up walls instead of building bridges. Over time, this survival mechanism reinforces the Mask of Cynicism, keeping us in a constant state of guardedness.

This explains why the voices of cynicism feel so compelling. They're rooted in the lizard brain's desire to shield us from pain. For example:

- The **dismissive voice** says, *Why bother?* to protect us from the sting of failure.
- The **defensive voice** whispers, *Expect the worst* as a way of bracing for disappointment.
- The **judgmental voice** mocks hopefulness in others, attempting to validate our own mistrust as wisdom.

While these instincts might feel protective, they often misfire, treating emotional risks like life-threatening dangers. Relationships are a common battleground for the lizard brain. It perceives vulnerability—letting someone in—as a risk too great to take. But the same mechanism that helps us survive true danger also keeps us from experiencing trust, intimacy, and connection.

By becoming aware of when this primal part of the brain takes over, we can start to reframe our reactions. Instead of immediately dismissing or mistrusting, we can pause and ask ourselves: *Is this situation truly dangerous? Or is my lizard brain overreacting? What might happen if I approached this with curiosity instead of fear?*

This shift doesn't mean ignoring caution or pretending hurt never happened. It means finding balance—allowing room for both skepticism and hope to coexist. It's about learning from the past without letting it dictate your entire future.

THE CYNICISM TRAP

While we often label cynicism as wisdom, true wisdom acknowledges the complexities of life—the joy and the pain, the hope and the uncertainty—without shutting out its possibilities. Cynicism, by contrast, narrows our view. It reduces everything to a negative expectation, leaving little room for growth, change, or connection.

> **The Mask of Cynicism acts as a shield, protecting a heart that still longs to believe in goodness, love, and possibility but is terrified of the pain that hope may bring.**

In keeping the world at bay, we also keep away the very things we need to heal and grow: connection, trust, and hope, as the following story demonstrates.

Mike came to me looking for help with his relationships—both romantic and personal. He was in a place many of us might recognize: worn out, frustrated, and deeply cynical. For Mike, it started with a few letdowns in the dating world. Plans were canceled at the last minute. Messages went ignored. And then came the ghosting—those abrupt, unexplained disappearances that left him feeling unseen and unworthy.

Over time, these repeated disappointments hardened into a worldview: *Everyone's the same. All gay men are the same.* Mike's Mask of Cynicism became his armor, shielding him from the vulnerability of hoping for something better. He stopped believing that relationships were even possible for him.

When we first started working together, his cynicism was palpable. He described every new person he met with skepticism, expecting them to let him down. He'd say things like, "Why bother? They're just going to ghost me like the rest of them." This mindset didn't just affect his romantic life; it seeped into his friendships, too. He stopped reaching out, stopped putting effort into plans, assuming they'd fall through anyway.

Mike's story isn't unique. Many of us have experienced the sting of disappointment—being let down by friends, partners, or even strangers. Over time, these experiences can pile up, making it feel safer to expect the worst than to risk being hurt again.

Mike's breakthrough didn't happen overnight. Like many who wear the Mask of Cynicism, he had spent years reinforcing it. It felt safer to hold on to his belief that "everyone's the same" than to risk being vulnerable and hopeful again. But during one of our sessions, I asked him a simple question that planted the seed for change:

"What would happen if you were wrong?"

Mike looked at me, confused. "Wrong about what?"

"About people. About the idea that they're all the same, that they'll always let you down."

At first, Mike resisted. He brought up the ghosting, the cancellations, the rejections. He pointed to the long list of reasons why his cynicism was justified. But as we dug deeper, we uncovered something important: his mask wasn't protecting him from people; it was protecting him from the fear of being unworthy.

He admitted, for the first time, that every canceled plan and unanswered message felt personal—like a reflection of his own inadequacy. "It's easier to believe that everyone's the same than to believe that something's wrong with me," he said quietly.

This was a pivotal moment. By naming that fear, Mike began to see his cynicism for what it was: a shield against rejection, but also a barrier to connection.

Once Mike acknowledged this, we worked on small, manageable steps to challenge his worldview. His first task was to question his assumptions. Instead of immediately writing someone off as unreliable or insincere, I asked him to approach interactions with curiosity.

For example, after a new match on a dating app didn't respond for a few days, Mike's initial reaction was to delete the conversation and tell himself, *Here we go again—they're just like the rest.* But instead, he paused and thought about the question we'd discussed: *What if I'm wrong?*

Rather than assuming the worst, he sent a simple follow-up message. To his surprise, the person apologized, explaining they'd been dealing with a busy workweek but were still interested in getting to know him. They scheduled a coffee date for the weekend, and, for the first time in years, Mike felt hopeful.

The biggest shift for Mike came when he started reframing the disappointments he had experienced in the past. Instead of viewing every canceled date or ghosted message as a reflection of his own worth—or proof that everyone was the same—he began to see them as isolated events.

"Not every person is going to be a match," he told me one day. "And that's OK. But that doesn't mean I stop trying."

By the end of our work together, Mike's transformation was evident. He hadn't shed the Mask of Cynicism entirely—after all, unlearning deeply ingrained patterns takes time—but he had loosened its grip. He no longer approached every interaction with distrust or skepticism. Instead, he chose to stay open, even when it felt risky.

"I still get disappointed sometimes," he admitted. "But I'm learning that disappointment is part of life—it doesn't mean I should stop trying."

The journey to shedding the Mask of Cynicism isn't about pretending everything is perfect or ignoring life's difficulties. It's about choosing how you show up. It's about taking a leap of faith and daring to hope again, even after being hurt. It's about embracing vulnerability as a strength that connects you to others. By letting go of this mask, you open yourself to a life where hope, trust, and love can take root once again.

STEPS TO REMOVE THE MASK OF CYNICISM

Removing the Mask of Cynicism doesn't mean becoming naive or blindly optimistic. It's about finding balance, where skepticism and hope can coexist, and learning from your past experiences without letting them define your future.

1. **Recognize the root cause:** Acknowledge that cynicism is often a result of past hurts or disappointments. Identifying specific moments or relationships where trust was broken or expectations weren't met can help you understand why you've adopted a cynical mindset as a form of protection.
2. **Allow for vulnerability:** Begin to practice vulnerability in small steps. Allow yourself to hope, trust, or engage emotionally in situations where you might usually shut down or distance yourself. By allowing space for vulnerability, you open yourself up to deeper and more meaningful connections.
3. **Challenge negative assumptions:** Consciously work to challenge cynical thoughts by asking yourself whether your assumptions are based on facts or past experiences. For instance, when you catch yourself assuming the worst about a person or situation, pause and question whether this expectation is rooted in the present or in past disappointments.
4. **Practice optimism:** Deliberately focus on positive outcomes and look for the good in people and situations. While this may feel uncomfortable at first, practicing optimism allows you to experience hope and joy without the constant fear of being let down.
5. **Seek positive reinforcement:** Surround yourself with people and situations that encourage positivity and trust. Engaging with optimistic, supportive individuals can help you reframe your outlook on life and reduce the habitual reliance on cynicism.

REFLECTIONS AND LEARNINGS: THE MASK OF CYNICISM

Approaching Each Moment with Curiosity

Learning (Mike's story): For Mike, cynicism became his way of shielding himself from the hurt of being let down—by friends, dates, and the world around him. But in trying to protect himself, he also blocked opportunities for meaningful connection.

Reflection: When have you used cynicism as a shield to avoid vulnerability? How might this be keeping you from experiencing joy or connection?

Exercise: Think of one situation where you dismissed someone's efforts to connect with you or doubted their intentions. How might you approach a similar moment with curiosity instead of cynicism?

Thinking Before Reacting

Learning: The lizard brain, designed to protect us from danger, can overreact to emotional risks, reinforcing the Mask of Cynicism.

Reflection: When have you felt the instinct to pull back or avoid something because it felt risky? Was the risk as significant as it seemed at the time?

Exercise: The next time you feel yourself withdrawing or dismissing something out of fear, pause and ask, *What's the real risk here? What's the potential reward?* Write down your response.

Rebuilding Trust and Connections

Learning: While the Mask of Cynicism shields us from disappointment, it also blocks joy, trust, and intimacy.

Reflection: How has cynicism impacted your relationships? Have there been moments where it prevented you from forming or deepening connections?

Exercise: Identify one relationship where you've held back due to mistrust or fear of disappointment. Commit to taking one small step—like opening up about your feelings or showing vulnerability—to rebuild trust.

Allowing Yourself to Hope

Learning (my story): Even as cynicism sometimes took hold, I held on to a flicker of hope that my mom could change. This balance between hope and skepticism allowed me to set boundaries while still keeping the door open for possibilities.

Reflection: Where in your life could you allow more room for hope without losing sight of reality? What might shift if you find a balance between protecting yourself and staying open?

Exercise: Choose one situation where you've been overly skeptical. Write down three potential positive outcomes of allowing yourself to hope. Reflect on what steps you can take to pursue one of those outcomes.

Reframing Damaging Beliefs

Learning (Mike's story): Mike's cynicism made him believe that all his dating experiences would end in rejection and disappointment. Through our work together, he learned to reframe those beliefs, seeing past disappointments not as proof of failure but as stepping stones to finding the right connections. By shifting his perspective, Mike opened himself to new possibilities.

Reflection: Think of a belief you hold that's rooted in past disappointments. How could reframing that belief change the way you approach similar situations in the future?

Exercise: Choose one recurring thought tied to your cynicism—like, *People always let me down* or, *Things never work out for me*. Write it down, then reframe it into something more balanced and hopeful, such as, *While I've been let down before, there are people who have shown me kindness and care*. Reflect on how this reframe could influence your actions moving forward.

MASK OF CYNICISM KEY TAKEAWAYS

- **Cynicism is a shield, but also a barrier:** While the Mask of Cynicism may protect us from disappointment, it also isolates us from joy, connection, and growth. By shielding ourselves from pain, we unintentionally block the possibility of hope and love.
- **The lizard brain plays a role:** Our primal instincts to avoid emotional risks often reinforce cynical thinking. Recognizing when these instincts take over allows us to challenge them and respond with curiosity instead of fear.

- **The voices of cynicism reflect pain, not truth:** The dismissive, sarcastic, or judgmental voices that accompany cynicism are often rooted in past hurts. They feel protective but keep us stuck in negativity and mistrust.
- **Reframing is key to letting go:** Shifting our perspective on past disappointments—from proof of inevitable failure to learning experiences—can open the door to new possibilities and healthier relationships.
- **Hope and vulnerability require courage:** Taking off the Mask of Cynicism means daring to trust again, even when it feels risky. Vulnerability isn't a weakness but a strength that fosters deeper connections and a more fulfilling life.

CHAPTER 15

THE MASK OF
CONTROL

CONTROLLING TO FEEL SECURE

The Cycle of Control

The moment I realized I was done … I was sitting in my car, hands gripping the steering wheel, staring at the house where my mother lived, where chaos had become the norm. But I wasn't angry. I wasn't sad. I felt nothing—just a hollow, heavy emptiness that spread through my entire body.

I had no fight left.

For years, I'd poured every ounce of energy into trying to control what couldn't be controlled. I thought if I tried hard enough—cleaned her house, set boundaries, managed her emotions, begged her partner to care—I could fix her. But nothing worked. No matter how tightly

I held on, the chaos kept slipping through my fingers.

The Mask of Control often starts with good intentions. We think if we can manage the chaos around us, we'll feel safe, grounded, and strong. For me, that meant trying to protect my mother from herself, clinging to the belief that I could somehow save her. But this mask doesn't protect us—it consumes us. It convinces us that we're responsible for fixing everything, and when we can't, it leaves us feeling powerless and empty.

A FRESH START ... OR SO I THOUGHT

After obtaining my visa, I began the next chapter of my life by preparing to move to Brisbane. It was a fresh start. I applied for an apartment in Fortitude Valley, a buzzing hub of nightclubs and restaurants. I was drawn to the amenities of the building: an infinity pool, a spa room, a private theatre, and one of the best gyms I'd ever seen.

Meanwhile, our little dog Bentley began showing signs of illness. He was shivering constantly, his energy fading day by day. We chalked it up to the stress of all the packing and the changes happening around him. David took him out for extra walks to keep him calm while I focused on getting everything ready for the move. Our cat Brodie, however, seemed to thrive in the chaos, playfully investigating the boxes and "helping" in his curious feline way.

Then the dreaded news came: a week prior to the move, Queensland was closing its borders due to a rise in COVID cases.

After years of fighting for control over my future, the universe had once again thrown chaos into my carefully laid plans. I was left staring at my packed boxes, wondering how I had ended up here. For so long, my life had been dictated by external forces—first the visa, now the pandemic. No matter how hard I tried to manage every detail, it felt like the world kept reminding me of one harsh truth: there are things you simply can't control.

THE MESSAGE I ALWAYS FEARED

A couple of days later, I was walking with my friend Shaun in Centennial Park when I received a text message from my uncle. Without even unlocking my phone, I caught the first line on the screen: *Rob, your mom's been taken to hospital in an ambulance.* My heart stopped. This was the message I had feared for so long—the one I'd braced myself for over the last 10 years. Could this be it? Could this be the call I'd been dreading, the one that would change everything?

Opening the message, I read on. My mom had been taken to the hospital due to breathing problems. That alone was terrifying, but the situation was far worse than I could have imagined. Through more conversations with my uncle and sister, I learned that my mom's condition had escalated. She'd been diagnosed with severe liver cirrhosis—years of drinking had finally taken their toll. The doctors had to drain over six liters of fluid from her abdomen. She had developed swelling in her legs and stomach, side effects of her failing liver. The increased pressure in the portal vein had caused fluid to accumulate, leading to conditions known as edema (fluid in the legs) and ascites (fluid in the abdomen). This wasn't just a scare—it was serious.

On the phone with my uncle and sister, the question hung in the air: "Should I come home?"

My sister didn't hesitate—she urged me to return, saying, "It might be the last time you see her."

WHEN WE SEEK TO CONTROL THE UNCONTROLLABLE ...

As I planned my trip home and sought approval to travel, I stayed in constant contact with the nurses who were caring for my mom. They were kind and understanding, going out of their way to keep me informed about her condition. At one point, they even helped organize a Zoom call so I could speak with her.

When the camera turned on, I was unprepared for what I saw. Mom looked frail, her face flushed and drawn. Her once-vibrant presence had faded, replaced by someone who was barely recognizable. She had a deep, jagged scar across her forehead, the result of a fall I hadn't even known about. True to form, she'd been reluctant to go to the hospital after the fall, letting it heal on its own—or at least, heal as much as it could. The scar was now a permanent reminder of her struggles, visible to anyone who looked at her.

The reality of my mom's condition hit me hard. Watching her waste away, barely able to walk, and seeing the scar on her forehead, I felt powerless. No matter how many calls I made to the nurses, no matter how many updates I received, I couldn't fix this. I couldn't control the choices she had made or the damage they had caused. And yet, for years, I had tried.

Many of us wear the Mask of Control without realizing it. We believe that by controlling everything around us—our circumstances, our environment, and even the people in our lives—we can avoid pain, disappointment, or failure. For me, that mask was firmly in place as I tried to manage my mom's drinking, her health, and even her relationship. Control became my way of creating certainty in an uncertain world, a shield to protect me from the chaos of her addiction.

But control is often an illusion. No matter how tightly we grip the reins, life has a way of reminding us that much is beyond our control. Sitting there on that Zoom call, looking at my mom's frail body and hearing the nurses describe her condition, I realized how little I could actually do.

In relationships, this mask can show up as trying to manage how others think, feel, or act, all in the name of maintaining harmony. According to the 2016 Personal Safety Survey (PSS), 23 percent of adult women (2.2 million) and 16 percent of adult men (1.4 million) in Australia reported experiencing some form of emotional abuse by a partner since the age of 15. These behaviors are often characterized by an individual's intent to manipulate, control, isolate, or intimidate a partner and can include repeated patterns of psychological, social, financial, and verbal abuse.[12] This is the darker, uglier side of the Mask of Control—where the need for dominance becomes harmful and destructive.

In careers, this mask manifests as micromanaging every detail, which might give us a fleeting sense of satisfaction but often leads to burnout and frustration. I saw this firsthand with one of my clients in Canada. His need to control every outcome led him to take on more and more work without delegating tasks to his team. Eventually, the stress and workload caught up with him, leading to complete burnout and exhaustion.

This behavior is particularly prevalent in corporate settings where deadlines and targets create immense pressure. Of course, a certain level of supervision and guidance is essential for any organization, but excessive micromanagement can have detrimental effects on both individuals and overall team dynamics.

According to one study, close to 59 percent of people surveyed reported feeling micromanaged at some point in their careers. Of those, 55 percent said it hindered their productivity, and 68 percent said it decreased their morale. While micromanagers often have good intentions, their behavior can drive employees away. In fact, 39 percent of employees surveyed admitted to changing jobs just to avoid working with a micromanager.[13]

For me, the Mask of Control was rooted in the fear of losing my mom. I thought if I could just do enough—say the right things, put the right systems in place—I could protect her from herself. But when the reality of her condition stared me in the face, it became clear: control wasn't the solution. It never had been.

For many of us, the need for control doesn't come out of nowhere—it's a response to past hurts or traumatic experiences. If we've felt powerless or vulnerable before, controlling our present can feel like a way to protect ourselves.

However, when we constantly seek to control our surroundings, we lose something essential. Spontaneity, creativity, and authenticity begin to disappear—not just in ourselves, but in those around us.

> **My mom didn't need my micromanaging; she needed connection, compassion, and someone to simply be there with her, not trying to fix her. The same was true for me. In my visa journey, every small setback felt like a personal failure, because I had tied my sense of worth to my ability to manage every detail.**

What makes the Mask of Control so insidious is how easily we mistake it for strength. Like independence, control can feel aspirational—something we strive for because we believe it will keep us safe. But in reality, control often stems from fear: fear of uncertainty, fear of vulnerability, fear of the unknown. For me, it was the fear of losing my mom, the fear of losing my footing in Australia, the fear that everything I had worked so hard for could crumble in an instant.

MORE DEVASTATING NEWS

On the morning of July 22, the day I was flying back to Canada to see my mom, David's phone rang at 3 a.m. Half-asleep, I watched him get up to take the call—it was his dad. A few minutes later, he crawled back into bed, leaned into me, and hugged me tightly.

"My mom just passed away," he said softly.

The words hit me like a freight train. My heart broke for him. His mom had been like a mom to me too, and I knew how deeply connected he was to her. We held each other for the rest of that early morning, lost in shared grief.

The mental conflict was overwhelming. *Do I stay and support David, who just lost his mom? Or do I go back to Canada to see my mom, who continues to drink and put herself in these states?*

As torn as I was, I knew deep down that I had to go. Leaving that day was heavy. The guilt, sadness, and grief felt unbearable. I hugged David tightly before walking out the door, my heart torn in two.

A SIMPLE YET MEMORABLE MOMENT

After a long, emotionally draining trip, I arrived at the tiny Smithers airport, still wearing my mask as required and to protect my mom. I saw Dad standing near the luggage claim. The space was small, just one big room. As I approached, he greeted me with a handshake and said, "You can take off the face diaper now. We don't wear those here." Let's just say he wasn't on board with the whole COVID thing.

Instantly, I felt uncomfortable. It was like he couldn't grasp the severity of the situation—the severity of my mom's condition. She was high-risk, and I was taking every precaution I could to protect her. His dismissal of that, of everything I was working to do for her, made my stomach churn.

After an uncomfortable car ride with Dad, I finally arrived at my mom's house, feeling a small sense of relief. I had organized for Gary to stay elsewhere during my stay. I didn't trust him to care for her properly, and I needed to know she was safe. Also, due to the pandemic, I was required to isolate for two weeks, and I didn't want to do it in a hotel room away from my mom while she needed me.

As I approached the house, Mom greeted me at the door. She was as frail as I'd ever seen her, but her smile told me how happy she was to see me. She clung to the walls for support, barely able to walk, her body weakened from months of inactivity and illness. I gave her a big hug, careful not to overwhelm her fragile frame, and helped her into the living room, where she settled into her favorite chair.

Immediately, I sprang into action. Every room needed attention—the kitchen, the bathroom, her bedroom, and even the loft. The cleaning wasn't just about tidying up. It was my way of showing love, of doing something tangible in a situation where so much felt out of my control. It was also about reclaiming a sense of order amid the chaos of her illness, her addiction, and the years of neglect that had built up around her.

During the first couple of days, when I wasn't cleaning, I spent time with Mom in the living room—the same room where I'd heard her laugh, cry, and share countless memories over the years, both good and bad.

Out of the blue, I asked her, "Mom, do you still smoke weed?" I only asked because I knew she was a pretty big stoner back in the day.

She paused for a moment, then smiled and said, "Yes, but I haven't in a while." There was a brief silence before she added, "Did you want some?"

I thought about it. I know the benefits of marijuana and its ability to relax the mind, but, in that moment, it wasn't about the weed—it was about sharing a bonding experience with my mom. "Sure," I replied.

Mom's face lit up as she directed me to her room to retrieve her little box of goodies. As I sat back on the couch and rolled a joint, the atmosphere began to feel lighter.

We moved out to the porch, sitting together and sharing the joint while chatting and telling stories. Mom, relaxed and more at ease than

I'd seen her in years, began reminiscing. She told me about a time when she had a bunch of friends over for drinks and a barbecue. Back then, she had two identical chocolate labs. Her friends were all sitting on the back porch, drinks in hand, while one of the labs lounged among them. When a new guest arrived, he came to the porch, said hello to everyone, and then walked around to the front door. There, he saw what he thought was the same dog sitting calmly by the entrance. Confused, he came back to my mom, marveling at how fast her dog had gotten to the other side of the house. It wasn't until he saw both dogs together that he realized his mistake.

For me, time stood still. It was the first time I'd seen my mom laugh—truly laugh—in over 10 years. I sat there, watching her, soaking in the moment. Seeing her smile, hearing her laugh, it was beautiful. I felt a lump in my throat as I tried to hold back my emotions. This moment, simple as it was, is one I'll never forget.

THE TOUGH MOMENTS CONTINUE

While cleaning up Mom's house, I kept uncovering so much junk—and so many empty wine bottles and vodka. They were everywhere, a constant reminder of the life she had been living. One morning, during my usual walk, I decided to check out the trailer that was sitting in the driveway. Mom and Gary used it for camping occasionally, and I wasn't surprised when I opened it up and found a stash of alcohol: a full bottle of Crown Royal, half a bottle of wine, and half a bottle of vodka.

I didn't even hesitate. I poured most of it down the drain. The only exception was the bottle of Crown, which I decided to give to Dad.

As I returned home from my walk, I told Mom what I had found and that I'd dumped most of it. She brushed it off, saying, "That's Gary's."

"So what?" I shot back. "He shouldn't be having alcohol anywhere near the house."

Of course, she defended him.

The tension was already high that day. It was the day of David's mom's funeral, and I knew how tough it was going to be for him. It broke my heart that I couldn't be there for him, to support him during one of the hardest days of his life. The funeral was being broadcast live from Newcastle, scheduled for 6 p.m. my time, so I spent the day trying to prepare myself emotionally.

As I was setting up outside to watch the service on my laptop, Mom called me over. "I spoke to Gary," she said. "I told him about the alcohol, and he's not happy."

"You told him?" I snapped. I couldn't believe it. Here I was, trying to help her, trying to create a better environment for her recovery, and she went straight to the one man enabling her behavior.

I lost it. I couldn't hold back my frustration and anger. I stormed out and sat outside, trying to calm myself and focus on the funeral. But the tears wouldn't stop. I felt gutted, betrayed, and let down. My emotions were raw and unfiltered as I buried my face in my hands, letting the tears flow freely.

When the funeral started, I pulled myself together and watched as people began entering the church. The ceremony was beautiful, but I couldn't take my eyes off David. He sat there the entire time with his head down, staring at the floor. My heart broke for him.

At the end of the ceremony, everyone took their turn going up to the coffin to lay a flower. When David's turn came, he stood there for a moment, his shoulders tense, and then broke down. Even now, as I write this memory, I have tears running down my face. Watching him from so far away, unable to hold him, to comfort him, was one of the hardest moments I've ever experienced.

THE COST OF CONTROL

My final day in isolation came to an end. I had made the most of the two weeks with my mom, but I was exhausted—physically, mentally, and emotionally. As much as I loved her, I knew I needed to get out of that house. Living with her full-time wasn't something I could imagine—it was like living with a child who was stuck in her ways.

As exhausted as I was, I knew I'd made a difference. I couldn't fix everything—my mom's health, her choices—but I could at least leave her with a home that felt clean, cared for, and a little closer to what it used to be.

Even though I was leaving Mom's house, I was still navigating the complexities of my relationship with Dad. One day, we got into a heated argument about COVID, but I quickly realized there was no point arguing. Dad was so set in his views that no reasoning or conversation would ever change his mind. The distance between us grew even further. All these little interactions with him were making me retract further into myself, and I started to become that anxious little boy again where the thought of seeing him or being around him triggered anxiety and stress.

It was a lot to process. Between my mom's condition, the strained relationship with my dad, and the sheer amount of work I'd poured into the house, I felt emotionally drained. As much as I'd accomplished,

I couldn't shake the heaviness that lingered.

The Mask of Control convinces us that if we work hard enough, plan perfectly, or manage every detail, we can shield ourselves—and the people we love—from pain and chaos. It makes us believe that we're responsible for holding everything together, even when it's not within our power to do so.

But control comes at a cost. As I scrubbed and cleaned, I could feel the weight of it all pressing down on me. I wasn't just cleaning a house—I was fighting against years of pain, frustration, and helplessness. The Mask of Control gave me something to focus on, something tangible I could do in the face of so much uncertainty, but it also kept me from being fully present with my mom.

AN ILLUMINATING CONVERSATION

Eventually, Gary moved back in with my mom, and I organized a meeting with me, him, and a counselor.

When Gary arrived at the counselor's office, I could see the tension on his face. He probably expected me to come at him with anger, but I kept my tone calm and focused on solutions. No surprise, he was dressed in sweats, a loose shirt, and his hair was messy. He looked unkempt, like he had just rolled out of bed.

I stood to shake his hand and greeted him before starting the conversation. I thanked him for showing up and reassured him that I wasn't there to attack or blame him for anything. I explained that over the past few weeks, I'd gotten a glimpse of what it was like living with my mom—a glimpse of what he'd been dealing with for the last 15-plus years.

It took a lot of strength for me to get to this point. I had been carrying so much anger toward him for so long, but I knew I had to put it aside and focus on what mattered most: my mom. I told him I understood that he had checked out emotionally and I didn't blame him. Being around someone with an illness like hers is hard. Honestly, it was impossible to understand how he had stayed as long as he had.

For so long, my feelings toward Gary had been black and white. I saw him as the enabler, the problem, the one standing in the way of my mom's recovery. But as the conversation unfolded, I started to see the shades of gray. He wasn't perfect—far from it—but he wasn't the monster I'd built him up to be in my mind. He was tired, drained, and just as lost as the rest of us.

Gary opened up and shared some stories. He told me he had known about my mom's drinking early on in their relationship. He said that the first time he met my grandpa, the very first thing he was asked was, "How's her drinking been?" Not exactly the kind of question you'd hope for when meeting your partner's parents.

He also shared the countless times she'd fallen and hit her head but refused to go to the hospital. That explained the scars on her head—ugly reminders of her stubbornness and the toll of her drinking.

I found myself shifting from rage to understanding, putting myself in his shoes for the first time. I started to sympathize with him, even though it was hard to admit. This was a man who had been living with the chaos of my mom's drinking for years, trying to manage the unmanageable. It didn't excuse his actions—or lack of action—but it made me realize that he was human too, struggling under the weight of a situation none of us knew how to fix.

As much as I appreciated hearing Gary's perspective, I needed to know one thing: "What's your plan?"

He was adamant that this was the last straw. He said if she drank again, he was leaving her, which was perfect. Maybe she would finally hit rock bottom and get the help she needed.

> **We live in a world full of ego, where setting aside our pride to consider a different perspective— or to emotionally understand what someone else might be feeling—can be incredibly difficult.**

Even now, I struggle in some situations where I'm faced with people or opinions that challenge me. But in this instance, I knew I had to take a different path than the one I'd always known.

RELINQUISHING CONTROL, LEARNING TO TRUST

Over the next few weeks, I prepared to move to Vancouver, deciding to pick up massage therapy again, as I needed something that would allow me the flexibility to look after my mom if she needed me.

I secured a great little one-bedroom apartment on Barclay Street, just west of Denman, in the West End. It was a quiet street within walking distance of everything I needed. It turned out to be exactly what I needed—fully furnished, with everything ready for me to move in. It even had enough space to set up my massage table.

Before leaving Smithers, I wanted to leave my mom with something meaningful—a small gesture to remind her how much I believed in her and loved her. I printed one of the latest photos we'd taken together, framed it, and wrote her a letter. It wasn't just any letter; it was a deeply personal message expressing everything I felt—the pride, the love, the hope, and the fears that had been weighing on me.

Dear Mom,

I want to start by saying how proud I am of you for being where you are today. Over two months sober is a huge accomplishment. I also want you to know that everything that has happened to you is not your fault.

I'm so grateful and glad I came home because for the first time in years, I got to see a glimpse of who my mom used to be. Happy, laughing, telling stories, smiling. I need you to know I would do anything for you.

But it hasn't always been easy. From the very first time I rode with you in the ambulance to the hospital to now, it has been mentally taxing. In and out of rehab, checking yourself out early, and not committing to the help that has been offered. I've been living my life over the last 10 years in fear that one day I'm going to get the phone call that you've killed yourself, and when I got that text from Dave this time, I was certain that was the one. Over the years, whenever I've visited home, I've had to spend my entire time helping you get out of bed or cleaning your house. I would love to bring a partner home one day and meet you without him having to help me clean your house.

I understand me being home has stressed you out, but I

know that you do appreciate my help. I know this change is scary, but it is needed more than ever if you want to beat this disease. Things cannot remain the same, and that goes for both you and Gary. I packed up my life and put it on hold to come back and help you—and to be clear, I was the only one that stepped up to do so. I didn't even hesitate, but everyone else, including Gary, has checked out.

Being here I have felt a strong pushback and huge lack of trust from you whenever I have suggested certain help. There have been days when I just wanted to walk out and leave and say fuck it, but at the end of the day, you've raised me to be a fighter and a healer. You're my mom, and I'm not ready to lose you at the same age that you lost your mother.

I'm terrified of leaving this week, as I'm scared that you will not get the proper help to help you long-term to work on these demons of yours. You've been battling this for 20+ years to the point where you've nearly killed yourself a couple of times. I know you want to be independent and do this on your own, but in reality, you just can't. You've spent years avoiding it. This is going to require a lot of work and dedication, and you'll need the proper support. I don't know if this is all an act until I leave. I just don't know. I believe you want to beat this, but I don't believe you want to face your demons.

I love you more than you know, and this has been really hard on me, but you are worth it. I want to see you fighting for this as hard as I am right now. This trip has taken it all out of me, and I'm mentally exhausted. I know you can fight this. I have plans for us in the future. I want you to have grandchildren, and I would love for you to come to my wedding one day and walk me down the aisle.

You are my mom, and I will fight to the end with you.

I love you—stay strong and stay committed.

You Got This!!

On the morning of my departure, I folded the letter, attached it to the framed photo, and slid it under her pillow for her to find later. Leaving her was one of the hardest things I've ever done. Walking away meant stepping back and letting go, trusting that she would stay sober without me there to keep an eye on her. For the last month, I had been there to support her, take her places, and keep her on track. I knew it wasn't my responsibility, but I also knew how serious the situation was.

Her doctors had made it clear—her body was shutting down, and she couldn't have another drink without catastrophic consequences. But I couldn't control the situation anymore. I had to let go.

I had to trust her.

I had to trust Gary.

I had to trust that everything I had done—the time I spent, the conversations I had, the support I gave—would mean something. I had to trust that Gary, after everything, would step up and have my mom's back when I couldn't be there.

As I left Smithers, there was a weight in my chest, a mixture of hope and fear. I had done all I could. Now, it was up to her.

LIKE A PUNCH TO THE GUT

One weekend, my friend Doug and I decided to escape the city and go camping on Vancouver Island. Doug had one of those trucks with a pop-up tent attached to the back—a perfect setup for an impromptu getaway. Armed with snacks, drinks, and enough overconfidence to avoid making a reservation, we set out for the beach.

On the third day of the trip, the carefree vibe came to a screeching halt. Mom had been trying to call me, but because we were in a spotty area of the island, none of her calls came through. When I finally saw her voicemail, I already had a sinking feeling in my stomach.

I pressed play, and the voice I heard hit me like a punch to the gut.

It was *that* voice. The one that took me back to countless other nights, filled with worry and dread. The little-girl tone she used when she'd had too much to drink. The one that told me, without a shadow of a doubt, that she was drinking again.

My chest tightened as I listened, the familiar mix of emotions bubbling up. Anger. Sadness. Frustration. Anger toward Gary for enabling her. Sadness because I knew what this meant—that the fragile progress she'd made was unraveling. And frustration because no matter how much I tried, no matter how much I sacrificed, I couldn't control this. The voicemail didn't even need words to convey what was happening. The slur in her speech, the forced cheerfulness—it was all I needed to hear.

When I returned to Vancouver, I called her. She admitted to having "just a couple of red wines," but I knew better. I'd heard this story too many times before.

Hearing that voice again broke something in me. I wanted to yell, to cry, to demand answers—but I knew it wouldn't change anything. It was the same cycle, over and over, and I was powerless to stop it.

ONE BLOW AFTER ANOTHER

Later in September, I sent David a text to check in on him, asking about him and Bentley. His reply was short, and it hit me like a tonne of bricks: *I had to put Bentley down.*

There was no buildup, no explanation—just the stark reality of it. I sat there staring at my phone, feeling a wave of emotions crash over me. I knew how much Bentley meant to David. That dog wasn't just a pet; he was David's family, his source of comfort and stability, especially during lockdown.

Bentley's health had declined rapidly. He had stopped eating entirely, lost all his energy, and had become painfully skinny. David, in his typical fashion, had done everything he could. He'd taken Bentley to the vet, tried consultations with a naturopath, and put him on new routines and treatments in a desperate attempt to improve his health. But nothing worked.

I immediately called David, but he didn't pick up. I texted him again, offering my condolences and asking if he wanted to talk, but he simply replied that he needed time. I couldn't blame him. He'd just lost his mom, and now he had lost Bentley too—all while being completely alone in the middle of lockdown. The thought of him going through all of that without me there to support him made my heart ache.

FLOW, NOT FORCE

Following the news about Bentley, I threw myself into work, catching up with friends, and planning for an upcoming visit from my mom. Despite my efforts to stay in control, the last four months had taught me one undeniable truth: sometimes you have to let go.

This theme kept circling in my mind, like a mantra: *flow, not force*. It was a constant reminder to trust the process, to stop forcing outcomes, and to accept that if something didn't work out, it was for a reason. Dwelling in anger or sadness wouldn't change the path ahead—it would only keep me stuck.

It felt like the universe had been pushing me toward this lesson. Everything I'd planned over the last four to five months had fallen apart, replaced by new paths I hadn't anticipated. It was a frustrating but humbling realization that life often has its own plans.

NO MORE FIGHT

My mother was planning to stay with me in Vancouver for Christmas. Given her health condition, I had this gnawing feeling that it might be our last Christmas together. She was adamant about having a real tree in my apartment. "None of that fake stuff," she insisted.

Alongside the festivities, she would be undergoing a minor eye surgery in Vancouver. She had been dealing with epiretinal membrane, a condition where scar tissue forms on the retina, blurring her vision.

During the first weekend of December, I called my mom, and it didn't take long to notice something was off. I knew the signs—she'd been drinking. Eventually, she admitted that Gary had supplied the alcohol. Just a few months earlier, doctors had found six ulcers in her esophagus that could have ruptured at any moment, causing fatal internal bleeding. Her body wasn't capable of handling alcohol anymore. How could he, of all people, enable her like this?

The next morning, I had a call with my uncle and Mom's doctor. We discussed her drinking and the risks it posed, especially with her upcoming surgery. The concern was real: if she went into withdrawal during or after the procedure, it could have devastating consequences. We decided the best course of action was for me to fly up to Smithers immediately to ensure she didn't drink before coming to Vancouver.

Then, I sent Gary a message:

Hi Gary, just letting you know I'm flying back tomorrow to ensure that my mom doesn't drink before her surgery. I'm highly disappointed that you have been supplying her alcohol again, from what she told me last night. You both have lost complete trust in me. I'm asking you to find a place to stay until I leave back for Vancouver with her.

His reply:

Hi Rob, I don't blame you and I fucked up. I'm disappointed in myself and Kathy. I gave in to her incessant whining, which is not an excuse. Don't know if it means anything, but I'm sorry I've put you through this.

I was beyond angry. I had lost all faith in the man my mom called her boyfriend. To me, he was nothing more than a leech. He'd checked out years ago, but he stayed—why? My mother didn't love him; she loved the idea of not being alone. Her dependency on him was sickening, and his apathy toward her health was even worse. It broke me to see my mom being taken advantage of, and even more to see her blind to it. How could someone continue to poison the person they supposedly care about? And why would she defend him so fiercely, even as he contributed to her decline?

I felt defeated. Broken. The fight I had in me was dwindling, and an enormous sadness coursed through my body. This was it, I thought to myself—it was time to cut all ties and say goodbye to my mom. As much as it tore me apart, I couldn't keep fighting a battle that felt like it would never end.

That evening, I took myself out for dinner, hoping it would help me process everything. But as I sat at the table, all I could feel was sadness. Tears began streaming down my face as I thought about going home and what I was about to do. I texted Wayne, asking if he could meet me. More than anything, I needed a hug.

I left to meet Wayne on the street, and the moment I saw him, I completely crumbled. I fell into his arms, breaking down and crying uncontrollably. I couldn't hold back the tidal wave of emotions—shattered, defeated, hopeless. He held me for what felt like five minutes as I let it all out.

We walked to a nearby café and sat down. Wayne talked while I mostly listened, tears silently rolling down my face. He was there for me when I needed someone most, as I wrestled with the decision I had been avoiding for so long. I had to let go of my mom for my own mental health. It was the one thing I never wanted to do, but the time had come.

The next morning, I woke up and packed my things. I felt so empty and numb. The entire morning was filled with feelings of failure and guilt. In my heart, I felt like I was giving up—the very thing I swore I would never do.

As I sat on the plane waiting to take off, I was overwhelmed by emotion. I was just a few hours away from seeing my mom, and I was doing everything I could to hold back the tears. The exhaustion of the past 24 hours was catching up with me. Trapped in the small plane, surrounded by people, I forced a polite smile at those walking past my seat. But mostly, I stared out the window, lost in thought.

* * *

As I drove, in my aunt's truck, along the long highway to my mom's house, which was only about 10 minutes out of town, my mind raced. How was this conversation going to go? What would I say? Would I yell at her? At Gary? The truth was, I didn't even have the energy to fight anymore. I was drained, defeated, and so far past caring. All I knew was that I had to say what needed to be said. Whatever happened next was out of my hands.

When I pulled up to Mom's house, Gary's truck was gone. I supposed he didn't want to face me, knowing how angry I was. Mom greeted me at the door, and the look in her eyes said it all—she knew she had messed up. I walked in, said a quick hello, made my way to the living room, and sat on the couch. Mom settled into her favorite lounger chair beside me.

"Where's Gary?" I asked.

"He got a hotel room for a few nights," she replied.

I nodded. "I let him know I wasn't staying here." I was calm—or at least I appeared calm. In truth, I felt empty. The fight had left me entirely.

"I'm sorry," she said quietly, her voice trembling.

"I put my life on hold to come back here. I put all my stuff in storage so I could help you, and you both just stabbed me in the back," I responded, my voice steady but cold.

Her immediate response was to fall into her familiar victim mode. "I know, I'm a screwup. I can't do anything right."

"Mom, he doesn't love you. He's practically assisting in killing you. You call that love?"

I reminded her—again—how close she had come to dying and how she couldn't keep risking her life like this.

"I know, I know," she said, her voice breaking.

"Do you, though?" I shot back. "Does he? Does Gary even care? How messed up do you have to be to keep giving someone alcohol when you know it's killing them?"

She had no response. In that moment, I realized I had to accept their relationship for what it was. From the outside looking in, it was toxic, unhealthy, and deeply messed up. But it was their relationship, and no matter what I did or said, Mom wasn't going to leave Gary. She wasn't going to see him for what he truly was. She was completely consumed by him, fully dependent on him, and clinging to him like he was all she had left.

As I sat there, I felt nothing. No anger, no sadness—just numbness. My voice was hollow as I said the words I never thought I'd say.

"Mom, I need you to know that when I go back to Australia, after you visit me for Christmas, it will be the last time you hear from me or see me again."

Usually, saying something like this would stir some emotion in me, but there was nothing left to feel. This situation, this betrayal—it had stripped me of every ounce of energy and hope I had left for my mom and her survival.

Sometimes, the hardest thing to do is accept the relationships and people in our lives for who they are, no matter how difficult it is to watch. For so long, I felt guilty being the only family member trying to help my mom. Everyone else had set their boundaries long ago, but I kept fighting. Now, though, the guilt was gone. There was just nothing left.

Not many words were spoken after that. Mom's eyes welled up, and tears ran down her cheeks.

"I just can't do this anymore," I said softly. "I love you, but I'm done trying to help this situation. I'm going to go now."

She walked me to the door, and I gave her a hug.

"I love you, and I'm sorry," she said.

"I love you too," I replied.

As I got into the truck and drove down the dark driveway onto the highway, I felt dead inside. It was the worst kind of emptiness I'd ever experienced. This moment, this situation—it had taken everything from me. I wasn't sad, angry, guilty, or ashamed. I was nothing. For the first time in my life, I felt like a broken man. It was a long drive back to my aunt's house that night. Time seemed to stand still as I sat in that space of emptiness.

I felt like my purpose was gone. I felt alone. What remained was a hollowed-out version of myself, and I wasn't sure if I'd ever feel whole again.

* * *

Over the next couple of days, the feelings didn't subside. I moved through life like a zombie, numb and detached, even when I was out in public with my aunt. I found myself staring into space, lost in thought. I wasn't the man I used to be. I was someone with no purpose, no drive. The battle I had been fighting for years felt like it was finally over—but had I lost? Or had I just given up? At that point, it didn't matter. All that remained was the empty space where my resolve used to be.

Conversations became a blur. Words passed through me, going in one ear and out the other. The smiles I managed to give were forced, barely masking the void I felt inside. I didn't even have the energy to pretend to be happy anymore. I didn't recognize myself. Who was this version of me? This hollow, defeated person? It was so far removed from the fighter, the optimist, the healer I had always been. But now, I was stuck in this space, unsure of how to move forward or if I even wanted to try.

A CHRISTMAS TO REMEMBER

As Mom and I settled into Vancouver for the Christmas break, we spent the next few days decorating the Christmas tree together and having small, quiet chats while she recovered from her eye surgery. She still needed my assistance walking around, holding on to my arm as we made our way through the city. Every morning, we'd head to the coffee shop down the street, Blenz Coffee. I introduced my mom to lattes—a completely new experience for her. She was so used to pot coffee and wasn't familiar with all the other options on the menu.

Later that night, she took a call from Gary, moving into the bedroom to talk. I couldn't help but overhear her describing our day. She shared how I'd taken her to the coffee shop and ordered her a latte. What made the moment so sweet was how she said "latte," almost like it was a foreign word, something exotic and unfamiliar to her. It was endearing, a small but meaningful experience for her—one of the little things about being in a big city she got to enjoy, along with endless shopping.

* * *

When Christmas came, we made a deal to cook a full turkey dinner, complete with stuffing, mashed potatoes, honey-glazed carrots, and broccoli with cheese—just like my mom used to make for us as kids. It turned out to be a beautiful little Christmas, one I got to truly enjoy with my mom. It was a brief reprieve from everything else, a moment of peace and connection that I knew I'd hold on to.

LETTING GO, ACCEPTING REALITY

As the day arrived for her to return to Smithers, it was also the day I had to let go of the reins. I needed to trust that she'd be OK—that she could do this on her own. But even as I told myself this, doubt crept in.

We were sitting on the couch, just 30 minutes before her ride would arrive to take her to the airport. I looked at her—the light from the window reflecting on her face, making her blue eyes shine.

There was a slight look of nervousness on her face, and I felt it too. A wave of fear washed over me, the relentless "what-ifs" crashing into my mind. *What if this is the last time I see my mom?*

I broke the silence and told her I was scared—scared of leaving her, scared of being so far away on the other side of the world. Just making it back this time had been a huge ordeal, but I made it happen. For 17 years, I'd been the one stepping up to help my mom. And why wouldn't I? She was my mom. She brought me into this world and raised me to be the man I am today. She passed on traits and values I'll forever be grateful for. But she was also battling an illness, and one of the hardest lessons life has handed me is this: sometimes, you have to let go.

I wanted her to be better. I wanted to believe she wanted to be better too. But her actions had often told me otherwise. She was strong—stronger than most people gave her credit for. Even family, doctors, and friends were amazed she'd lasted this long. She had stood at death's door more times than I could count, and each time, she had managed to pull through. It had been incredibly hard to watch, but she was still here.

And yet, this was the biggest lesson I'd faced to date. How do you let go of someone who brought you into this world? Someone who raised you, who you love deeply? How do you step back and not help when you know times will get tough again? I cried more times than I could count just thinking about it. Every experience we shared over those two weeks had been colored by the thought: *Could this be the last time?* I cherished every moment, lived in each second as fully as I could, taking in the details of her face, her laugh, her joy.

Before she left, I asked her a few questions—questions I hoped might give me some peace. Her answers weren't what I was hoping for, but they gave me something else: a sense of acceptance. Acceptance that the situation was what it was. I had to trust her, trust that she'd be OK, and trust that I'd done everything I could.

Letting go of the reins wasn't easy. But it was necessary. I'd learned that I couldn't always be there to save her, and I needed to respect my own boundaries. This was the lesson I needed to learn before starting the next chapter of my life. To let go, to trust, and to focus on building my future while holding on to the love and hope I had for her.

This was my hardest lesson yet, but I knew it was the one I needed to learn to move forward.

PLAN AFTER PLAN DERAILED

As February rolled around, I started planning my return to Australia, clinging to the hope that Pete might meet with me. Maybe we could finally talk, and I could explain everything. Before New Year's, I had sent him a routine holiday message—just a simple "Merry Christmas" and an update about being in Canada to care for my mom. To my surprise, he replied. But his response wasn't what I had hoped for.

Pete acknowledged how good it was that I had gone home to help my mom, saying she must truly appreciate it. But then came the part that crushed me: he asked me to stop messaging him, to stop trying to contact him altogether.

I had no choice but to act quickly. I poured everything into an email—a page and a half that held all my feelings, all my love, and all my truth. I told him how much I still loved him, how I wanted to be with him, even marry him. It was my final attempt to win him back, my last shot at salvaging what I believed we still had.

Then, I waited.

Days turned into weeks, and still, no response. I clung to hope for as long as I could, checking my inbox incessantly. But nothing came. I had given it everything I had, and if that wasn't enough, I had to find peace in knowing I'd done all I could. Still, a small part of me remained hopeful—maybe once I returned to Sydney, we could meet for coffee. Maybe then.

During this time, life threw me another curveball. My friend Axel, who had been caring for my cat while I was away, called me with some concerning news. Brodie, my blue-eyed, cross-eyed companion, was breathing abnormally and wasn't eating as much.

Two weeks before my departure back to Sydney, Brodie's health rapidly declined. Axel rushed him to the vet, where they decided to sedate him for further testing. But while under sedation, Brodie had a heart attack and passed away.

Axel called me in tears, devastated. He had bonded deeply with Brodie and was gutted by the loss. I was shattered. I had been looking forward to starting my life in Queensland with Brodie by my side, but now he was gone too. First David's mom. Then our dog Bentley. And now Brodie.

Control had always been my armor, my way of creating stability in an unpredictable world. But now, as I faced loss after loss, I realized that no matter how tightly I gripped the reins, life had its own plans.

And I was powerless to stop it.

STEPS TO REMOVE THE MASK OF CONTROL

While the Mask of Control can help us bring order to the chaos in our lives, it becomes harmful when we seek to control the uncontrollable. Understanding that not everything is within our control is crucial to dropping the mask.

1. **Recognize the mask:** Identify where and how the Mask of Control appears in your life. Is it at work, in relationships, or within your family dynamics? Reflect on situations where you feel the need to micromanage, dictate outcomes, or hold on to control tightly.
2. **Understand the underlying fear:** Control often stems from fear—fear of unpredictability, failure, or vulnerability. Explore what you're afraid of losing or facing. This self-awareness can be uncomfortable but is necessary for growth.
3. **Practice acceptance:** Acknowledge that not everything is within your control. Life is unpredictable, and trying to micromanage every aspect can lead to burnout and disconnection. Begin practicing phrases like "I accept what I cannot change."
4. **Learn to trust others:** Control often masks a deep mistrust in others. Practice trusting people with small tasks or emotional vulnerabilities. Understand that things may not always go according to plan—and that's OK. Trust can be built over time by allowing others to step in.
5. **Accept imperfection:** Perfectionism and control often go hand in hand. Understand that things won't always be perfect—it's a fact of life. Accepting imperfection will help you release the

need to micromanage every detail.
6. **Practice letting go in small ways:** Start with small acts of surrender. For example, let someone else plan an event or handle a situation, even if it's not done exactly as you would like. These small moments of letting go can help you build tolerance for uncertainty.

REFLECTIONS AND LEARNINGS: THE MASK OF CONTROL

Approaching Each Situation with Trust

My story: My attempts to control my mom's actions—like throwing away Gary's alcohol or trying to manage her recovery—came from a place of love, but it often pushed her away or led to conflict. I realized that my need to control was driven by fear, not trust.

Reflection: Think about a situation where your desire to control was rooted in fear rather than trust. How did this impact your relationships? How might things have shifted if you had approached the situation with trust instead?

Exercise: Write a letter to someone (real or hypothetical) where you acknowledge the fear driving your actions. Practice replacing fear-based thoughts with trust-based affirmations. For example: "I trust you to make the right decisions for yourself."

Releasing Control

My story: Whether it was planning my life in Australia around the visa, or trying to craft the perfect email to Pete, I clung to the belief that controlling every detail would guarantee success. But the reality was that outcomes were out of my hands, no matter how much I planned.

Reflection: Consider a time when you believed meticulous planning would ensure success but still didn't achieve the outcome you wanted. What did you learn about letting go of control in that moment?

Exercise: Identify one current goal where you're overplanning or obsessing over details. Let go of one part of the process—delegate it, simplify it, or leave it to chance—and observe how it feels to release control.

Stepping Back, Creating Space

My story: Deciding to step back from my mom's situation was one of the hardest decisions I've ever made. It felt like giving up, but it was a necessary step to preserve my own mental health and well-being.

Reflection: Where in your life are you holding on too tightly, even though it's draining you emotionally? How might stepping back help you regain your strength?

Exercise: Write down a situation or relationship where stepping back feels impossible. Now list three potential benefits of creating space. Commit to one small step to establish healthier boundaries.

Dropping Responsibility

My story: I spent years trying to control my mom's drinking, Gary's behavior, and even the relationships in my life, believing that, if I just did enough, I could fix everything. But the constant effort left me emotionally drained and feeling like I had failed when things didn't go as planned.

Reflection: Think about an area of your life where you're trying to "fix" everything. How has this affected your emotional well-being? How might you find peace in letting go?

Exercise: Spend five minutes journaling about a situation you've been trying to fix. End by writing one sentence to release responsibility: "It's not my job to fix this, and I release myself from the burden."

Accepting What Can't Be Changed

My story: It took me years to accept my mom's relationship with Gary for what it was. My constant fight against their dynamic only drained me further and delayed the peace that comes with acceptance.

Reflection: Is there a situation or relationship in your life that you struggle to accept as it is? What would acceptance look like, and how might it bring you peace?

Exercise: Write a list of things you've resisted accepting. Choose one and write a short mantra to practice daily, such as: "I accept [person/situation] as they are, and I release myself from the need to change them."

MASK OF CONTROL
KEY TAKEAWAYS

- **Control often comes from fear:** The need to control is often driven by fear—fear of uncertainty, failure, or vulnerability. Recognizing this fear is the first step to releasing it.
- **Letting go is not giving up:** Releasing control doesn't mean giving up; it's about trusting others and the process of life while focusing on what you can influence—your own actions and emotions.
- **Acceptance brings peace:** Accepting people and situations as they are, instead of fighting to change them, brings clarity and emotional freedom.
- **Boundaries are healthier than control:** Setting clear boundaries allows you to protect your well-being without imposing control on others, fostering healthier relationships.
- **Trust is the antidote to control:** Choosing to trust, rather than control, creates space for connection, growth, and unexpected possibilities.

CHAPTER 16

THE MASK OF INVULNERABILITY

SHIELDING FROM FEAR OF VULNERABILITY

The Cycle of Invulnerability

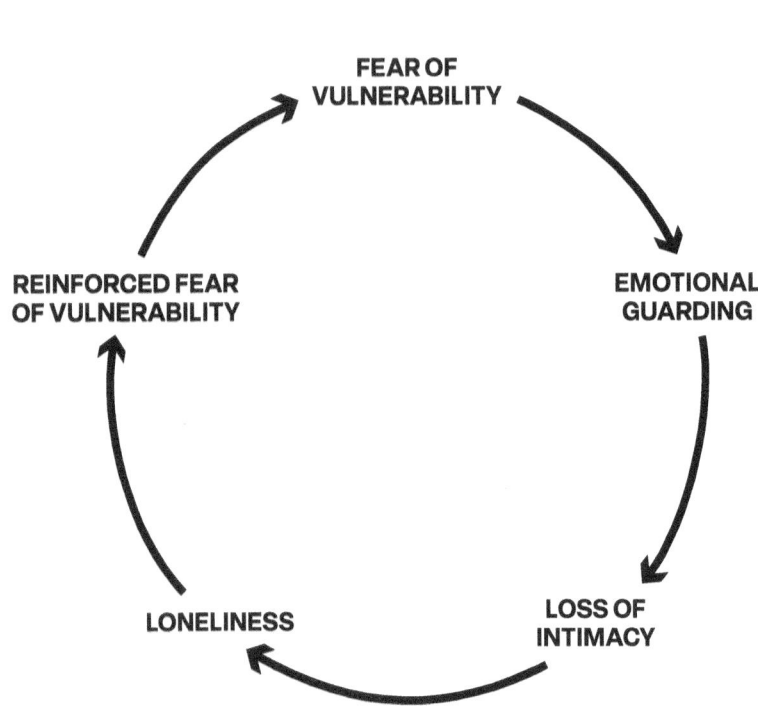

The Mask of Invulnerability is a common one, and if you've followed me for some time, you've definitely seen me post "VULNERABILITY IS SEXY." But let me be honest—being OK with not being OK was something I had to learn the hard way.

THE PHONE CALL I ALWAYS FEARED

March 11 had arrived. After 10 months of the most intense emotional roller coaster of my life, and being tested on so many levels, even to the point of being broken, I was finally heading back to Australia. This was supposed to be the beginning of my fresh start—the chapter I'd been waiting to write for nearly a year.

The morning after my return, I had a call with my mom. She was checking in, doing her usual routine of telling me about her day and what she'd been up to.

"Did you meet up with Pete?" she asked. I'd talked about him when I was back in Canada, telling her how I was still in love with him and wanted to try and make it work now that I was out of the visa mess. I'd shared my plan to get in touch with him, have a proper chat, and tell him everything—how I still loved him and all that I'd been through.

"No," I replied, feeling a pang of disappointment. "I don't think it's going to happen before I head up to Brisbane."

"Aww, I'm sorry, dear. That's too bad," she said, her voice soft with sympathy.

"I'll call you from Brisbane once I'm settled, OK, Mom?"

"OK, love you."

"Love you too."

* * *

The next day, I made the move to Brisbane, moving in with my friend Shaun in his apartment.

On the evening of March 14, Shaun and I were making our way home from a day's drive, and the sun was setting in the distance, painting the sky with soft hues of orange, red, and gold. It was one of those sunsets that seemed too perfect to be real, the kind that makes you pause and appreciate the moment. I was dozing in and out, letting the rhythmic hum of the car soothe me as I sat in the passenger seat.

Shaun broke the silence.

"How are you feeling since being back?" he asked, glancing over at me.

"It's nice," I replied, pausing for a moment before continuing. "But, to be honest, it's a mix of emotions. I'm happy to be back, excited about starting this new chapter up here in Queensland, but …" I trailed off, staring at the streaks of color still lingering in the sky. "I still have this worry about my mom in the back of my mind."

Shaun stayed quiet, letting me gather my thoughts.

"It's hard being so far away from her, you know? Not being able to help as much. Every day, I wake up with this fear, wondering if today will be the day I get that phone call—the one telling me my mom has passed away. I can't help but think … will today be the day?"

* * *

The following morning, I was sitting on the couch watching the news, while Shaun was in the kitchen, making something to eat. Suddenly, my phone rang. It was a FaceTime call from my uncle. The moment his face appeared on the screen, I knew something was wrong. His expression gave it all away.

"Hey, buddy," he said, his voice heavy.

"What's going on?" I asked, already feeling a lump forming in my throat.

"She's gone, buddy. Your mom passed away last night."

My body froze. I didn't know how to respond. It was like my mind was trying to compute the words, but they didn't make sense. And then it hit me. The rush of emotion. My eyes flooded with tears, and a sharp, unbearable pain gripped my chest.

The reality of losing someone you love, even when you know it's coming, crashes over you like a tidal wave. Nothing can prepare you for the moment when the fear becomes real.

"I love you, buddy. Stay strong," my uncle said before we hung up.

I crumbled, sinking into myself, overwhelmed by the sheer weight of the loss. Shaun had overheard the conversation and immediately came over to hold me as I cried uncontrollably in his arms. The weight of it all crushed me—I had just spoken to her a few days ago.

After the initial wave of waterworks, I called my sister. Both of us were crying on the phone, the grief so heavy that we could barely manage more than five words to each other.

Next, I called Gary. His voice was somber as he filled me in with what little detail he had. He told me that, the night before, he had said goodnight to her at 8 p.m. before heading to the couch where he usually slept. In the morning, just before leaving for work, he decided to check on her, as he hadn't heard a sound. That's when he found her—slumped over the bed.

That night, something extraordinary happened. Mom visited me in my dreams. We were having a conversation, though the exact details were fuzzy. But one thing stood out clearly—she told me she was OK. I woke up crying, the emotions from the dream spilling into reality.

THE CRACKS IN THE MASK

After Mom passed, I went straight into planning mode. I think it was my way of coping, of keeping myself occupied so I didn't have to sit with the heaviness of it all. I told everyone I was fine. I convinced myself I was fine. I told myself Mom's passing was a good thing because she was finally at peace. And yet, there were moments when the grief would sneak up on me, completely uninvited. Watching a commercial where someone mentioned hummingbirds—a symbol my mom adored—set me off. Another time, Shaun and I were watching *Life After Death* with Tyler Henry, the celebrity medium. Probably not the smartest choice post Mom's death. Within minutes, I had to tell Shaun to turn it off. I ran into the bathroom, sat on the toilet, and bawled my eyes out.

This is what the Mask of Invulnerability does. It tells us to keep it together, to stay strong, to not let anyone see the cracks. Vulnerability, after all, involves risk and emotional exposure—which many of us find daunting. It asks us to show the parts of ourselves that aren't polished, the parts we're not sure others will accept.

The Mask of Invulnerability often forms as a response to early experiences of emotional pain or disappointment. For those who've been betrayed, rejected, or abandoned, vulnerability starts to feel like a weakness—a doorway to more pain. So, we develop an emotional armor, a way to shield ourselves from further hurt. This mask helps us maintain control over how much of our true selves others can see. It lets us avoid situations where we might feel exposed, where our softer side might be laid bare. But the truth is, this mask keeps us stuck.

For me, grief didn't care about the mask I was wearing. It found the cracks, no matter how much I tried to convince myself I was fine. It reminded me that vulnerability isn't weakness—it's strength. It's human. And it's the only way we truly connect with others and heal.

EMBRACE THE GAME

The next few days were a whirlwind of planning. After doing some research online and hearing suggestions, I decided to create something meaningful for everyone attending the memorial. I designed a bookmark—something practical, yet symbolic of her love for reading. Along with the bookmark, I planned to include envelopes of seeds from four of her favorite flowers for people to take home and plant. It felt like a fitting tribute, something that would continue to grow and bloom in her memory.

As I planned my trip home, I kept reminding myself, *This is going to be hard. It's going to hurt. But you will emerge stronger.* By this point in my life, I had adopted a mindset of leaning into challenges.

> **I truly believe that every difficulty we face holds an opportunity for growth, no matter how painful or overwhelming it might seem at the time.**

Life isn't meant to be easy—if it were, where would the growth come from? The challenges we encounter are there for a reason: to shape us, to help us develop confidence, resilience, and empathy. They force us to rise, to adapt, to become better versions of ourselves.

Think of life like a video game where you're the main character. Each level presents a new obstacle or challenge—a "boss" you have to beat to move forward. These bad characters are your life's struggles and obstacles. When you beat one, you get to the next level, unlocking new superpowers, tools, and opportunities. But what happens if you don't beat the boss? Do you throw down the controller, storm off, and give up? Maybe, at first. But eventually, most of us come back, determined to try again until we succeed. The game of life has infinite levels and infinite rewards. The real question is: are you willing to keep playing for those rewards?

Going back to my mom's house after her death felt exactly like one of those life levels. I mentally prepared myself for every "boss" I might face: landing in my hometown and knowing she wouldn't be there to greet me, walking into the house where she died, stepping into her bedroom where she was found, sorting through her belongings, cleaning her room, hosting the wake—even dividing her ashes into three separate bags. Each of these moments felt like a challenge, one I could easily avoid if I let fear or sadness take over. But I refused to back down. I wanted to face it.

THE MASK MY MOTHER WORE

My mom, sadly, had worn the Mask of Invulnerability. Because she never dealt with the pain she carried, alcohol consumed her. It became her way of shielding herself from the emotions and memories she didn't want to face. Even in her final months, when I gently tried to talk about the past, she'd cut me off with a familiar refrain: "I don't want to talk about it." It was her armor, her way of protecting herself from reopening wounds that she feared would never heal. Over the years, ignoring and avoiding her pain became her normal. It was heartbreaking to witness because I could see the toll it was taking on her—physically, mentally, and emotionally. The mask may have shielded her from her past, but it also blocked her from the healing and connection she desperately needed.

I didn't want to follow that path. I didn't want to let the Mask of

Invulnerability define my story the way it had hers. I wanted to face the hard times, confront the pain, and grow through it. I believed that embracing vulnerability, rather than hiding from it, was the only way to truly heal. And this—the grief of losing her—became my hardest challenge yet.

The question we all need to ask ourselves is, *If not now, then when?* How much time are we going to give ourselves to feel "ready"? Days? Months? Years? How long will we let this heavy burden sit on our shoulders, whispering, "Are you ready to deal with me yet?" Sure, we might convince ourselves we've handled it. But life has a funny way of proving otherwise.

STRENGTH IN VULNERABILITY

Men have historically been conditioned to embody what we often term "stoic masculinity"—the idea that to be a man, you must remain strong, composed, and emotionally guarded. In the past, vulnerability didn't exist in a man's world. To express emotion openly, to show weakness, meant risking ridicule. You were called names like "pussy" or "faggot." The message was clear: if you weren't strong, you weren't a man. As someone who grew up feeling different, this expectation was isolating.

In 2011, researcher Kristen Springer conducted a study revealing that men who conformed to rigid masculine beliefs were significantly less likely to seek preventive health care compared to those with more moderate views.[14] This avoidance of help, driven by the Mask of Invulnerability, often comes at a profound cost.

Even athletes like Michael Phelps, who seem untouchable, have spoken about the pressures of stoic masculinity. In a 2024 interview, he shared how vulnerability was seen as a weakness, especially in competitive sports. Opening up about struggles felt like giving his competitors an edge, so he kept everything bottled up. Over time, though, he learned that vulnerability isn't a weakness but a strength.[15]

In school, the word "faggot" was tossed around so casually, and phrases like "stop being gay" and "that's so gay" were thrown about by siblings and peers. Equating weakness or stupidity with being gay was normalized. And you know what? I said those words too. Why? To blend in. To make myself invisible, to avoid drawing attention to the parts of me that didn't fit the mold. That's the power of the Mask of Invulnerability—it convinces you to hide your true self to avoid the pain of rejection or judgment.

And now, here I was, telling everyone I was fine after losing my mom, while my inner voice screamed, *"LIAR."* I wasn't fine, but I felt like I had to be. Why? Maybe because admitting I wasn't OK felt like failing the very narrative I'd been raised to believe: men are strong; we don't cry; vulnerability is weakness. It was exhausting. And it wasn't true. I made a choice that day to shed some of the mask. I decided that when someone asked me if I was OK, I would just be honest. I didn't want to carry the weight anymore. The truth was, I felt like shit. Plain and simple. My mom had just died, and I was walking around trying to convince everyone—including myself—that I was fine, that I had it all together. But I didn't. I was heartbroken, exhausted, and overwhelmed by grief.

I realized that by pretending I was OK, I wasn't fooling anyone—especially not myself. More than that, I was denying myself the chance to heal. I needed to release the pressure, let people in, and allow myself to feel. So when the next person asked how I was doing, I didn't plaster on a fake smile or give them the "I'm fine" line. I told them the truth: **"I'm not doing great, but I'm trying."**

It felt strange at first, like I was exposing myself in a way I wasn't used to. Vulnerability is scary—there's no denying that. But in that moment, it also felt freeing. The weight I'd been carrying began to lift, little by little, as I let myself be honest about how I was really feeling.

FACING THE CHALLENGE HEAD-ON

When I arrived at my mom's house, I sat on the couch alone for two hours, letting myself feel every ounce of the pain. I didn't force myself to move or distract myself. I just *was*. But there was one place I wasn't ready to face yet—her bedroom. The room where she was found. The room where I had found her drunk and in some of the worst conditions I'd ever seen her. I couldn't go in there alone.

At around lunchtime, Gary's sister Rachel arrived to help and support me. She had always been there for my mom, helping out whenever she could, and her presence felt comforting amid the heaviness of the day.

We started upstairs, sorting through boxes of old photos and organizing belongings. As we sifted through hundreds of pictures, I began envisioning how I wanted to celebrate my mom's life during her memorial. A giant wall of photos on the fireplace seemed perfect, capturing her story—from childhood to motherhood, her passions, partners, and everything in between. Some of the photos were completely new to me, showing parts of her life I'd never known. It felt bittersweet—piecing together the timeline of her life while mourning her absence. I set aside photos that felt like they truly represented her essence, wanting her vibrancy and strength to shine through for everyone to see.

Then came the moment I'd been mentally preparing myself for. Rachel gently asked if I was ready to go into my mom's room. I said yes. I had to do it—I couldn't avoid it just because it was going to be difficult. As I walked in, I was hit with a rush of familiarity and discomfort. The room smelled exactly as I remembered—musty, with faint traces of alcohol lingering in the air. The mattress was stained, and the space felt stagnant, like it had been closed off from the world for far too long. It wasn't just a room; it was a reflection of my mom's inner world—a dark cave where she hid, consumed by her past trauma and too afraid to emerge.

I stood there in silence, taking it all in.

*　*　*

The next day, Rachel and I returned to continue cleaning and organizing. This time, I focused on my mom's room. It felt like an essential step, not just for me but for Gary too. I wanted to change the energy of the space, to make it feel different from how he'd last seen it—the haunting image of my mom slumped on the bed, her life taken by an aneurysm. I knew the room had become a source of trauma for him, and I wanted to soften the pain, even if just a little.

I rearranged the furniture, put on fresh sheets, and deep-cleaned the space. I scrubbed the carpet and laid down an area rug to cover lingering stains. Slowly, the room began to feel less like a shrine to tragedy and more like a fresh start. It was a small gesture, but one that carried so much weight.

Then came the drawers and closets. As I opened each drawer, I uncovered pieces of her life that told a story beyond the pain. There were old passports, her nursing certificates, and graduation photos from when she became a nurse. Then, tucked away in a drawer, I found her journals from her rehab days. Leafing through the pages, I could feel her struggle, her hope, her fight. But one discovery stopped me in my tracks—a letter.

It was a letter addressed to me, one she had written but never sent.

It was *the letter I never got.*

June 27th

Dear Rob,

I'm really sorry I let you down. I'm really sorry I let myself down too. I'm very angry and disappointed in myself. I have been doing so well until Tuesday. The problem is I have been overdoing it with activities. I had so much energy. I cleaned the whole house, even the closets and cupboards (except the basement). I spent hours gardening and planted over 200 flowers. I had a friend over several times for dinner and overnight. She helped me clean the upstairs. Then Barry came last week for three days. Then the candle/spa party, which I wanted to cancel, but I had already invited everyone. Laurie, from our meetings (she's wise) said to be careful because I was doing too much, setting my expectations too high and should slow down and relax more. Any kind of stress has the potential to set me back. For the past two months everyone commented on how good I look. My blood pressure is perfect.

I've also been stressed waiting for my drivers license, it's been hard getting rides to meetings. However I have been making it to 3-4 meetings a week. So this was a very short relapse, which is over and will never happen again. A lot of our members have had them. I'm going to talk about myself at the Monday meeting. Everyone will be supportive. I am going to slow down and not have anymore company over and learn different ways to handle stress.

June 29th

I went to the meeting last night. There were 23 people there. I was really nervous but I told them I had relapsed. They were very supportive and said it had happened to them too. They said "keep coming back."

I called my counselor this morning and told her. She was very supportive and didn't put me down. She was proud that I admitted to her and the group. She said I've come a long way. Before I would hide everything and pretend life was perfect. My counsellor at Aurora (rehab center) called me Princess Kathy and said I candy coated everything. Not Anymore!

Beth and I talked about my plan
- Don't take on more than you can handle
- Keep life simple
- Be honest with myself, my counsellor, my sponsor and the group, they are there to support me.
- Attend meetings
- Call if I need help. I have a list of names by my phone

Gary had nothing to do with this. He has been very supportive. He could have left me now but he didn't. I love you so much Rob! I'm really sorry!! My ride's here for my noon meeting so I must go.

Love Mom

I broke down. A wave of emotion flooded over me as I held the letter in my hands. It was too much, too raw. I walked out of the room to cry in private, hoping to compose myself before returning. After a few minutes, I gathered the strength to go back in, but it didn't last long. As I started looking through the drawers again, another wave of grief hit me, this one stronger than the last. I rushed out of the room once more, tears streaming down my face.

From the other room, Rachel called out, "Pull yourself together, you big baby!" Her sarcasm cut through the heaviness, and I couldn't help but laugh. As emotional as it all was, her comment brought a moment of levity, and I kept chuckling at how much I was falling apart.

THE MASK HE MADE, THE MASK I WORE

I've done this dance with my dad for as long as I can remember—the one where I take off the mask, expose my feelings, only to have it forced back on. Ever since I was a child, I'd reached for connection, for acknowledgment, only to be met with indifference, dismissal, or silence. It was a constant chase where my expectations were never met. The pattern was familiar: I'd let my guard down, hoping this time would be different, only to be reminded why I built walls in the first place.

The Mask of Invulnerability is armor—something we wear to shield ourselves from pain, disappointment, or rejection. For years, I had hidden behind it, suppressing emotions and avoiding vulnerability, especially with my dad. It was easier to pretend I didn't care than to risk being dismissed.

I had carried a letter for 10 months, afraid to send it. Afraid of being vulnerable, afraid of what his response—or lack thereof—might mean. For 10 months, I simmered in my feelings, anger and sadness swirling together like a storm I couldn't calm. In that letter, I laid bare the ways his actions had made me feel, hoping for acknowledgment—just once.

Looking back now, I see it clearly: I was wearing the Mask of Invulnerability. I had built emotional walls between us, convinced they would protect me from the hurt that always followed his lack of acknowledgment or emotional support. Vulnerability had come to feel like weakness, as if opening up would only give him more power to hurt me. And I knew why. The mask had its roots in my childhood—where criticism, silence, or distance planted the seeds of self-protection.

When I finally sent the letter, I felt everything at once—fear, relief, vulnerability, and a flicker of hope. It was my attempt to bridge the gap, to say what I had held inside for years. But as I pressed send, the familiar fear returned. What if he ignored it? What if he brushed it aside? Vulnerability felt like a gamble, one where the stakes were my emotional well-being.

His response landed like a punch to the gut. Instead of addressing my pain, he focused on a minor correction—how many times he had messaged me after my mom passed—and then casually suggested dinner.

The anger hit instantly. It wasn't just his words; it was what they represented. Another moment of being unseen, another reminder that my feelings didn't matter to him. I had placed expectations on someone incapable of meeting them, and yet, the rejection still stung. Once again, I felt the pull to retreat behind my mask, to protect myself from further hurt. But the truth was, I was tired. Tired of pretending.

A couple of days later, Wayne and I arrived at Dad's for dinner. I barely spoke. I forced a handshake, avoiding eye contact, feeling like a stranger in my own family. Every moment at the table was a silent battle between my anger and my unspoken longing for connection. I wanted to say something, to call out his dismissal, but the fear of another rejection kept me quiet.

Later, as we rode across the lake on a four-wheeler—my dad on one side, Wayne on the other—I felt trapped. The wind bit at my face, the rumble of the engine filled the silence, but inside, I was screaming. I stared at the ground, letting the mask do what it always did—keep me from breaking down, keep me from saying what I needed to say.

The Mask of Invulnerability convinces you that you're protecting yourself, but in reality, it isolates you. It trades vulnerability for control, connection for self-preservation. That night, I wanted one thing—acknowledgment. Instead, I was left with the same hollow truth: the gap between us wasn't going to close. And yet, for the first time, I saw the mask for what it was. If I wanted to heal, I had to start taking it off.

MOM'S MEMORIAL—SIMPLE YET DEEPLY MEANINGFUL

In the lead-up to Mom's memorial, Wayne was there to help me finish cleaning the house. We cleaned everything, arranged the space, and laid out the details that would make the event special—a memory book, the envelopes filled with Mom's favorite flower seeds, the bookmarks, with her favorite author, Danielle Steel, prominently featured, and the photo collage on the fireplace.

It was a simple day yet deeply meaningful. Seeing the love and laughter in the room reminded me of how much of an impact my mom had on those around her. The memorial wasn't about grand gestures—it was about honoring her spirit, her stories, and the love she left behind.

A NEW CHAPTER, A NEW ME

Two days later, Wayne and I rose early to begin our trip home. The air was crisp, and the morning light cast a soft glow over the house. This was it—goodbye. Years of memories, both joyful and painful, were now being left behind. As we pulled away, I felt the weight of everything that had happened here start to lift, replaced by a bittersweet ache. It wasn't just a goodbye to the house—it was a goodbye to a chapter of my life. This was the end of one story and the beginning of another.

For years, I had been caught in a cycle of trying to protect myself. I wore the Mask of Invulnerability as my shield, thinking it would keep me safe. And in many ways, it did. It kept me from reopening deep emotional wounds; it gave me the strength to carry on, and it helped me stay independent through it all. But it also came at a cost.

The mask created a barrier between me and the people who cared for me. It left me feeling isolated, unable to share my pain, and disconnected from my own emotions. I had convinced myself I was fine when, deep down, I wasn't. Vulnerability felt like weakness, and the thought of exposing that weakness terrified me. But what I've come to realize is that true strength comes from being open, from letting the walls down, from letting others in.

The road ahead was uncertain, but, for the first time, I wasn't trying to control every twist and turn. Instead, I leaned into the discomfort, trusting that this journey would lead to growth. This wasn't just the start of a new chapter—it was the start of a new me. A me who could embrace both the joy and pain of life. A me who could finally shed the mask and step into the light, fully and authentically.

With the car humming beneath us and the sunrise painting the sky, I felt the weight of the past lift a little more. This was an ending, but it was also a beginning. The healing had already begun. And for the first time in a long time, I felt ready to truly let it in.

STEPS TO REMOVE THE MASK OF INVULNERABILITY

The Mask of Invulnerability is an armor many of us wear to protect ourselves from pain, disappointment, or rejection. However, by shielding yourself from vulnerability, you also shut yourself off from the possibility of connection and healing. Only by embracing vulnerability can we begin to shed the mask.

1. **Acknowledge your fears:** Start by recognizing what you're truly afraid of. Is it rejection? Is it appearing weak? Dig deep into the root causes of why you feel the need to protect yourself. Journaling about these fears can be a helpful tool.
2. **Practice vulnerability in safe spaces:** Start small by sharing your emotions with people you trust. It doesn't have to be your deepest fears right away—small steps, like admitting you're having a tough day, can be a starting point for practicing vulnerability.
3. **Reframe vulnerability as strength:** Understand that vulnerability isn't weakness. In fact, it takes incredible courage to be vulnerable. Try to reframe your perspective by thinking of vulnerability as a path to deeper connections and greater emotional health.
4. **Accept that being hurt is part of growth:** No matter how thick your armor, life will present situations that may hurt you. Accepting that pain is part of the human experience can help soften the edges of your emotional armor. True growth happens when we allow ourselves to feel, even when it hurts.
5. **Seek support:** If letting down your guard feels overwhelming, consider seeking help from a therapist, counselor, or even myself. We can provide tools and a safe environment to practice vulnerability without fear of judgment.

REFLECTIONS AND LEARNINGS: THE MASK OF INVULNERABILITY

Practicing Openness

My story: For years, I believed that being vulnerable was a weakness. Whether it was telling others I was struggling after my mom's death or expressing emotions with my father, I hid behind the Mask of Invulnerability. When I finally started to open up—by admitting I wasn't fine—I realized it took far more courage to share my true feelings than to suppress them.

Reflection: Think about a moment when you avoided showing vulnerability. What were you afraid might happen? What might you gain if you allowed yourself to be honest in similar situations?

Exercise: Identify one person in your life you trust. Share something small but personal with them—how you're feeling today, a challenge you've faced, or a memory that's important to you. Notice their response and how it feels to be open.

Sitting with Uncomfortable Emotions

My story: My mom avoided her pain by drowning it in alcohol, and, in some ways, I avoided mine by pretending to be fine. But I learned that real growth comes from sitting with the discomfort. Whether it was grieving Mom's death or confronting my father, facing my pain allowed me to process and move forward.

Reflection: Think of a situation where you've avoided pain or discomfort. How has avoiding it impacted your emotional health or relationships? What might shift if you allowed yourself to sit with the pain?

Exercise: Set aside 10 minutes in a quiet space to sit with an uncomfortable emotion you've been avoiding. Write down how it feels in your body and mind. End the exercise by writing one positive lesson this experience might be teaching you.

Allowing Others to Truly See You

My story: When I opened up to Wayne about my grief, he held me as I cried, and I felt an emotional release I didn't know I needed. These moments reminded me that true connection happens when we allow others to see us as we are—messy, emotional, and human.

Reflection: When was the last time you allowed someone to truly see you? How did they respond? What would it feel like to let someone into your emotional world today?

Exercise: Choose someone close to you and share a story or feeling you've been keeping to yourself. Pay attention to how they respond and how it impacts your relationship. Reflect on the experience in a journal.

Dropping the Facade

My story: Pretending to be fine all the time was draining. I found myself emotionally detached and constantly battling my inner voice that called me a liar. The energy it took to maintain the Mask of Invulnerability came at the cost of my own emotional well-being.

Reflection: Think about a time when you felt exhausted from pretending to be something you're not. What did that feel like? How might your life change if you let go of the need to appear "fine"?

Exercise: Take five minutes to sit quietly and ask yourself, "Where in my life am I pretending to be fine?" Write down your answers, then commit to sharing your honest feelings with one trusted person this week.

Expressing Vulnerability Without Judgment

My story: I spent so long hiding behind the Mask of Invulnerability, avoiding my feelings and the fear of being judged for not having it all together. But I realized that allowing myself to cry, to grieve openly, and to admit I wasn't OK was freeing. Acceptance of my own vulnerability didn't make me weaker—it made me feel lighter, more authentic, and more connected to myself and others.

Reflection: What emotions or parts of yourself have you been hiding behind a mask? How might your life change if you begin to embrace and share them with others?

Exercise: Choose one vulnerable thought or feeling you've been suppressing and write about it in detail. Then, share it with someone you trust or explore how it feels to accept it without judgment. Reflect on how this process impacts your emotional state.

MASK OF VULNERABILITY KEY TAKEAWAYS

- **Vulnerability is a strength, not a weakness:** The courage to show your true emotions fosters deeper connections and authentic relationships,

dismantling the isolation caused by the mask.
- **Suppressing emotions takes a toll:** Over time, hiding your pain or pretending to be "fine" can lead to emotional burnout, numbness, and even physical health issues. Addressing your feelings is necessary for holistic well-being.
- **True growth comes from emotional risk:** Allowing yourself to feel and share difficult emotions—even at the risk of being hurt—opens the door to personal growth, healing, and stronger relationships.
- **Fear of judgment is a barrier, not a reality:** Most people are more accepting of vulnerability than we assume. By letting down your guard, you might find unexpected compassion and support.
- **Authenticity starts with self-acceptance:** Removing the mask begins with acknowledging and embracing your fears, flaws, and emotions. By being honest with yourself first, you pave the way for authentic connections with others.

THE LAST CHAPTER

MOVING
FORWARD

Healing isn't about erasing the past—it's about learning how to carry it. Every step I've taken in recent times has been a lesson in grief, growth, and surrender. This chapter isn't just about closing the book on my past—it's about stepping into the next version of myself with the wisdom I've gained.

TIME

"Healing isn't linear. It's messy, personal, and requires self-compassion."

When I returned to Brisbane, it felt as though everything had aligned for me to start the next chapter of my life fresh and properly, without any burdens holding me down. Even though there was a heaviness from having just lost my mom, there was also a strange sense of weightlessness. My year of healing, my year of firsts, was about to begin. I was starting over from scratch on every level—physically, emotionally, spiritually, and financially.

I'd spent my meagre savings flying back to Canada and organizing Mom's memorial, and my weight had slipped to a beautiful 102 kg, thanks to my emotional eating and enjoyment of margaritas, pizza, and chicken wings.

When you go through something as intense as what I experienced over 10 months—blow after blow—it's hard to believe it won't break you. And for a while, I let it knock me down. I checked out. I stopped trying to fight what the universe was throwing at me. I gave myself full permission to go through whatever I needed to go through over the next few months. I indulged in food, drank more than usual, and sometimes drinking was accompanied by cocaine. It was never excessive—I've never had an addictive bone in my body—but the imbalance of that lifestyle without any physical training or self-care showed on my body.

Shaun, who I was staying with, was patient with me. He let me go through what I needed to, never rushing me. But my weight gain started affecting me deeply. I became so self-conscious that I wasn't even comfortable having my shirt off around him, despite knowing he would never judge me. It wasn't just about how I looked; it was about how I felt. Walking up hills and being out of breath. Struggling to tie my shoes. Clothes not fitting. Going shopping and realizing I was now a size 36 in shorts—it was demoralizing. It sent me further into a cycle of self-pity.

But I kept reminding myself that when I was ready to come out of this *poor me* phase, I would know.

Through all of this, I still surrounded myself with motivation. I flooded my social media with inspirational posts and words of encouragement—the kind that gives you glimmers of hope and reminds you that everything will be OK. And I continued to put out my own content, trying to help others. Some people didn't understand that. They questioned why I wasn't, in their eyes, *grieving properly*. Why was I on social media? Why was I still trying to inspire others? But the truth was, that *was* part of my healing journey.

Knowing that I was still making an impact—even if it was just one person a day—made me feel like I still had purpose. I wasn't avoiding my own journey, but I was choosing who I let in. And if that's not a full-circle moment, I don't know what is.

Time didn't heal me. Time just moved.

What healed me was the decision to sit with my grief, to give myself space, and to eventually choose to rise again.

Healing doesn't happen *to* you—it happens *through* you.

We always hear, "Time heals all wounds," but the truth is, time just gives us the space to decide what we do with our pain. Some people bury it. Some people let it define them. Others use it as fuel.

I chose to sit with it. To feel it. To allow it to shape me, but not break me.

I didn't rush it. I didn't force it. I let it unfold in its own way, on its own timeline.

Because healing isn't a race. There's no finish line. No perfect formula. No right way to move through grief.

There's only your way.

And the moment you stop resisting and start trusting your process—*that's* when healing truly begins.

PAIN

"You can't outrun what you haven't faced."

The funny thing about pain is it has a way of forcing you to feel, whether you want to or not. It doesn't ask for permission. It doesn't wait for the right time. It just *is*. And when you don't face it, when you push it down or try to numb it, it finds another way to show up.

I knew all about pain. I had seen it firsthand in my mom. I watched her for years, trying to escape it—running from her past traumas, burying the weight of what she had been through. The sexual abuse. The loss of two children. The divorces. She drowned it all in alcohol, avoided the hard conversations, changed the subject whenever I tried to discuss her struggles. But where did that get her? Stuck. Consumed. Trapped in a cycle that eventually took her life. She carried so much pain behind that beautiful, kind smile. And I saw it in other family members too—generations of pain being avoided, numbed, or passed down.

Pain has a way of feeling *endless* when you're in it. Like the world is crumbling around you, like there's no way out. It's this overwhelming force, like it's going to swallow you whole. You don't see hope. You don't see light. You just see the pain.

But here's what I learned—**pain doesn't stay the same. It moves.**

It shifts. It changes shape. And the only way through is to let it *move through you.* That means sitting with it. Feeling it. Letting it exist without trying to fight it.

One of the biggest lessons I learned is this: **Pain is inevitable, but suffering is a choice.** Pain is what happens to us. Suffering is what happens when we resist it. As Tony Robbins says, "Change happens when the pain of staying the same is greater than the pain of change." I use this quote often in my coaching work, and it's absolutely true.

My mom suffered because she never let herself *face* her pain. She numbed it, avoided it, hoping it would go away. But the truth is, pain only gets louder when you don't listen. And for my mom, that cycle never ended. So many of us are stuck in situations that are *causing* us pain—whether it be relationships, careers, or our own self-worth—but the fear of facing the truth, of actually *dealing* with it, feels too great.

I could have stayed stuck too. I could have let the weight of those 10 months—of losing my mom, David's mom, Bentley, and Brodie—*consume* me. But I made a different choice. I let myself feel every ounce of it. I let it *break me open.* And in doing so, I realized something: **Pain isn't here to destroy us. It's here to *transform* us.**

Pain makes us stronger. It makes us more resilient. It prepares us for the next challenge life will inevitably throw our way. When I reflect on everything I've been through—the losses, the heartbreaks, the grief—I see how it all led me to this moment. Pain *taught* me how to rise. It knocked me down, but it also showed me that I could get back up. Again and again and again.

Many of us see pain as something to fear, something to avoid at all costs. But what if we view it differently? What if we see pain as a *teacher*—something that reveals where we need to heal, something that strips away what we thought we needed and forces us to rebuild from the ground up? What if we look at pain as an *opportunity* for growth? Instead of seeing it as a never-ending cycle of hurt, what if we recognize that pain, no matter how heavy, always has a light at the other end?

Because what I've learned going through my journey is—**when you stop fighting it, stop fearing it, and start *listening* to it, pain has the power to set you free.**

STRENGTH

"True strength isn't holding it all together—it's having the courage to be real."

Strength isn't just about physical endurance or pushing through challenges—it's about the resilience to stand back up after being knocked down, again and again. It's about redefining what strength *actually* means.

For the longest time, I thought strength meant not breaking, not showing weakness, and being the person who had it all together. But after everything I'd been through—the loss, the setbacks, the moments where I truly felt like I had nothing left—I realized that real strength isn't about holding it all in. It's about choosing to keep going *even when you feel broken.* Strength is allowing yourself to sit with the pain without letting it consume you. It's looking in the mirror and deciding, *I'm not done yet.*

The Power of the High Five

A massive shift occurred for me when I read Mel Robbins's *The High 5 Habit*. I devoured the entire book in two days, and I've since recommended it to many of my clients who were feeling stuck or in a tough place. The book dives deep into understanding the universal language of the high five—how we spend most of our lives cheering others on, supporting friends, teammates, coworkers, and even strangers with a simple high five. *"Way to go." "Well done." "Keep going."* We do it in schools, workplaces, sports, and everyday life. It's a universal gesture of encouragement. But how often do we *high-five ourselves*? Not often—if at all.

At first, I brushed off the idea of high-fiving myself in the mirror. It sounded silly. But as Mel explained the psychology behind it, sharing her personal stories, I started connecting on so many levels. It forced me to take a good look at myself—not at the physical things I'd been fixated on, like my weight or the changes in my body, but *at the person standing there.*

The Science Behind the High Five Habit

What makes this practice so powerful isn't just the action itself—it's the way our brains respond to it. Mel Robbins explains that when we raise our hand for a high five, the brain *automatically* associates it with positivity, celebration, and encouragement. This is because, throughout our lives, we've been conditioned to view a high five as a positive reinforcement. Whether it was on the sports field, in a classroom, or at work, a high five was always connected to success, support, and camaraderie.[16]

When we give ourselves a high five in the mirror, we're *rewiring* our brains to direct that same level of encouragement and support inward. Even if, in that moment, we don't believe in ourselves, the physical action alone triggers our brain to release dopamine—the "feel-good" hormone. This isn't just self-help talk; it's backed by neuroscience. Studies show that positive reinforcement and celebratory gestures activate the brain's reward system, helping to shift our mindset and boost resilience.[17]

There's also the mirror effect: when you look into your own eyes and acknowledge yourself, you create a *moment of connection* with yourself. So many of us, especially in moments of struggle, look in the mirror with self-judgment. We criticize our bodies, our failures, or what we think we lack. But this practice flips that. It forces you to see yourself with compassion.

My Experience with the High Five Habit

In her book, Mel takes you through an exercise: You stand in front of the mirror and really *see* yourself. Not just your exterior. Not just the imperfections. You look into your own eyes, acknowledging everything you've been through, all the battles you've fought, and the fact that you're still here. It's about recognizing your victories, the milestones, and the obstacles you've overcome. And then, you raise your hand and give yourself a high five, saying out loud: "Keep going. You've got this. Here's to another great day."

I won't lie—the first time I did it, I cried. Standing there, looking at myself, remembering the past 10 months, remembering all the grief, the setbacks, the moments where I felt like I had nothing left—it all came flooding in. Tears rolled down my face as I processed the weight of it all. But then, as I lifted my hand to give myself that high five, something shifted. It was as if I was finally telling myself, *I see you. I'm proud of you. You're still standing.*

That moment was the push I needed to take back control of my life. It was time to stop feeling sorry for myself. Time to stop letting my health spiral. Time to rebuild—not because I hated where I was, but because I *deserved* to feel better. My time of sitting on the couch, indulging in chicken wings and pizza, had served its purpose—it was a part of my healing. But now, it was time for change.

Redefining Strength

Strength isn't about never falling. It's about deciding to get back up. And for me, that high five was the first step.

So often, we think of strength as pushing through pain, as never showing weakness, as handling everything alone. But real strength is in allowing yourself to *be human*. It's in acknowledging your struggles without letting them define you. It's in choosing to keep moving forward, even when the weight of the world is on your shoulders.

As my own experience demonstrates, strength isn't something you're born with—it's something you *build*. And sometimes, it starts with something as small as looking at yourself in the mirror and saying, *I believe in you.*

PEOPLE

"The right ones will lift you. The wrong ones will weigh you down."
I used to really struggle with breaking a connection with someone because I valued relationships and connections so much—so much that I would sacrifice my own emotional and mental well-being just

to maintain them. But as I learned to value myself more and worked on my own growth, I became more aware of the energies I wanted near me and the ones I didn't. Learning to remove certain people—whether temporarily or permanently—wasn't easy. At first, there was resistance. It was a muscle I had to develop. But over time, it got easier. And with each person or energy I let go of, I created more space for myself—for my healing, my peace, and whatever journey I was on.

If there's one thing this journey has crystallized for me, it's that who you surround yourself with *matters*.

As I moved through my healing journey, I came to understand that people come and go. Relationships can unexpectedly grow out of hard times, and some will end because of them. I learned to view friendships differently—to adjust my expectations of people, to recognize that not everyone is capable of showing up in the way I would—and that's OK. I stopped expecting certain friendships to be something they weren't and instead accepted them for what they *could* be. And in doing that, I found more peace.

Some people will call it cutting people off. I call it *protecting my peace*.

> **We outgrow people. We evolve. We recognize when certain relationships no longer align with who we are or where we're headed. And that's not something to be afraid of—it's something to embrace.**

The people who are meant for you, the ones who truly *see* you, will always be there. And the ones who aren't? Letting them go is just another way of making space for something better.

CONTROL

"Letting go is where freedom begins."

Control was something I had clung to for most of my life. Whether it was managing my mom's recovery, throwing away Gary's alcohol, or trying to force my dad to acknowledge my pain—I had convinced myself that if I could just control things enough, I could prevent bad things from happening.

I saw it clearly in how I structured my life. The way I planned my future in Australia around my visa, meticulously crafting every step to ensure I wouldn't have to leave. The way I wrote and rewrote that email to Pete, believing that if I said the right words, I could control the outcome. The way I held on so tightly to the fantasy of my family being different, of my dad finally showing up in the way I needed him to.

But the thing about control is, it's an illusion.

No matter how hard I tried, I **couldn't control** my mom's choices. I **couldn't control** how Pete would respond. I **couldn't control** my father's ability to give me the emotional validation I craved. And the tighter I held on, the more I felt everything slipping through my fingers.

At one point, I had to face it—**my need for control wasn't about strength, it was about fear.**

Fear of loss. Fear of pain. Fear of things not going the way I needed them to.

And the irony? The more I tried to control things, the more out of control I felt. I exhausted myself trying to control the uncontrollable.

Remember, **flow, not force.**

I took this lesson so deeply to heart that I had it tattooed on my body.

I wanted the reminder etched into my skin—a symbol of surrender, of trust, of allowing life to unfold without constantly trying to manipulate it. The tattoo represents everything I've learned about control: **when you force things, they break. But when you flow with life, things have a way of working out.**

The moment I let go, things started falling into place in ways I never expected.

Life moves whether we try to control it or not. The question is, are we going to exhaust ourselves fighting the current, or are we going to let go and trust that we'll find our way?

WORDS

"The way you speak to yourself matters."

The way we speak to ourselves can either build us up or tear us down. After my mom passed, I found myself falling into a loop of self-criticism. The weight gain became my focus, and the words I spoke to myself were brutal. *You've let yourself go. You look disgusting. How did you get here?*

The thing is, our subconscious mind doesn't argue with us. It simply listens and absorbs. When you tell yourself something enough times, you start to believe it, and then it starts to shape your actions.

That's why words matter.

To change my mindset, I had to make a conscious shift. I had to stop tearing myself down and start reframing my thoughts. Not in a delusional way—not by pretending everything was fine when it wasn't—but by recognizing that the words I chose could either pull me further into despair or help me find my way out.

The Power of Reframing

Neuro-linguistic programming (NLP) teaches us that how we frame an experience determines how we feel about it and how we respond to it. I had unknowingly been doing this when I told myself, *This will be hard, but you'll be OK* when my mom passed away. That's an example of a *presupposition*—a technique where you phrase something in a way that assumes a positive outcome.

Another powerful NLP tool is **reframing**—the ability to shift the meaning of an experience by looking at it from a different angle. Here's an example:

- Instead of, *I've let myself go,* I started saying, *I gave myself permission to grieve in the way I needed to. Now, I get to rebuild with intention.*
- Instead of, *Look at these back rolls, I've let myself go,* I told myself, *My body has carried me through the hardest year of my life—now, I get to take care of it with love, not punishment.*

Reframing isn't about lying to yourself. It's about shifting your focus so you don't get trapped in a narrative that keeps you stuck.

The words we choose shape our reality. We can use them to bury ourselves in shame and limitation, or we can use them to create the path forward.

FORGIVENESS

"It's not about them. It's about you."

I spent years **waiting for an apology** from my dad.

Years hoping for Pete to **give me closure.**

Years **wishing my mom had chosen differently.**

Forgiveness didn't come easy. I was holding on to so much anger and sadness—not just toward my family, but also toward people I once considered friends. Betrayal from those I trusted cut deep, and the feeling of being let down by the people I love is something I've never handled well.

As my journey back to health began, I started with the physical. I lost 20 kg, focused on my mental and emotional health, and got my body back on track. But I knew that wasn't enough. The emotional weight I was carrying—the resentment, the hurt, the disappointment—was still there, dragging me down. Forgiveness was the next step, but I wasn't ready.

After Mom's memorial, I didn't speak to my dad for at least two years. The anger I felt toward him was still fresh, still consuming me. I couldn't have him in my life—it was that simple.

At first, the separation worked. But as time passed, as the second year crept in, I felt it all bubbling back up. The emotions I had buried—the sadness, the resentment, the disappointment—started showing up in different ways.

> **That's the funny thing about emotions we refuse to deal with. They don't just disappear. They linger, waiting for the cracks in our armor. And when they find them, they seep through.**

The unresolved pain between Dad and me, and even with some other family members, wouldn't let me go. I found myself longing for the relationship I wished I had with them, grieving the fantasy family I had always chased.

And it wasn't just sadness. The anger was still there too. Every time I thought about the past—about his absence, his dismissiveness, the way he brushed off my emotions—it fueled the fire inside me. I was stuck in a loop. It was affecting my energy, my work, and my personal life. I wasn't my usual self. I was moody, short-tempered, and completely disconnected from my creative side. Even my ability to inspire others felt drained.

I needed help.

One of my brilliant mentors and coaches, Jo, was guiding me and a group of other students through our Master NLP training. I had only met Jo a week before our training, but she already saw straight through me. She could read me like a book, pinpointing exactly what I needed to work through.

She had this gift—the ability to challenge you, to flip your perspective in ways that forced you to look inward instead of outward. I'd approach her like a lost puppy, desperate for guidance, saying, "Jo, I need help. I don't know how to deal with this."

And every time, she'd give me the same response: "Yes, in time, we'll work through it."

She never rushed me. She never let me off the hook either. She knew that real change wouldn't happen just because I wanted it to. I had to *do the work*.

I didn't know what was about to hit me.

As we went deeper into our NLP training, emotions began to

surface. I wasn't the only one—tears flowed all around the room as we all faced our own battles. But then came the day I hit a wall.

I was paired with a partner to go through a particular technique. But I wasn't connecting with it. There was a block. That's when Jo recognized that what I really needed was *Timeline Therapy*.

Timeline Therapy is a technique that helps you deal with deeply embedded emotions, guiding you back to the root cause—the moment in your subconscious where those emotions first took hold. It's about identifying when that emotion *began*, whether that was in childhood, in the womb, or even generationally passed down. Once you find that root, you can process it, understand its purpose, and finally release it.

My partner, though well-meaning, was rusty. As he tried guiding me through, I felt frustrated. I wanted it done *right*. I kept snapping back into coaching mode, critiquing his delivery in my head rather than allowing myself to be the client. At a certain point, I just started making up answers to move the process along, pretending it was working.

But it wasn't.

I left the room feeling worse than before, frustrated and angry. I pulled one of the assistant coaches aside and told her my partner needed more practice. She looked at me and asked, "Were you in client mode or coaching mode?"

I knew the answer.

When I walked back into the room, Jo took one look at me and said, "You're angry. Good."

"It didn't work," I muttered.

She didn't react with sympathy. She didn't coddle me. Instead, she handed me a piece of paper with *three more emotions* she had added to my list—fear, shame, and guilt.

"Sit down and do it again."

She got right in my face, her finger pointed straight at me.

"I'm not here to fucking save you, Rob. No one is. It's not anyone else's responsibility to do this work for you. If you want to change, you need to make it happen."

Tears started rolling down my face.

She was breaking me, but, in all truth, I *needed* to be broken. I needed that tough love, that no-bullshit approach. I had been waiting for someone to fix me, but Jo wasn't going to let me take the easy way out.

We started again. This time, I was fully in it.

Facing the Root of My Pain

When you go through Timeline Therapy, your subconscious takes you back to your earliest memory of the emotion you're exploring.

The first stop was *anger*. My subconscious took me straight back to my dad. I was five years old.

I don't even remember what he did in that moment, but I remember the feeling. That small, helpless, powerless boy who was absorbing everything—his father's energy, his absence, his presence that felt more like a storm than a shelter.

That anger had never left me. It had just grown, layer by layer, building up over the years. It had turned into resentment, into expectations unmet, into disappointments that stacked upon each other like bricks in a wall.

I sat there, floating above my five-year-old self, watching the scene play out.

And then I was guided to step further back—to view it not just as a son, but as an observer. And that's when the shift began.

Because I saw him differently.

For the first time, I didn't just see *my dad*. I saw *a man*. A flawed, wounded man who had his own traumas, his own upbringing that shaped him into who he became.

He wasn't just *my dad who let me down*. He was *a human being who didn't have the tools to show up the way I needed him to*.

That didn't erase the anger. But it loosened its grip. Because when you see someone as a whole person rather than just the role they played in *your* life, something changes.

I let go of some of that anger. And in its place, something unexpected crept in: *compassion*.

As I released the anger, something shifted. And then, the sadness hit. I broke down, sobbing uncontrollably. I must have sat there for 10 minutes, my face buried in my hands. The sadness wasn't just about my dad. It was about *everything*. My mom. The pain she carried. The losses she endured. The relationships I had longed for that never materialized. The childhood wounds I had buried so deep I didn't even recognize them as wounds anymore.

For sadness, shame, and guilt, my subconscious took me somewhere I never expected.

I was in a hospital room. My mom was making the hardest decision of her life—choosing not to keep her six-month premature baby. I wasn't even born yet. But I was there, in that room, reliving her pain, her grief, her sadness. And not just once—both times she had to make that decision, my subconscious took me there. This was *her* trauma. *Her* pain. Pain she never worked through. And somehow, I had been carrying it, long before I even took my first breath.

As my partner guided me through, I kept going, layer by layer. Next came *guilt*. And shame wasn't far behind.

My subconscious mind took me back to that same hospital room. I watched my mom lying in her hospital bed, lying in a space meant for healing, yet carrying her own silent wounds. She was making the hardest decision of her life. And even though I wasn't born yet, I *felt* her torment, her heartbreak, her impossible choice, and perhaps my father's too

For years, I had unknowingly held on to that guilt as if it were my own. But in that moment, hovering above it, I saw it differently. She wasn't a failure. She wasn't broken. She wasn't weak. She was *doing the best she could with the tools she had*. She was making the right choice—the only choice she could make at the time. And that realization lifted the weight I didn't even know I had been carrying. I had spent so much of my life trying to fix things, trying to control outcomes, trying to save people from their own pain—especially my mom. But in that moment, I saw the truth: *it was never my responsibility to save her*. I could love her. I could support her. But I could never carry her pain for her. And just like that, I let go of the guilt. I let go of the shame. I let go of the idea that I needed to hold on to it all.

By the time I had gone through every emotion—three hours later—I was exhausted. But something was different. Something had *shifted*. There was no more anger associated with the thought of my dad. For two years, I had carried it. Let it fuel me. Let it dictate my emotions, my reactions, my expectations. I had held on to it like armor, believing that if I let go, it would mean I was excusing him, letting him off the hook for everything he did or didn't do. But in that chair, after going through *everything*, I realized something.

It wasn't about him anymore.

It was about *me*.

I didn't need his apology to move forward. I didn't need him to acknowledge the pain he had caused for me to heal. Because I had done the work. *I* had acknowledged it. *I* had sat with it. *I* had faced it head-on. And in doing so, I had taken away its power over me. There was no more anger. Just peace. And *that* was the real forgiveness. It wasn't a conversation. It wasn't a moment of closure where everything was tied up neatly with a bow. It was an *internal shift*.

> **I finally understood—the past wasn't something I had to keep dragging with me. It was something to learn from, not live in.**

And the biggest lesson of all?

Forgiveness isn't for them—it's for you.

It doesn't mean forgetting. It doesn't mean excusing. It means releasing yourself from the weight of what was. And for the first time, I was truly free. Free to move forward without resentment anchoring me. Free to let go of the anger that had kept me in a cycle of pain. Free to create space for something new—peace, healing, and maybe even reconnection.

Because in the end, forgiveness wasn't about rewriting the past. It was about reclaiming my future.

GROWTH

"Every challenge prepares you for the next."

As I wrote this book and reflected on my past—on all the masks I've worn, the relationships I've encountered, the highs and the lows—it allowed me to see the lessons that came from each and every experience. Every obstacle, every heartbreak, every moment of grief—they weren't just roadblocks. They were lessons. They shaped me, strengthened me, and forced me to grow in ways I could never have imagined.

Even though I didn't consciously start my true self-development journey until 2018, the growth I've experienced since then has been immense. I've pushed myself to do better, to be better, and to show up as a better human for those around me. I'm not perfect, nor do I ever plan to be, but I continue to do the work.

But growth isn't comfortable. In fact, it's painful. It requires sitting in the discomfort, staring at yourself in the mirror, and asking, *Who do I want to become? How do I want to show up in this world?*

While writing this book, I read *Emotional Repatterning* by Lisa Samet, and one chapter stayed with me—the chapter on gifts. It explores how the universe sends us gifts in the form of lessons, often wrapped in difficult experiences.[18] This resonated deeply with me because, as I reflected on the masks we wear, I realized that the masks themselves are also gifts.

What if we looked at the masks not just as shields, but as mirrors? They show us where we hurt, where we need healing, and where we can grow. They reflect each challenge we've faced, each heartbreak we've endured. They're the universe's way of gifting us a lesson, asking us to unwrap it with curiosity and courage.

Of course, these gifts aren't always easy to receive. Sometimes they come disguised as pain, disappointment, or loss. They challenge us, frustrate us, even break us. But as I've learned, it's often the hardest lessons that hold the greatest gifts. The masks we wear may protect us for a time, but they also teach us where we've been, where we are now, and where we have the potential to go.

For much of my life, I was caught between two illusions—the past I wished had been different and the future I hoped would finally bring me love, acknowledgment, or closure. I spent years chasing fantasy futures in my family and relationships, believing that if I just said the right thing, did enough, or waited long enough, things would change.

The future with Pete never came, and I made peace with that. There was a time I held on to hope that love could rewrite the ending, but some futures aren't meant to be lived—they're lessons, not destinations. Letting go freed me.

With my dad, hope still lingers. Maybe it always will. Despite the distance, there's a part of me that believes in the possibility of something more. But hope doesn't mean waiting. I can hold it while living fully, without being stuck in unmet expectations.

The truth is, growth isn't about waiting for something outside of you to change. It's found in surrender—accepting that some people will never give you the closure you seek, that some relationships won't become what you hoped. Real growth asks you to be here, now, in the present—where healing happens. It means accepting relationships for what they are, rather than focusing on what they aren't. Because when you're always looking behind you or too far ahead, you miss the life unfolding right in front of you. When we're ready to look beyond the surface, to face the lessons and the truths hidden behind the masks, we can see them for what they truly are—opportunities for growth, resilience, and transformation. And when we unwrap these gifts, we can begin to shed the masks that no longer serve us, stepping closer to the most authentic version of ourselves.

The deeper I dove into my healing, the more I realized—growth doesn't come from clinging to what was. It comes from stepping into what *could be*. Growth is a never-ending journey. When you stop growing, you stop *living*. It's not something you reach and check off a list—it's an ongoing process, a commitment to becoming more than you were yesterday. And that commitment? It takes courage.

Because real growth demands that you let go.

Let go of the past versions of yourself that you've outgrown.

Let go of the stories that kept you small.

Let go of the pain that shaped you but no longer needs to define you.

It means stepping into the unknown, into discomfort, into the spaces that stretch you. It means walking forward even when you don't have all the answers. It means accepting that you'll stumble, that you'll question yourself, that, at times, you'll wonder if you're even making progress at all.

But growth isn't linear. It's messy. It's uncomfortable. And it doesn't always come with immediate rewards. But every time you choose to push forward instead of retreating, every time you choose to do the work instead of avoiding it, you're expanding. You're evolving. And one day, you'll look back and see just how far you've come.

The masks we wear serve a purpose. They're there when we need them. But they're not meant to stay on forever. It's up to us to recognize when they no longer serve us, when they become unhealthy, when they start suffocating our authenticity, damaging our relationships, or limiting our potential.

Growth isn't just about surviving your past.

It's about *thriving* in your future.

It's about giving yourself permission to *become*.

Because you're not who you were.

And you're not yet who you will be.

But every step forward, every challenge faced, every layer shed—brings you closer.

FINAL MESSAGE

Healing doesn't mean erasing the past. It means learning how to carry it differently.

I won't ever "move on" from my mom's passing. I won't ever "forget" the lessons of this journey. But I've grown, healed, and stepped into a new version of myself. And as I stand here now, reflecting on everything—the pain, the love, the loss, the growth—I see it for what it truly is: a transformation.

Every piece of my story, every mask I once wore, every challenge that pushed me to my limits—it all brought me here. And now, as I step forward, I do so knowing this:

- ✓ Control is an illusion—trust the process.
- ✓ Vulnerability isn't weakness—it's strength.
- ✓ The right people will love you as you are.
- ✓ Forgiveness sets you free.
- ✓ Healing is lifelong.

But most importantly—I'm still here. Still growing. Still becoming. And that? That's enough.

THE NEXT STEP OF YOUR JOURNEY

This isn't just my story. It's all of ours. The masks we wear, the pain we carry, the growth we fight for—it's a universal journey.

So now, I ask you: **where are you in your journey?**

Are you holding on to something that no longer serves you?

Are you stuck in a cycle, afraid to let go?

Are you ready to take the first step toward healing, growth, and stepping into who you're meant to be?

If this journey has resonated with you, if you see yourself somewhere in these pages, I encourage you to take a moment for yourself. Journal. Reflect. Have the conversations you've been avoiding. Take off the mask you've been hiding behind.

And if you're ready for guidance, for support, for a space where you don't have to do it alone—**reach out**.

Your next chapter starts when you decide to write it.

Are you ready?

ACKNOWLEDGEMENTS

Looking back on life, it's easy to focus on the traumas and challenges—the struggles that life threw my way, the pain inflicted by family, or the hardships I faced alone. It would be simple to dwell on blame, to point fingers at circumstances or people. But the truth is, every experience, every relationship, and every interaction has shaped me into the person I am today. Without them, I wouldn't have the understanding, resilience, or perspective I now hold.

Writing this book has been a three-year journey—one that began with a simple intention: to share my struggles, to make sense of the hardships, and to highlight the growth that emerged from them. But through this process, it has become so much more. It has been a journey of reflection, of uncovering patterns, and of seeing my life in ways I had never fully understood before. Revisiting some of the darkest times was painful; there were moments I had to step away because the emotions were still too raw, the memories too vivid. At times, the mental and emotional exhaustion felt overwhelming. Yet, within those moments of hardship, I also rediscovered some of the most beautiful times of my life—my greatest achievements, cherished memories, and the moments that shaped me in profound ways.

For that, I say thank you—to every person who has been a part of my life, in any capacity. Every interaction, whether fleeting or long-lasting, has contributed to my growth and my understanding of myself.

Writing this book, *Behind the Smile*, has been one of the most transformative and humbling experiences of my life. It has required me to dig deep, revisit old wounds, and find the courage to share stories I once kept hidden. This journey would not have been possible without the support, encouragement, and love of so many incredible individuals.

I want to start by thanking my parents. My mom, despite facing her own battles and demons, never stopped being a source of love and kindness. Her struggles did not define her; rather, she showed me what resilience looks like in the face of adversity. She taught me the importance of empathy, of showing up for others even when you're struggling yourself. Mom, your love never wavered, and that is something I will always carry with me.

To my dad, our relationship wasn't always easy, but through the challenges, you taught me invaluable lessons. You shaped me into the man I am today—strong, reliable, adaptable, and determined. You instilled in me the importance of perseverance, of pushing forward even when the road is unclear. Thank you for the ways you showed up, for the lessons that have helped me navigate life's challenges.

To my uncle Dave, you have been my rock through thick and thin. You stepped in when I needed support the most, offering wisdom, guidance, and a space where I could simply be myself. You have been more than an uncle—you have been my best friend, my mentor, and my greatest supporter. Thank you for always being there, for the countless conversations, and for reminding me that I was never truly alone in this journey.

To my sisters, thank you for challenging me, questioning my actions, and allowing me to see different perspectives. Your presence in my life has been invaluable. Through our disagreements, our laughter, and our shared experiences, you have taught me patience, understanding, and the importance of family. You have been my sounding board, my source of wisdom, and my reminder that I am never alone in this journey. I appreciate your unwavering support and love more than words can express.

Wayne and David, my past partners—you both played significant roles in my life during times of immense change and growth. Your support was not just about standing by me in difficult moments; it was the way you uplifted me, challenged me, and provided comfort when I needed it most. You were there during some of the hardest and most transformative periods of my life, offering patience, understanding, and care. Your willingness to help shoulder the burden of caregiving for my mother, as well as your unwavering encouragement through my personal struggles, will always hold a special place in my heart. I am forever grateful for the impact you had on my journey and the lessons we shared along the way.

To my friends, who have come in and out of my life through different stages of my journey, our interactions—whether brief or ongoing—have left an impact. To those who stood by me through some of the toughest times, offering a shoulder to lean on, a listening ear, or simply their presence when words failed, I am forever grateful.

Your support carried me through moments of deep struggle, and your belief in me gave me strength when I needed it most. Thank you for being there in the darkness and celebrating with me in the light. To those who saw through my masks and still offered me a safe space to be myself, thank you for your understanding, your compassion, and for sharing countless moments of joy. No interaction has ever gone unnoticed or unappreciated.

To my clients, whom I've had the pleasure of working with over the last 10 years in my health and wellness journey, thank you for trusting me with your experiences. Each of your stories has allowed me to grow, gain knowledge, and gain experience in what I do today. Working with you has been fun, insightful, and challenging—whether it was making you do ridiculous workouts in the park, listening to your personal stories during a massage, or helping you break through personal barriers. Witnessing your transformations has fueled the fire in me to continue walking this path.

To those who have followed me on social media throughout my journey, even though we may have never met in person, I extend my deepest gratitude. You have supported me through thick and thin, even when those closest to me did not. You have seen my darkest times and my best moments through what I've shared, and you have continued to show your unwavering support.

To my mentors and coaches, who have shared their knowledge, challenged me to think outside the box, and picked me up when life knocked me down, thank you. Your wisdom has been a guiding force in my journey, pushing me to dig deeper, confront my fears, and embrace my potential. Each of you has played a crucial role in shaping not just my career, but my personal growth as well. Your unwavering support and belief in me have been instrumental in moments when I doubted myself. Whether through powerful conversations, thought-provoking lessons, or simply leading by example, you have shown me the power of resilience, adaptability, and purpose. I am eternally grateful for your guidance, your encouragement, and the invaluable lessons that continue to shape my path.

And a heartfelt thank you to my editors and publishing team at Dean Publishing. From the very beginning, you saw the vision for this book and helped shape it into what it is today. Your guidance, insight, and patience through the countless drafts and revisions have been invaluable. You not only helped refine my words but also provided me with the support and encouragement to keep going when the process felt overwhelming. The dedication and passion you bring to your craft have made this journey not just possible but deeply fulfilling. Thank you for believing in me and in this story, for your unwavering commitment, and for being partners in bringing this book to life.

Lastly, to every reader who picks up this book—thank you. Thank you for your curiosity, your willingness to explore vulnerability, and your openness to peeling back your own masks. My hope is that these pages provide you with comfort, insight, and perhaps the permission to embrace your true self. This book is for all of us who have worn masks to protect or hide. Together, may we find the courage to take them off when needed and step into the light.

In Loving Memory ...

ABOUT THE AUTHOR

Rob Goddard is an author, Master NLP Practitioner, and Life Coach, as well as a health and wellness advocate with over a decade of experience in coaching, bodywork, and personal development.

As the founder of Lifting Stones Coaching, he specializes in helping individuals shed emotional masks and navigate major life transitions, including career shifts, relationships, or stepping into a new chapter of self-discovery. Through hard-earned wisdom and psychological insights, he empowers individuals to break free from limiting patterns and beliefs, achieve personal breakthroughs, and embrace their authentic selves.

Beyond coaching, Rob finds inspiration in nature, thrives on deep conversations, and is committed to continuous learning and growth—both for himself and those he guides.

www.liftingstones.com.au

TESTIMONIALS

"I developed a clearer sense of purpose and direction, enabling me to make informed decisions aligned with my values."
Wayne D., VP

"I've emerged much stronger with a true sense of freedom. I'm living my life authentically with such clarity, purpose and intention now."
Ted R., Creative Director

"I thought I knew myself inside and out before working with Rob, but I soon realised there was still much to discover about the elements driving my daily decisions, career choices, fears, and joys."
Nicholas T., Scientist

"My experience with Rob, a personal coach, has been transformative. He helped me move beyond excuses and inaction, placing me on a trajectory towards the next phase of my life. Instead of merely talking or dreaming about the future, I'm now taking concrete steps towards meaningful change."
Craig L., HR

"Working with Rob, we delved deeper to uncover the origins of my behaviours and insecurities. We explored past traumas and negative experiences and by shifting my perspective, I developed a deeper understanding of the multi facets of every situation."
Craig S., Executive Director

"Over the past 12 weeks, working with Rob transformed my life. This collaboration bolstered my confidence, helping me counter negative self-talk and perceive challenges in a fresh light. This new perspective enabled me to take risks, like attending an event I'd previously avoided and initiating more candid conversations with my partner."

Corey M., Teacher

"Working with Rob has been nothing short of amazing. Despite my initial doubts, I felt an immediate connection with him. His attentive listening and understanding provided a safe space for me to open up and grow. This coaching journey has set me on a path of self-discovery and growth that I feel will benefit me for the rest of my life."

John H., Retiree

"Rob has helped me tremendously. I've been getting my life together and learning how to save money, how to make more money and I'm about to go into a medical assistant program this fall which I'm excited about."

Steve S., Nurse

"Rob was flexible around my schedule and was able to not only help with pinpointing my longer term goals but also identify why I was having struggles both articulating and achieving them."

Matt P., HR

"Through Rob's guidance, I learned tools and techniques that not only allowed me to rise above negativity but also to value myself more. The pivotal shift was realizing that it's crucial to surround myself with positive influences, a change that took years but was achieved with Rob's help."

Kel K., Nurse

"Rob made me feel comfortable from day one, and I never felt like I was being judged throughout our time working together. It was great having Rob provide me with an objective and sincere perspective on what my issues were (and are—as I am still working on bettering myself) and he was able to really help me dig deep to get to the root cause of many of my problems."

Maurice, Physio

"Rob's unique blend of empathy, insight and practical advice helped me navigate some very challenging experiences and guide me into a new phase of my life. Rob is very gifted and has an incredible ability to listen deeply, ask the right questions and provide guidance that is both profound and actionable."

Scott B., Real Estate Agent

ENDNOTES

1 McLeod, Saul. 2024. "John Bowlby's Attachment Theory." *Simply Psychology*, January 24. https://www.simplypsychology.org/bowlby.html.

2 Wong, Y. J., A. J. Horn, and S. Chen. 2013. "Perceived Masculinity: The Potential Influence of Race, Racial Essentialist Beliefs, and Stereotypes." *Psychology of Men & Masculinity* 14 (4): 452–464. https://doi.org/10.1037/a0030100.

3 Cherry, Kendra. 2023. "The Asch Conformity Experiments." *Verywell Mind*, November 13. https://www.verywellmind.com/the-asch-conformity-experiments-2794996.

4 Listening Partnerships. n.d. "About the Drama Triangle – And How to Escape It." Accessed May 5, 2025. https://www.listeningpartnership.com/insight/about-the-drama-triangle-and-how-to-escape-it/.

5 Center for the Empowerment Dynamic. n.d. "About the Empowerment Dynamic." Accessed May 5, 2025. https://theempowermentdynamic.com/about/.

6 Center for the Empowerment Dynamic. n.d. "About the Empowerment Dynamic." Accessed May 5, 2025. https://theempowermentdynamic.com/about/.

7 Dariotis, Jacinda K., Francis R. Chen, Ye Rang Park, Montana K. Nowak, Katherine M. French, and Anisa M. Codamon. 2023. "Parentification Vulnerability, Reactivity, Resilience, and Thriving: A Mixed Methods Systematic Literature Review." *International Journal of Environmental Research and Public Health* 20 (13): 6197. https://doi.org/10.3390/ijerph20136197.

8 Fang, Siqi, Man Cheung Chung, and Yabing Wang. 2020. "The Impact of Past Trauma on Psychological Distress: The Roles of Defense Mechanisms and Alexithymia." *Frontiers in Psychology* 11. https://doi.org/10.3389/fpsyg.2020.00992.

9 Shetty, Jay. 2019. "True Friends and True Love by Jay Shetty." Ashrafz Etiwh. June 4. https://youtu.be/lYySH-N_O1w.

10 Newport Institute. n.d. "What Is Hyper-Independence Trauma in Young Adults?" Accessed February 25, 2025. https://www.newportinstitute.com/resources/mental-health/hyper-independence-trauma/.

11 Mills, Candice M. and Frank C. Keil. 2005. "The Development

of Cynicism." *Psychological Science* 16 (5): 385–390. https://doi.org/10.1111/j.0956-7976.2005.01545.x.

12. Australian Bureau of Statistics. 2016. "Personal Safety, Australia." Accessed February 27, 2025. https://www.abs.gov.au/statistics/people/crime-and-justice/personal-safety-australia/2016.

13. Accountemps. 2014. "Survey: More Than Half of Employees Have Worked for a Micromanager." *PR Newswire*. Published July 1. https://www.prnewswire.com/news-releases/survey-more-than-half-of-employees-have-worked-for-a-micromanager-265359491.html.

14. Springer, Kirsten W. and Dawne M. Mouzon. 2011. "'Macho Men' and Preventive Health Care: Implications for Older Men in Different Social Classes." *Journal of Health and Social Behavior* 52 (2): 212–227. https://doi.org/10.1177/0022146510393972.

15. NBC News. 2024. "Michael Phelps Reflects on Depression and Mental Health: 'I Saw It as a Sign of Weakness.'" Published May 10. https://www.nbcnews.com/meet-the-press/video/michael-phelps-reflects-on-depression-and-mental-health-i-saw-it-as-a-sign-of-weakness-210641477876.

16. Robbins, Mel. 2021. *The High 5 Habit: Take Control of Your Life with One Simple Habit*. London: Hay House UK.

17. Morris, Bradley J. and Shannon R. Zentall. 2014. "High Fives Motivate: The Effects of Gestural and Ambiguous Verbal Praise on Motivation." *Frontiers in Psychology* 5 (August). https://doi.org/10.3389/fpsyg.2014.00928; Ladouceur, Cecile D., Michael W. Schlund, and Anna-Maria Segreti. 2018. "Positive Reinforcement Modulates Fronto-Limbic Systems Subserving Emotional Interference in Adolescents." *Behavioural Brain Research* 338: 109–117. https://doi.org/10.1016/j.bbr.2017.10.019.

18. Samet, Lisa. 2021. *Emotional Repatterning: Healing Emotional Pain by Rewiring the Brain*. O-Books.

www.ingramcontent.com/pod-product-compliance
Lightning Source LLC
Chambersburg PA
CBHW022025290426

44109CB00014B/749